SUMPTUOUS ACCLAIM FOR FULL-FLAVORED MEALS THAT LEAVE OUT THE MEAT!

"An entirely new approach to meal planning....Recipes are easy to execute, and ingredient lists are short....If more vegetarian efforts were like *THE OCCASIONAL VEGETARIAN*, few Americans would have trouble giving up meat altogether, let alone for a few nights a week."

—*COOK'S ILLUSTRATED*

"Covering the basics and then some...stinting on neither ingredients nor technique...keeping practicalities in mind."

—*PUBLISHERS WEEKLY*

"Clear and concise."

—*NEW YORK TIMES*

"An appealing book....The idea of an entrée surrounded by a side dish and a potato is replaced by an array of dishes that make up a well-balanced meal."

—*NEWSDAY*

"Lee...gives dishes a rounded, full flavor....Helpful to those used to building dinner around a hunk of meat."

—*MILWAUKEE JOURNAL*

"The book is full of [Ms. Lee's] genius for creativity with ingredients."

—*SOUTHAMPTON PRESS*

"If the test of a good cookbook is that it tempts you to try the recipes, Lee's book accomplishes that...we found no losers."

—*AUSTIN AMERICAN-STATESMAN*

"Lee understands that to eat vegetarian, one has to do more than substitute a vegetable concoction for daily meat."

—*PHILADELPHIA INQUIRER*

"Don't skip reading this book if you're not a vegetarian."

—*KNOXVILLE NEWS-SENTINEL*

"What is obvious is Lee's passion for fresh, robust flavor....
With its preponderance of innovative recipes based on the use of fresh ingredients, this book is a joy of vegetarian cooking."

—*KITCHEN GARDEN* (CT)

THE OCCASIONAL VEGETARIAN

More Than 200 Robust Dishes to Satisfy Both Full- and Part-time Vegetarians

KAREN LEE

with DIANE PORTER

WARNER BOOKS

A Time Warner Company

Grateful acknowledgment is made for permission to use the following recipes, which are reprinted, adapted, or derived from the sources below.

Fresh Beet Salad with Oranges and Fried Onions, Richard Faron, Long Island Chef
Barefoot Contessa's Low-Fat Ginger Cake, Barefoot Contessa
Porcini Vinaigrette, Lynn Burnett, friend and caterer
Artichokes with Mustard Vinaigrette, Rolande Circurel, friend and artist
Roasted Portobello Mushrooms, Jamie Leeds, chef
Fresh Sweet Pea Soup, Jean-George Vongerichten, chef and owner of JoJo
Eggplant Torte à la Provençal and *Couscous Salad with Mint,* Sigun Coyle, friend
Parmesan Toast, Robert Sanford, manager of E.A.T.
Cabbage Vinaigrette, Middle Eastern Rice and Lentils, and *Middle Eastern Rice and Spinach,* Janis Carr, chef at Grace's Market
Split Pea and Lentil Soup, Joan Snyder Lewisohn
Slow-Cooked Rice Pudding, Ken Korsh, Chef de Légumes
Creamy Polenta with Marscapone and Gorgonzola, Danny Meyer and Michael Romano, owners of Union Square Cafe
Basmati Rice with Leeks and Cauliflower, Red Bean Sauce, and *Asparagus and Carrot Vinaigrette,* Dominique Richard
Year-Round Bruschetta, Restaurant Sette Mezzo

Grateful Acknowledgment is made for permission to quote from the following:
Pierre Franey, *New York Times*

Warner Books, Inc., 1271 Avenue of the Americas, New York, NY 10020
Visit our Web site at http://warnerbooks.com

 A Time Warner Company

Printed in the United States of America
First Trade Printing: October 1998
10 9 8 7 6 5 4 3 2 1

The Library of Congress has cataloged the hardcover edition as follows:

Library of Congress Cataloging-in-Publication Data

Lee, Karen.
The occasional vegetarian : more than 200 robust dishes to satisfy both full- and part-time vegetarians / Karen Lee with Diane Porter.
p. cm.
Includes index.
ISBN 0-446-51792-5
1. Vegetarian cookery. I. Porter, Diane. II. Title.

TX837.L4 1995
641.5´636—dc20
ISBN 0-446-67452-4 (pbk.)

94-35363
CIP

Cover and book design by Kathleen Herlihy-Paoli, Inkstone Design

This book is dedicated to my mother,
Trudy Korsh,
the first occasional vegetarian in my life

ACKNOWLEDGMENTS

My students have been a constant source of inspiration and motivation. Their demands for healthful and tasty food led to my search for the recipes in this book. I have learned a huge amount from them over the past twenty-two years of teaching, as I have grown from being years younger than my youngest student to now being the mother of the class.

Thanks to Rae-Carole Fischer for introducing me to Diane Porter. Thank you, Diane, for insisting on reducing the fat in every recipe. You were right—it is possible to have delicious food with less oil. Thank you for helping me write a book with recipes that I love to use daily.

Thank you, Sigun Coyle, for sharing so many of your cooking secrets. I love to cook with you.

Thank you, Liv Blumer, for being such a thorough, enthusiastic, and creative editor—the best I can imagine.

Thank you, Judith Weber, my agent, for your unflagging faith and guidance throughout this project.

CONTENTS

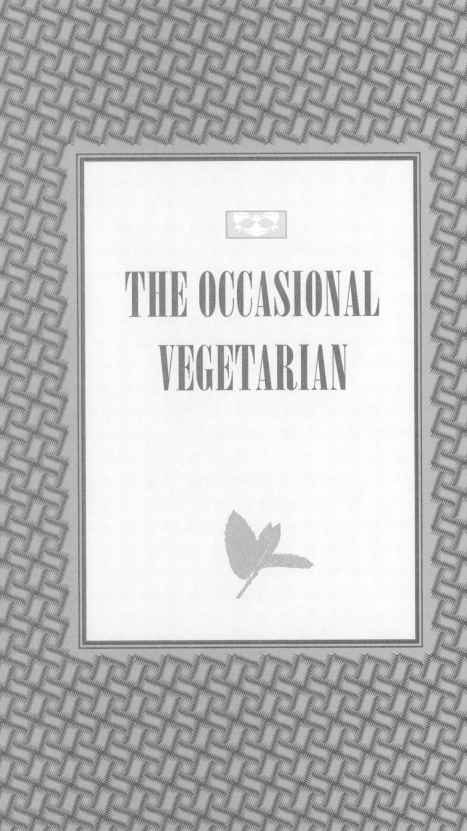

THE OCCASIONAL
VEGETARIAN

INTRODUCTION

"I'm Not a Vegetarian, but I Often Eat Like One"

This is the fifth cookbook I've written, and while I still love and use many of my older recipes, this book reflects the way I eat these days—low-fat, well-seasoned food made with familiar ingredients combined in new ways.

I'm a part-time vegetarian. I love meat, but I also love pasta with spicy tomato sauces, salads of all kinds, chunky vegetable soups, nutty, roasted grains, and white beans cooked with herbs or pan-roasted garlic. When I eat this way I like the way my body feels—light and energetic. I keep my weight down without a struggle. I know in my head—and I can feel it in my body—that it's good for my health. But mostly I like the tastes.

If you are trying to cut back on the amount of meat you eat, join the crowd. According to studies by the Department of Agriculture, so are more than 50 million of us. Our diets have improved over the past decade. We've shifted to lower-fat milk and less meat, and we've added more grains. Friends, neighbors, students, and relatives in New York and other cities—virtually everyone I told I was writing a cookbook for part-time vegetarians—exclaimed, "That's me!"

Meatless meals have even become fashionable. No longer do we apologize for not serving meat. The recipes in *The Occasional Vegetarian* have been created to offer meat-eaters and vegetarians alike delicious, satisfying, healthful food with only modest amounts of fat. After all, if you eat less meat in order to eat less fat, it's silly to eat a dish drenched in butter and cheese.

What *is* a vegetarian, anyway? Some people who call themselves vegetarians don't eat red meat but will eat chicken and fish; others will eat dairy products but not eggs; some will eat both dairy products and eggs. I've come to wonder if the word has any real meaning at all. I define a vegetarian as someone who eats no meat, chicken, or fish. By this and every other definition, I'm not a vegetarian. I never have been and never will be.

Vegetarian cooking has been a gradual shift for me. I'm probably best known for my traditional Chinese cooking and for creating new dishes by combining Eastern and Western ingredients and cooking tech-

niques. For the past twenty-two years, I've been a caterer, cooking teacher, and cookbook writer.

I began my formal cooking education back in 1967, in a class with Madame Grace Zia Chu, one of the earliest and most outstanding teachers of Chinese cooking in this country. During the five-year period that I studied with her, I became a traditional Chinese cook. For the next ten years, I taught, wrote about, and cooked Chinese food.

Twelve years ago I was hired by a company with over 500 employees to revamp its employee-lunch program. The company wanted to offer tasty, nutritious food that could be prepared by its existing kitchen staff. My specialty—elaborate Chinese banquets—was definitely out!

I had just begun to develop an interest in Italian cooking, and it was to this cuisine that I turned for dishes to answer the company's needs. Pasta, beans, grains, vegetables, and salads—these became the mainstays of their new lunch program.

As I explored Italian cooking, the similarities between it and Chinese cooking fascinated me: both emphasize pasta, grains, and vegetables; both use only minimal amounts of meat in many dishes. Combining the different seasonings, allowing the flavors to play off each other, became my hobby.

I let my imagination go, and my palate told me where to stop. I mixed Chinese soy sauce with Italian tomato sauce, I stuffed wontons with goat cheese, I seasoned leeks with five-spice powder. Knowing when to stop—never allowing the flavors and combinations of ingredients to seem contrived—is the essence of developing an original recipe. I recently heard of a restaurant serving, to the dismay of its customers, a raisin and asparagus ice cream—now that's contrived!

It Wasn't Just a Summer Romance

The first culinary seed was planted in me in 1961, when I was sixteen years old and my parents sent me to Marseilles, in the south of France. For three glorious months I lived with a French family, where I learned to speak French and fell in love with good food.

That summer my daily responsibility was to buy fresh milk and bread. Every morning I walked to the village with a large straw basket hanging on my arm. The dairyman filled the bottle I brought with fresh milk. When I returned, the family and I ate breakfast together.

Afterward I tagged along with Collette, the mother, and Jocelyn, the grandmother, as they walked to the market. There we planned lunch—the main meal of the day—based on which meats and vegetables looked best.

I remember stall after stall of intensely colored vegetables that had been picked that morning. *Haricots verts*, the tender young green beans so prized by the French, were perfectly aligned, stem ends all facing the same direction. Choosing the best was a major decision. The *haricots* had to be crisp and deep green, with no yellow or brown spots. Beads of moisture glistened on the taut, red skins of the vine-ripened tomatoes. The famous white peaches of France were slightly soft to the touch and smelled like a sweet intoxicating perfume.

These fresh ingredients went directly from the market to the skillet. We went to the market every day; the only foods this French family kept in the refrigerator were milk, butter, and beer.

At the table the conversation centered on the meal itself. I recall two melons being passed around. Each family member held, gently squeezed, and then sniffed them to see which one was *à point*—perfectly ripe. Only then did we slice into the chosen melon.

When I've returned to France on vacation, like most chefs on holiday I couldn't stop noticing foods, tasting dishes, and accumulating recipes. For me, it's as natural as taking in the sights. It hadn't just been a summer romance. French food remained as I remembered it: extraordinary breads and cheeses, the best quality and widest variety of fresh fruits and vegetables.

I particularly remember the bread in Cannes. Baked fresh twice daily, it was good enough to eat by itself. A coarse-grained sourdough loaf a foot in diameter and more than six feet long came out of the baker's wood-burning oven at four each afternoon. I lined up with twenty or more townspeople each day and waited for the crusty loaf to emerge. Unable to restrain myself until I got it home, I nibbled at the hot bread as I strolled down the street.

Over the years the varieties of cheese multiplied. Each town had its own *fromagerie* with its unique selection of local specialties. I especially enjoyed the vast variety of tangy goat cheeses. Their tastes ranged from mild to robust; their textures, from moist to dry. All had natural rind as their only wrapping.

Students often ask which of my dishes can be frozen. I tell them how I first learned about good food in Marseilles when I was sixteen—in a home where the natural bounty and the resulting dishes were never refrigerated, let alone frozen. That was food at its best. However, living in

New York City and needing convenience as much as the next urban dweller, today I not only refrigerate but also freeze stock, tomato sauce, and occasionally even soup or bread.

Yet without a doubt my exposure at sixteen to French country cooking influences how I feel today. I still prefer food in its freshest and most natural state, ideally picked and prepared the same day, unadulterated by chemicals and industrial processing.

USING THE BEST IS LIKE GETTING A HEAD START IN A RACE

I spend a lot of time in my cooking classes talking about the quality of ingredients. Using the best is like getting a head start in a race.

For most dishes fresh herbs are superior to dried. But where dried herbs can be successfully substituted, I've listed them in the recipe. Many supermarkets now carry fresh sage, thyme, marjoram, and coriander year-round.

I make it a point to buy fresh vegetables and fruits in season. I enjoy anticipating the first spring asparagus or June strawberry. And I prefer organically grown produce for its superior taste and nutritional value. For me, cooking without chemicals, finding food in its most natural state, is one of the greatest culinary challenges of the late twentieth century.

In order to have the best, I make my own stocks and tomato sauces. For bread crumbs, I use good bread and my own seasonings. I don't use canned beans, but yes, they can be substituted in equal amounts for cooked beans. I'll talk more about this in the chapter on beans.

Okay, I'll confess to being something of a purist. You may want to replace some of my homemade ingredients with store-bought. In large cities, it's possible to find specialty stores that carry excellent stocks, tomato sauces, and dried tomatoes. Soy sauce, chili oil, and even pickled ginger are now available in many supermarkets around the country. However, first explore the recipes in the Basics chapter. You may be surprised how little of your time it takes to make chili oil, bread crumbs, and even oven-dried tomatoes. When you make these yourself, you'll find they're fresher, cheaper, and far tastier than store-bought.

I Haven't Given up Butter, Cheese...

I feel light and energetic when I eat fresh, wholesome vegetarian meals. I sleep better, too. My body absorbs this food quickly and easily, whereas a meat meal takes six hours to digest.

My lunches are typically salads or bean soups; dinners are a second salad, pasta, and a vegetable. I haven't given up butter, cheese, cream, or sugar, but I use them only in small quantities. I don't count fat grams or calories, but I do watch the size of my portions. I almost never eat between meals or after dinner, and I drink lots of herb tea and water.

These days I eat chicken, fish, and meat about three times a week. Usually the red meat I eat is in stir-fried dishes where it plays only a small role. This isn't to say that I don't occasionally enjoy a veal chop or a few slices of roasted lamb.

I eat a sweet most days—sometimes a cookie or two. Lately, my favorite is plain yogurt topped with fruit poached in a sugar syrup. I'll certainly eat a couple of bites of a rich dessert when I make it for class or a catering event. That's because I don't believe in stringent low-fat diets. Many people who adopt them end up craving high-fat desserts because they feel deprived. Dining should be a joyful experience, a celebration of life, not a test of willpower.

Over the years, my cooking at home has evolved into a healthier, increasingly vegetarian cuisine. At first I served vegetarian entrees only to my vegetarian friends. Soon I was serving them to those who were watching their weight—almost everyone I knew. I got rave reviews, and to my surprise, no one seemed to miss the meat.

Eventually, these dishes became a significant part of both my catering business and my classes. Today, my clients and students demand more vegetable and grain dishes than in years past. They ask for lighter foods and fewer red-meat and fried dishes.

You Are What You Eat

I've always been interested in nutrition. I believe the old clichés: You are what you eat, and Your food is your medicine. While most part-time vegetarians begin to eat this way for health reasons, many of us find we prefer the lighter, fresher tastes.

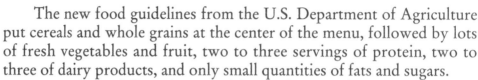

The new food guidelines from the U.S. Department of Agriculture put cereals and whole grains at the center of the menu, followed by lots of fresh vegetables and fruit, two to three servings of protein, two to three of dairy products, and only small quantities of fats and sugars.

It's easier to follow these guidelines when we choose at least a few vegetarian meals a week. Since most beans, pasta, grains, and vegetables are practically fat-free, I can add small quantities of high-quality, high-fat ingredients—imported Parmesan cheese, the best extra-virgin olive oil, a scattering of pine nuts, a few olives, or even a bit of cream—and still maintain a sensible intake of fat.

By combining a judicious amount of high-fat ingredients with interesting seasonings, rich stock reductions, and creative cooking techniques, you can produce outstanding dishes.

Because *The Occasional Vegetarian* is written for those who don't plan to give up meat as well as for vegetarians, I've included suggestions for using these recipes with meat, poultry, and fish. In addition, some recipes suggest nonvegetarian variations.

The biggest obstacle for many part-time vegetarians is their lack of confidence in putting together a satisfying vegetarian meal. Without meat at its center, many of us are at a loss as to where to begin. In Chapter 1, "Strategies for Creating Vegetarian Meals to Delight Meat-Eaters," I discuss the four ways I structure a vegetarian meal, and throughout the book I've given menu suggestions.

I'm convinced this book will persuade you that it's possible to eat in a healthful vegetarian style as often as you choose and love it as much as I do. I wish you good health and happy eating.

STRATEGIES FOR CREATING VEGETARIAN MEALS TO DELIGHT MEAT-EATERS

*L*ast Thanksgiving I was a guest at a dinner party in which more than a half-dozen excellent vegetable, grain, and fruit dishes were served alongside the turkey: squash fresh from the garden, pears and cranberries stewed with spices, green beans sautéed with butter and almonds, an aromatic basmati rice, a subtle fennel and onion confit, a superb casserole made from sourdough bread cubes and fresh sage, and a fresh apple chutney.

When this feast was over, we all sat back, stuffed, and exclaimed over the food. No one mentioned the fine turkey, most of which was left over. The hostess smiled ruefully and said that next year she didn't think she'd bother to make a turkey. Several traditionalists—including me—argued that we couldn't imagine a Thanksgiving without one.

No, I'm not going to prepare Thanksgiving dinner without the turkey, but I do frequently serve my guests vegetarian dinners. No longer do I feel the need to apologize or explain. Sometimes I think nobody misses the meat.

HOW TO BUILD A VEGETARIAN MEAL

*W*hile some dishes fit neatly into any course—"Cream" of Carrot Soup (page 71) is always soup and nobody would serve the Ricotta Torte (page 248) for any course but dessert—many of the recipes in this book can be used in numerous ways.

I use Chino Caponata (page 53) not only as an intensely flavored eggplant appetizer or hors d'oeuvre but also as a topping for pasta, as part of an antipasto, on a buffet, or as part of a composed plate (an entree made up of equal-size servings of three or more dishes arranged on a single plate).

Most of us are accustomed to designing meals around meat, chicken, and fish. However, now most nutritionists encourage us to think of meat as the side dish and to focus on grains and vegetables.

When we create a vegetarian meal, several possibilities present themselves. The "main course" could be Ginger Lentil Stew (beans; page 164), Mixed Wild Mushrooms with Grilled Polenta (grains and vegetables; page 179), Penne with Creamy Basil Tomato Sauce (pasta; page 145), or Stuffed Grilled Eggplant Rolls (vegetables and cheese;

page 196). Several "side dishes" could form a composed plate. Or there might be no "main course" at all.

I structure a vegetarian meal in one of four basic ways:

1. *WITH A FEATURED ENTREE*
2. *WITH A COMPOSED PLATE OF THREE OR FOUR SIDE DISHES AS THE ENTREE*
3. *AS SEVERAL SEQUENTIALLY SERVED DISHES*
4. *AS A BUFFET*

THE FEATURED ENTREE

By a *featured entree* I mean the star of the meal—the main course around which the rest of the meal is planned. For example, if you say, "I think we'll have steak for dinner," then you consider what to serve with it. The same is true for a vegetarian featured entree.

Examples of meals with vegetarian featured entrees (in italics) are:

MINESTRONE SOUP (PAGE 82)	ROASTED WINTER SQUASH SOUP (PAGE 74)	FRENCH LENTIL SALAD WITH GOAT CHEESE (PAGE 113)
ASPARAGUS AND CARROT VINAIGRETTE (PAGE 89)	FENNEL AND ORANGE SALAD WITH HERB-LIME VINAIGRETTE (PAGE 94)	*EGGPLANT TORTE À LA PROVENÇAL (PAGE 195)*
PASTA WITH MARSALA AND WILD MUSHROOMS (PAGE 134)	*ROASTED VEGETABLE CASSOULET (PAGE 158)*	SAFFRON HERB RICE (PAGE 187)
RICOTTA TORTE (PAGE 248)	BROCCOLI DI RAPE WITH GARLIC (PAGE 212)	SWISS CHARD WITH SHALLOTS (PAGE 216)
	CHOCOLATE SOUFFLÉ (PAGE 249)	PUMPKIN CRÈME BRÛLÉE (PAGE 252)

THE COMPOSED PLATE

A composed plate is an entree formed by comparable-size portions of three or more dishes on a single plate. The colors, textures, and flavors of the dishes chosen should create a harmonious whole rather than an impression that one food dominates and the others are subordinate to it.

The vegetarian composed plate resembles many meat-based main courses—typically a protein like beans, a starch like pasta or rice, and a vegetable. A Middle Eastern restaurant in my neighborhood specializes in composed plates. The customer is offered a list of fifteen to twenty dishes from which he may pick any three. Equal-size portions of the selected items are then arranged attractively on the plate.

Three examples of menus with composed plates (in italics) follow:

FRENCH GREEN LENTIL SOUP (PAGE 81)	BAKED TOMATO SLICES WITH GOAT CHEESE (PAGE 100)	FRESH BEETS WITH YOGURT DRESSING (PAGE 93)
CARROT AND RICE PUREE (PAGE 215)	*GREEK ROASTED POTATOES (PAGE 221)*	*STIR-FRIED SUGAR SNAPS WITH SHIITAKE MUSHROOMS (PAGE 230)*
FENNEL AND ONION CONFIT (PAGE 218)	*GREEN BEANS AMANDINE (PAGE 211)*	*WHOLE-GRAIN FRIED RICE (PAGE 182)*
ASPARAGUS WITH BROWN BUTTER AND LEMON (PAGE 211)	*RED-COOKED CABBAGE (PAGE 214)*	*BRAISED SPICED LEEKS (PAGE 67)*
PASTA RISOTTO (PAGE 142)	*WHITE BEANS WITH PAN-ROASTED GARLIC (PAGE 157)*	APPLE CRISP (PAGE 254)
CHOCOLATE ANGEL FOOD CAKE (PAGE 247)	SLOW-COOKED RICE PUDDING (PAGE 253)	

SEQUENTIALLY SERVED DISHES

*U*nlike a dinner with an entree, when dishes are *served sequentially* there is no one dish that you can cite as the focal point of the meal. The dishes are served one after the other in a series of mini-courses.

Often when I'm alone or with close friends, I test recipes. I serve small portions of each food separately. This better allows us to taste and discuss each one by itself. Vegetarian cooking lends itself to serving sequentially; a meat-based meal doesn't. I can't imagine serving a chicken dish, following it with green beans, and then offering a rice pilaf.

Three examples of sequentially served dishes follow:

WATERCRESS, ENDIVE, SNOW PEA, AND PEAR SALAD (PAGE 104)

BLACK BEANS WITH ROASTED PEPPERS (PAGE 160)

MIDDLE-EASTERN RICE AND SPINACH (PAGE 183)

CHOCOLATE CUSTARD (PAGE 251)

FRESH SWEET PEA SOUP (PAGE 73)

WHITE BEAN, ARUGULA, AND ONION SALAD (PAGE 109)

SPINACH SOUFFLÉ (PAGE 202)

POACHED PEARS AND CHERRIES IN PORT (PAGE 261)

ARTICHOKES WITH MUSTARD VINAIGRETTE (PAGE 60)

VEGETABLE SOUP WITH FRENCH PESTO (PAGE 84)

CREAMY POLENTA WITH MASCARPONE AND GORGONZOLA (PAGE 180)

STRAWBERRIES WITH RASPBERRY SAUCE (PAGE 261)

THE BUFFET

For a *buffet*, I lay out all the dishes, except for the desserts, which I serve after the food and plates have been cleared.

Buffets suit the way we live today. What better way to serve when you have eight or more coming for dinner and no help? Because you have little to do once the food is set out, you can relax and enjoy your company.

As a guest at a buffet, you can decide for yourself what goes on your plate. You can take a bit of everything at once, or try one dish at a time. You can choose a few favorites and leave the rest, or take only the vegetarian dishes and side-step the meat. You need never explain why you're not eating the beef or that the quiche doesn't fit your low-fat diet.

This has long been one of my favorite ways to serve a vegetarian meal at home and at the affairs I cater. My buffets typically include beans, pasta, and two or three vegetables and salads.

Many of the recipes in *The Occasional Vegetarian* can be prepared hours ahead and left covered on the table until your guests arrive. Following are three buffet menus:

SAFFRON HERB RICE
(PAGE 187)

*CHICKPEAS AND
SPINACH (PAGE 162)*

*ZUCCHINI
WITH FRESH HERBS
(PAGE 225)*

*BRAISED MUSHROOMS
(PAGE 219)*

*CHERRY TOMATO
AND ONION SALAD
(PAGE 101)*

*MOROCCAN ORANGES
(PAGE 258)*

*ANTIPASTO SALAD
(PAGE 111)*

*YEAR-ROUND
BRUSCHETTA (PAGE 62)*

*CHOPPED SALAD
(PAGE 102)*

*ORZO PRIMAVERA
(PAGE 141)*

*STIR-FRIED SUGAR
SNAPS WITH SHIITAKE
MUSHROOMS
(PAGE 230)*

*RICOTTA TORTE
(PAGE 248)*

*ROASTED BARLEY
SALAD (PAGE 119)*

*CANNELLINI SALAD
WITH RED WINE
VINAIGRETTE
(PAGE 108)*

*ORANGE, AVOCADO,
AND RADISH SALAD
(PAGE 98)*

*TOMATOES STUFFED
WITH HERBS AND
CHEESE (PAGE 68)*

*PEACH AND CHERRY
COBLER (PAGE 260)*

Chapter 2

BEFORE
YOU BEGIN

SHOPPING

Whether you shop for one meal at a time or the whole week, plan before you shop and bring a list. Without one you're bound to overlook an ingredient you need and buy food you'll end up throwing out. Bring a list, but remain flexible enough to substitute items for those that are unavailable, overpriced, or not of good quality.

Often, cauliflower can be substituted for broccoli, broccoli for broccoli di rape, and Swiss chard for escarole. Bok choy and Swiss chard can be used interchangeably. Any wild mushroom can be switched for another. If the watercress looks wilted, buy the arugula. If you're not comfortable making substitutions on the spot, write alternatives on your shopping list. You'll get the hang of it.

THE PANTRY

With a well-stocked pantry, you don't have to worry about last-minute meals. For those times when I haven't any idea of what I want for dinner, I look to see what vegetable catches my eye. I know that with a fresh vegetable and the ingredients I keep on hand, I'll be able to turn out a tasty meal.

THE FOLLOWING ARE THE ITEMS I CONSIDER ESSENTIAL TO MY PANTRY:

Red wine vinegar
Rice vinegar
Balsamic vinegar
Olive oil
Peanut oil
Oriental sesame oil
Long and short dried pasta
White rice
Brown rice
Cornmeal
White beans
Black beans
Dried oregano
Salt
Pepper
Sesame seeds

Almonds or pine nuts
Soy sauce
Tahini
Canned or boxed tomatoes
Dried mushrooms
Bay leaves
Indispensable, too, are these more
    perishable items:
Leeks
Carrots
Onions
Garlic
Parsley
Shallots
Parmesan cheese
Olives

ESSENTIAL EQUIPMENT

Like most home cooks, I wouldn't be without an assortment of pots and pans, measuring cups, wooden spoons, and a host of other kitchen basics.

The following are items I find essential but have frequently found my students don't own. You can always improvise, but I suggest owning as many of these as suit your budget and needs.

1. *A 12-inch iron skillet.* Excellent for roasting, baking, and sautéing. I use it in the oven as well as on top of the stove. It's good for roasting shallots and garlic and for sautéing vegetables. However, when adding wine or tomatoes, a nonreactive pan is called for.

2. *A 3- or 4-inch iron skillet.* Perfect for roasting a tablespoon or two of nuts. Of course, you can roast nuts on a cookie sheet, but this skillet is easier to clean and I like the way the heavy cast-iron evenly conducts the heat.

3. *A 14-inch flat-bottom steel wok.* One with a long wooden handle makes the wok easier to hold while stir-frying. Designed for American stoves, the flat-bottom wok sits directly on the gas or electric heat source, eliminating the need for the metal ring used to stabilize the round-bottom wok. (The ring keeps the wok elevated from the heat source, which is the opposite of what's needed in stir-frying, where the success of the dish is equal to the intensity of the heat.)

4. *A metal spatula or turner.* Sometimes known as an egg-flipper, these are needed for stir-frying. I prefer wok spatulas, those with curved edges that fit the contour of a wok.

5. *A shallow roasting pan.* Mine is 17$\frac{1}{2}$ by 13 inches and less than 3 inches high. I use it frequently for roasting vegetables and making double batches of Peach and Cherry Cobbler (page 260).

6. *Bamboo chopsticks.* I use chopsticks for everything from taking an olive out of a jar to beating an egg. I hold a pair in one hand and a metal spatula in the other to toss vegetables when I stir-fry. I use a single stick to measure the depth of oil. I use the square end to level dry ingredients when measuring them, to peel ginger, and to toss a salad. And of course I eat with them!

7. *A 2-quart enamel saucepan.* My first choice for cooking rice.

8. *A large stainless-steel pot with a colander.* Ideal for cooking pasta and stocks, and for steaming vegetables.

Most if not all of the above items are available at housewares and kitchen-supply stores throughout the country. However, should you be unable to find any of these locally, you can order them from Bridge Kitchenware Corp., 214 East 52 Street, New York, NY 10022; 800-274-3435 and 212-688-4220.

ADVANCE PREPARATION

*L*et's face it: vegetarian cooking is more work than throwing a steak on the grill. However, by having cooked soup, beans, and grains in the refrigerator, and stock and tomato sauce in the freezer, putting together a last-minute meal becomes a cinch. And when you're really in a bind, there's always canned beans and stock, and store-bought tomato sauces.

The time-consuming part of preparing most of the recipes in this book is the cleaning, peeling, and cutting of the vegetables. Here are some suggestions to cut down on last-minute preparation:

• As soon as you come home from the market, wash the leafy-green vegetables you plan to use that day or the next.

• Cut vegetables such as onions, ginger, and carrots early in the day and cover them separately with a plastic wrap. Refrigerate them until you're ready to cook.

• When an ingredient is used in a number of recipes, prepare it all at once. For example, if you're using chopped garlic in stir-fried vegetables, pasta, and salad dressing, peel and chop the garlic for all three dishes at the same time.

ORGANIZATION

*I*n real estate, only three things are said to matter: location, location, and location. In cooking, it's organization, organization, and organization.

The more organized you are, the calmer you are and the better the meal will be; there's less likelihood of negative surprises. When you're

late, rushing to get everything done, unable to find the pan you need or the spice you haven't used in weeks but can't make *this* dish without, you're setting yourself up for culinary disaster.

When I was apprenticing with Madame Chu, I was always amazed at how many dishes she could prepare simultaneously. I stood mesmerized as she completed four, five, even six dishes within minutes of each other. She never became flustered. Smoothly, calmly, with the grace of a ballerina, she glided through the preparation and cooking. *That's* organization!

I believe in the French phrase, *mise en place*: everything in its place. Before you begin to prepare the meal, have the pots, spatulas, and other equipment ready. The ingredients should be out of the cupboards and refrigerator. Line up *everything* you'll need.

Post the menu for yourself so you don't end up forgetting the bean salad you made yesterday. And don't undertake more than you're comfortable with.

It helps to enlist the aid of a friend to chop the vegetables as well as share the meal. Or if your budget allows it, hire someone to assist with the preparation if you're having a lot of people to dinner.

When I'm organized, I develop a rhythm, a flow. Time slips by. I like all the phases of preparing a meal: the planning and the shopping, the cutting and chopping. But most of all I enjoy the actual cooking . . . and eating.

Chapter 3

THE BASICS

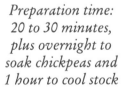

I cook stock in my two-part pasta pot so that I can easily remove the solids. The two-handled colander lifts out, leaving the liquid in the pot and making it easy to dispose of the herbs and vegetables.

This section contains the recipes that are essential to my cooking. Each cook has her own—those indispensable I-just-couldn't-cook-without basics. For me they include tomato sauce, roasted nuts, chili oil, roasted peppers, and stock. Many of these recipes are simple; a few are hardly recipes at all. I include them because in my twenty-two years of teaching I've learned to assume nothing. What may seem obvious often isn't. I've known a few excellent cooks who didn't know how to make bread crumbs, and many who didn't realize it takes only a few minutes to roast cumin.

I've included the three stocks I use extensively in my vegetarian cooking. Strong, flavorful stocks are essential to satisfying soups and stews. The only way to make a good stock is to use good ingredients. I would no more put bruised or wilted vegetables into a stock than I would serve them to guests. However, I do add the dark green ends of fresh leeks and scallions, parsley stems, and occasionally vegetables that are a few days old.

There's an essential truth in cooking that you can't escape: the ultimate success of a dish depends on the quality of its ingredients. If you don't have the time to invest in making your own tomato sauce, stock, and bread crumbs, locate a trustworthy source.

Yields 8 cups

Preparation time: 20 to 30 minutes, plus overnight to soak chickpeas and 1 hour to cool stock

Cooking time: 1 hour

Vegetable Stock

This stock is the basis for many of the soups in this book. Unless a particular stock is specified in a recipe, use any unsalted stock of your choosing. For those who are not vegetarians, a chicken stock can be used in any of the recipes, but be sure to taste and if necessary adjust the seasonings.

I add salt to the final dish, never to the stock. I sometimes reduce stocks to make the flavors more intense. If there were salt in the stock, once reduced, the stock might well taste too salty.

4 medium onions, coarsely chopped
4 medium leeks, white and green parts, cleaned (page 32) and coarsely chopped (about 5 cups)

1 unpeeled carrot, coarsely chopped

4 celery stalks, coarsely chopped
¼ cup chopped fresh parsley
¼ cup dried mushrooms, or 1 teaspoon Porcini Powder (page 42)
½ cup chickpeas, soaked (see page 153) and drained, or lentils, washed and drained (see Note)

2 or 3 sprigs fresh thyme, or
   1 teaspoon dried
1 bay leaf
1 tablespoon whole black
   peppercorns
4 quarts water

Scrub carrots well, but do not pare them. The peel is rich in vitamins.

1. Combine onions, leeks, carrot, celery, parsley, mushrooms or Porcini Powder, chickpeas or lentils, thyme, bay leaf, peppercorns, and water in a large stockpot. Bring to a boil over high heat; lower the heat and allow to simmer uncovered for 1 hour.

2. Remove the pot from the heat and allow the vegetables to remain in the stock for an additional hour. Strain the stock and discard the solids. Remove the bay leaf.

Stock can be refrigerated for 1 week; frozen for 3 months.

Note: Chickpeas make a light-colored stock similar to chicken stock; lentils add a rich, almost beefy taste.

HOW TO CLEAN LEEKS

There are two good ways to wash leeks that you're going to slice or chop. Whichever you choose, be sure to remove all the sand and dirt. Nothing ruins a dish quicker than the grit against your teeth from poorly cleaned vegetables. While it's obviously important to remove the dirt from all vegetables, leeks cause most cooks the greatest trouble.

Both methods call for cutting the leeks lengthwise. I haven't found any way to adequately clean leeks without cutting them, as the leaves are so tightly wrapped together that the water can't get between them.

The first method is to trim and discard all but one half inch of the hairlike roots. Cut the leek in half lengthwise up to the root. Attached at the root end, the leek will still be in one piece.

I spread the tightly wrapped leaves and, using a vegetable brush or my thumbs, gently rub the dirt off the leaves while holding the leek under a warm-water spray. I find that warm water dislodges the dirt better than cold. Now I'm ready to cut away the rest of the root and slice the leek into whatever size pieces I need.

The second method is to cut away the entire root end and then cut the leek lengthwise. Holding the two halves of the leek together, I slice the leek into pieces. I submerge the cut-up pieces in warm water. Using my hands, I gently rub them to loosen the dirt that clings to the leaves.

Finally, I put the leek pieces into a strainer and spray them well with warm water, and I check carefully to make sure they're clean.

MUSHROOM STOCK

Yields 8 to 10 cups

Preparation time: 10 minutes, plus 1 hour to cool

Cooking time: 1 hour

Use Mushroom Stock in any recipe that calls for stock when you want to add or intensify the mushroom flavor. Bean soups, Roasted Vegetable Cassoulet (page 158), and Fresh Pasta with Black Chanterelles (page 135) are dishes in which I sometimes use this stock.

For an even more pronounced mushroom taste, return the stock to a simmer after removing the solids and reduce by one-fourth. With a little soy sauce, this reduced stock makes a savory broth to drink by itself.

1 unpeeled carrot
1 medium onion, quartered
6 garlic cloves
3 celery stalks
3 cups stems and pieces of mixed
   fresh mushrooms—shiitake,

portobello, cremini, button—
   but don't use all button
   (see Note)
1 tablespoon whole black
   peppercorns
4 quarts water

1. Combine carrot, onion, garlic, celery, mushrooms, peppercorns, and water in a large stockpot. Bring to a boil over high heat; lower the heat and allow to simmer uncovered for 1 hour.

2. Remove the pot from the heat and allow the vegetables to remain in the stock for 1 to 1 ½ hours. Lift the solids from the pot. Press them firmly with the back of a ladle to extract all the liquid; discard solids.

Stock can be refrigerated for 1 week, frozen for 3 months.

Note: If you don't have enough bits and pieces of fresh mushrooms, soak a handful of dried mushrooms for 30 minutes. Strain the soaking water and then add both the mushrooms and the soaking water to the stock. Or add a teaspoon or two of Porcini Powder (page 42).

GARDEN SALAD STOCK

I make this stock as soon as I come home from the market. It's part of my routine of cleaning and putting vegetables away. The preparation time is short because I put the vegetables into the water either whole or in large chunks. Garden Salad Stock has a bright, fresh taste.

Green parts of 1 bunch medium
   leeks, well cleaned (see page 32)
3 plum tomatoes, cut in half
Handful of fresh coriander
   (cilantro)
Handful of fresh parsley
3 garlic cloves, smashed
1 small onion, quartered
2 celery stalks

1 unpeeled carrot
Handful of lettuce leaves
¼ cup stems and pieces of dried
   mushrooms, or 1 teaspoon
   Porcini Powder (page 42)
1 fresh thyme sprig
1 teaspoon freshly ground black
   pepper
6 quarts water

YIELDS 4 TO 5 QUARTS

*Preparation time:
10 minutes,
plus 1 hour to cool*

Cooking time: 1 hour

1. Combine the leeks, tomatoes, coriander, parsley, garlic, onion, celery, carrot, lettuce, mushrooms or Porcini Powder, thyme, pepper, and water in a large stockpot. Bring to a boil over high heat; lower the heat and allow to simmer uncovered for 1 hour.

2. Remove the pot from the heat and allow the vegetables to remain in the stock for 1 to 1½ hours. Strain the stock and discard the solids.

Stock can be refrigerated for 1 week, frozen for 3 months.

YIELDS 3 CUPS

*Preparation time:
15 minutes*

*Cooking time:
25 to 35 minutes*

BASIC TOMATO SAUCE

The leeks give this sauce its special sweet taste, while the absence of any distinguishing herbs allows this sauce to be used in any cuisine. As with a basic stock, you add the seasoning you want to the final dish.

I always keep a good homemade tomato sauce on hand. I use it in French and Spanish recipes that call for a few tablespoons of tomato sauce, and in Chinese ones that require catsup. This sauce is the base for many of my Italian pasta sauces. It can easily be doubled.

Keep in the refrigerator or freezer, or substitute a good-quality store-bought sauce if you choose not to make your own.

I prefer to store food in glass jars, as plastic acquires odors. However, I use plastic containers for freezing because glass can break.

When freezing stocks, soups, and sauces, leave 1 to 2 inches of space (known as headroom) at the top of the container to allow for expansion.

1 tablespoon olive oil
1 medium leek, white and green parts, cleaned (see page 32) and chopped (about 1¼ cups)
2 garlic cloves, minced
1 (35-ounce) can Italian tomatoes,

or 3 pounds peeled and seeded fresh tomatoes (see Note)
1 teaspoon sugar
1 teaspoon salt
½ teaspoon freshly ground black pepper

1. Heat the oil in a deep skillet. Add the leek and garlic, and sauté over low heat for 5 minutes or until the leek is wilted.

2. Empty the tomatoes with their liquid into a bowl. Squish the tomatoes thoroughly; I use my hands.

3. Add the tomatoes, sugar, salt, and pepper to the leek and stir to combine.

4. Bring the sauce to a simmer over high heat. Turn the heat to low and simmer uncovered until the sauce is reduced by half, usually 25 to 35 minutes. (The wider the skillet, the less time it takes to reduce.)

Sauce keeps stored in covered glass jars, for up to 1 week in the refrigerator, 3 months in the freezer.

Note: When I use canned tomatoes, I like to add a few chopped fresh ones, too. Cherry tomatoes or plum tomatoes work well here. If you're using all fresh tomatoes, dice them and add about ½ cup water—a little more or less depending on the juiciness of the tomatoes.

Simmer tomatoes and tomato sauce over low heat, as they become bitter when boiled.

BASIC WHITE BEANS

The two kinds of white beans I use most often are great northern, a small white bean, and cannellini, a large white bean. All white beans can be used interchangeably, but I prefer the smaller beans in some situations, the larger in others. For example, I might choose great northerns for the White Bean Salad with Tomatoes and Herbs (page 110) if I'm planning to stuff it into endive leaves. But I'm more likely to prepare this bean salad with cannellini if I'm going to serve it on an antipasto platter.

YIELDS APPROXIMATELY 2½ CUPS

In advance: 6 hours to overnight to soak the beans

Preparation time: 15 minutes

Cooking time: 1 hour

1 cup dried white beans
2 cups water
1 bay leaf
⅓ teaspoon freshly ground black pepper
1 unpeeled carrot, cut in half
1 Spanish onion, quartered

2 garlic cloves
A few parsley sprigs
A few thyme sprigs, or ½ teaspoon dried
1 teaspoon salt

1. The night before, spread the beans in a large pan and remove any small stones and bits of dirt.

2. Wash the beans by placing them in a bowl and covering them with cold water. Allow the beans to settle to the bottom of the bowl. This allows the dirt to float to the top. Pour off the water.

*R*inse cheesecloth under cold running water to remove the sizing. Substitute a double layer for a fine-mesh sieve when straining foods.

3. Cover the beans by 4 inches or more with cold water. Soak the beans for 6 to 8 hours, or overnight.

4. The next morning, pour off the water and place the soaked beans in a pot with a tight-fitting lid. Add the cold water, bay leaf, pepper, carrot, onion, and garlic. Tie the parsley and thyme in cheesecloth and add it to the pot.

5. Cover and bring to a simmer over high heat. Turn the heat to low and simmer slowly for 1 hour. Add the salt during the last 15 minute of cooking.

6. Remove the bay leaf, garlic, onion, carrot, parsley, and thyme. Wring the cheesecloth out over the beans to extract as much flavor as possible. Serve hot or at room temperature.

Beans can be prepared up to 4 days in advance. Refrigerate if you are keeping them for longer than a few hours.

Note: These beans are flavorful enough to eat just as they are or can be used in any recipe that calls for cooked white beans.

Basic Black-Eyed Peas

*Y*IELDS APPROXIMATELY 2 CUPS

In advance: 2 to 4 hours to soak the beans (optional)

Preparation time: 10 minutes

Cooking time: 45 minutes

*T*hese black-eyed peas can be eaten with rice just as they are or used as the basis for Fiery Black-Eyed Pea Salad (page 108) or Creole Black-Eyed Peas (page 166).

Although it's not necessary to soak black-eyed peas, I do when I have the time.

1 cup dried black-eyed peas
3 cups vegetable stock (see page 30), or stock of your choice
1 bay leaf
5 to 6 parsley stems

Branch of fresh sage with 3 or 4 leaves on it, or ½ teaspoon dried
Salt and freshly ground black pepper to taste

1. If soaking the beans ahead of time, wash and drain, then place in a bowl with water to cover by 4 inches. Let soak for 2 to 4 hours.

2. Drain the beans and combine with the stock in a large pot over high heat. Bring to a simmer, then add the bay leaf. Lay the sprigs of parsley and sage across the top of the beans. Partially cover and simmer until the beans are tender, about 45 minutes. (Increase the cooking time to 1 hour or longer if the peas were not soaked.)

3. Remove the bay leaf, parsley, and sage. Add salt and pepper if the beans are to be eaten without further preparation. Serve hot.

Beans can be refrigerated for up to 2 days.

EASY ROASTED PEPPERS

The primary difference between these peppers and traditional roasted peppers is that the skin is not removed. I use this method when I'm in a hurry and also when the peppers are part of an appetizer and I want them to hold their shape.

Red bell peppers, seeded, deribbed, and cut into 1-inch strips	*Freshly ground black pepper*
Olive oil	*A combination of fresh or dried oregano and thyme (or either herb by itself)*
Salt	

1. Preheat the oven to 375°F.

2. Toss the peppers lightly with a little olive oil, then with salt, pepper, and oregano and thyme.

3. Roast for 30 minutes.

Peppers can be refrigerated for 3 or 4 days.

Preparation time: less than 5 minutes per pepper, plus 10 minutes to cool

Cooking time: 30 minutes

CLASSIC ROASTED PEPPERS

I use roasted peppers frequently in my cooking, especially in bean dishes, salads, and pasta sauces.

I roast my peppers as many restaurants do—in the oven, rather than over an open flame—because you can roast many more peppers at one time.

Red bell peppers   : *Olive oil*

1. Preheat the oven to 400°F.

2. Rub the peppers lightly with olive oil. Place them on a cookie sheet or in a shallow roasting pan and put them into the oven. Turn every 10 minutes until the peppers are soft, wrinkled, and well charred, about 30 minutes.

3. Put the peppers in a paper bag, close the bag, and let the peppers cool for 10 minutes. (This makes them easier to peel.)

4. Holding the peppers over a bowl to catch the juices, peel the charred skin from the peppers and discard. Remove and discard the seeds. Save the juices. Never peel peppers under water; you'll lose much of the flavor.

Peppers can be refrigerated for 3 or 4 days.

ROASTED CHILE PEPPERS

To protect your skin, wear surgical gloves or other clean, thin rubber gloves when handling chile peppers. Never get their strong oils in or near your eyes.

Come January, I head for Rancho la Puerta in Tecata, Mexico, a rugged spa known for magnificent early-morning mountain hikes, challenging exercise classes, and marvelous fresh, low-fat vegetarian food.

It was here I first began to appreciate the value of roasting chile peppers. Roasting mellows the raw heat of the peppers while deepening and intensifying their flavor.

Poblano or jalapeño peppers   : *Olive oil*

1. Preheat the oven to 400°F.

2. Rub the peppers lightly with olive oil and place them on a cookie sheet or in a shallow roasting pan. Put the peppers in the oven and immediately reduce the temperature to 375°F.

3. Turn the peppers every 5 minutes until they're charred on the outside, about 10 minutes for jalapeño peppers and 15 minutes for poblano peppers.

4. Allow the roasted peppers to sit at room temperature until cool, about 15 minutes. Peel the charred skin from the peppers and discard. Remove and discard the seeds.

Peppers can be refrigerated for at least 3 days.

Preparation time: under 5 minutes, plus 15 minutes to cool

Cooking time: 10 to 15 minutes

ROASTED SHALLOTS

*S*hallots have long been the royalty of the onion family. They cook rapidly and have a mild garlicky flavor. As with all onions, roasting enriches their flavor and mellows their bite.

I use these shallots in pasta and cassoulets and as part of an antipasto plate.

YIELDS 24 SHALLOTS

Preparation time: 15 minutes

Cooking time: 1 hour and 15 minutes

24 shallots (see Note), about 1 pound
1½ tablespoons olive oil
1 teaspoon salt

¼ teaspoon freshly ground black pepper
2 bay leaves
A few sprigs of fresh thyme

1. Preheat the oven to 325°F.

2. Peel the shallots, leaving them whole. To keep them from falling apart, cut away only a small amount of the root end.

3. Toss the shallots with oil in an ovenproof pan. Spread the shallots out so they aren't touching. Sprinkle with salt and pepper. Add the bay leaves and the thyme. Cover with foil and bake for 30 minutes. Uncover, turn the heat up to 350°, and bake for an additional 30 minutes.

4. Turn the heat to 450° and roast for 15 more minutes, shaking the pan every few minutes to brown the shallots on all sides.

Shallots can be prepared up to 2 days in advance and refrigerated.

Note: Large shallots can be separated into two parts by cutting off the outer layer; you'll find two bulbs inside.

YIELDS ½ CUP

*Cooking time:
5 minutes*

ROASTED CUMIN

O nce you've used roasted cumin, you'll never settle for the unroasted. Take a moment to smell the cumin before you roast it so you can recognize the difference.

This pungent spice is used to enhance the taste of many bean dishes; the dry roasting and grinding intensifies cumin's flavor and aroma.

When cumin is used unroasted in Middle Eastern, Latin, and Indian cuisines, it's usually fried to remove its raw taste. But when the cumin has been roasted, frying is unnecessary.

½ cup cumin seeds

1. Place a wok or iron skillet over high heat for 1 minute. Add the cumin seeds.

2. Turn the heat to low and roast, stirring every 30 seconds, until the seeds lose their greenish tinge and just begin to turn brown, 3 to 5 minutes. Be careful not to burn them.

Roasted cumin seeds can be kept in a pepper mill and ground as needed.

B oth *Roasted Cumin and Roasted Sesame Seeds can be ground in a coffee grinder kept solely for the purpose of grinding nuts, spices, and seeds. Store in the refrigerator in a tightly covered jar for up to 2 months.*

If you don't have an extra coffee grinder, you can use a food processor.

ROASTED SESAME SEEDS

R oasted Sesame Seeds can be kept for up to one month. But since it only takes a few minutes to roast them, I prefer to do it weekly or as needed.

¼ *cup sesame seeds (see Note)*

Heat a wok or iron skillet over high heat for 1 minute. Turn the heat to low and add the sesame seeds. Stir frequently. If the seeds begin to pop, the heat is too high. Lower the heat and remove the wok from the heat for a few seconds until the seeds stop popping. Roast the sesame seeds until they turn a few shades darker, 5 to 7 minutes.

If the roasted sesame seeds are to be stored for longer than a week, keep refrigerated.

Note: If you roast less than ¼ cup seeds at a time, reduce the cooking time; if a larger amount, increase it.

OVEN-ROASTED NUTS

*R*oasting accentuates the flavor and aroma of nuts. As an example, just a tablespoon of roasted pine nuts sprinkled across the top of pasta or vegetables can transform a simple dish into a treat. Nuts are high in fat, so I use them sparingly.

Nuts can be roasted either dry or with a bit of oil or butter. I roast them the day I use them because I love the smell and they're virtually effortless to make. If you prefer you can prepare a week's supply at a time.

Preheat the oven to 325°F. Spread the nuts in a shallow pan. For dry-roasted: pine nuts, roast for 5 to 7 minutes. For dry-roasted almonds, roast for 6 to 7 minutes.

For oil-roasted peanuts, mix ½ cup peanuts with ½ teaspoon peanut oil and roast for 10 to 12 minutes. For oil-roasted walnuts, mix ½ cup walnut pieces or halves with ½ teaspoon butter; roast for 5 to 12 minutes depending on their size.

Store nuts in a covered jar at room temperature for up to a week.

Porcini Powder

Preparation time:
5 minutes

The intense flavor and aroma of dried porcini mushrooms cannot be equaled. Use this Porcini Powder in pasta, bean soups, and stocks. It's a fast and easy way to get mushroom taste into a dish. It does not need to be reconstituted.

Grind the small bits and pieces and the dregs of dried porcini mushrooms—the powdery stuff at the bottom of the container—in a clean coffee mill. (I prefer to save the bigger pieces, but you can grind them too if you want.)

Keeps for 1 year in a glass jar at room temperature.

Yields 1 cup

Preparation time:
10 minutes, plus 6 to 8
hours to steep

Cooking time:
5 minutes

Herb-Infused Oil

Substitute Herb-Infused Oil for olive oil in salad dressings, on pasta, and in pasta salads. I also use it in Seasoned Dipping Oil (page 43). Only fresh herbs will produce the heady aroma of this oil—no dried substitutes here!

1 cup olive oil
¼ cup chopped fresh herbs—a mixture of basil, oregano, and thyme

1. Heat the olive oil gently over medium heat, until it is hot but not yet at frying temperature, 2 to 3 minutes.

2. Add the herbs. Remove from the heat. Steep uncovered for 6 to 8 hours.

3. Strain and discard the herbs. Put the oil into a glass jar.

Use immediately or refrigerate for up to 3 months.

Seasoned Dipping Oil

YIELDS ¼ CUP

*Preparation time:
5 minutes*

*Cooking time:
5 minutes*

A great substitute for butter. Whenever I have a dinner party, unless the menu is Chinese—in which case I don't serve bread—I prepare this dipping oil. I put a small amount in front of each guest in the tiny dishes designed for soy sauce.

*¼ cup Herb-Infused Oil
(page 42)*
1 tablespoon chopped garlic

*1 tablespoon roasted sesame seeds
(see page 40)*

Gently warm the olive oil over low heat. Add the garlic and sesame seeds. Sauté until the garlic turns golden, 2 to 3 minutes. Serve warm or at room temperature.

Chili Oil

YIELDS 1 CUP

*Preparation time:
2 hours to steep*

*Cooking time:
2 to 3 minutes*

Homemade Chili Oil is more flavorful than store-bought because the oil you use is typically fresher and of a higher quality. It's easy to make and inexpensive. If you choose to buy it, find a source where the stock turns over quickly.

I prefer to use Chili Oil in many recipes where other chefs might use Tabasco or another hot sauce.

1 cup peanut oil

*⅓ cup crushed dried chile peppers
or hot red pepper flakes*

1. Heat the oil in a wok until waves form on the surface of the oil, 2 to 3 minutes.

2. Stick a chopstick straight down into the center of the oil. When bubbles rapidly form around the chopstick, the oil is hot enough (see Note). Remove the oil from the heat and set aside for 1 minute.

3. Add the chile peppers or pepper flakes. Stir and set aside for 2 hours. Strain the oil through a double layer of washed cheesecloth or through a fine-mesh sieve. Discard the solids.

Ready to use in 1 week. Store in the refrigerator for up to 1 year.

Note: You may question this unscientific method, but it works. If you prefer, insert a deep-fat frying thermometer when you see the beginning of waves on the surface of the oil. Remove the oil from the heat when the temperature reaches 350°F.

Oven-Dried Tomatoes

Preparation time: 20 minutes for each tray of tomatoes

Cooking time: 4 to 8 hours

In the past tomatoes were air-, sun-, or oven-dried. Today most are dried in large commercial ovens and dehydrators.

Slices of small dried tomatoes from California, delicate and almost transparent, are usually sold in plastic bags. They can be reconstituted directly in a sauce or blanched for 1 minute and stored in olive oil.

Dried tomatoes from Italy should be soaked in warm water for 10 minutes and either used immediately or stored in olive oil. When stored in oil, they're ready to eat in a week. You can also buy them already packed in olive oil.

I prefer to make my own oven-dried tomatoes. They're moister, with a softer consistency than the Italian and not nearly as salty. Oven-Dried Tomatoes take little time to prepare. The tomatoes you dry should be ripe but firm, but not as ripe as those you'd use for tomato sauce.

Well-ripened plum tomatoes

1. Cut the tomatoes in half lengthwise. There's no need to remove the small spot where the stem was attached. Using a grapefruit spoon, a *demitasse* spoon, or a teaspoon, scoop out the seeds. Put the tomato halves on a cookie sheet, cut side up.

2. Preheat the oven to 225°F., and place the tomatoes in the oven. Start checking the tomatoes after 4 hours. Usually they take 6 to 8 hours, but some ovens run hotter than the set temperature. The tomatoes are done when they are dark red, have dried shriveled skins, yet are still slightly moist inside. Don't let them scorch.

3. Allow the tomatoes to cool. Pack them into a glass jar and cover with olive oil.

The tomatoes can be refrigerated in a glass jar for 6 months.

THE GINGER STORY

Ginger is the pungent, aromatic root of the *Zingiber officinale*, a member of the lily family. It's available year-round at virtually all supermarkets. Choose a large, fat, smooth-skinned hand of ginger. Hawaiian is the best.

Use a natural-bristle vegetable brush to wash the ginger. Peeling isn't necessary if you're going to use it within the next couple of weeks. Simply store it uncovered in the vegetable bin of your refrigerator.

If you're going to keep the ginger for up to a few months, peel it with a vegetable peeler, a sharp knife, or the square end of a chopstick. Place whole or in large chunks in a glass jar and pour in enough medium-dry sherry to cover the ginger. Store at room temperature.

Each time you use the ginger and sherry in a recipe that calls for both, use the sherry from the storage jar, then replace it with fresh sherry. Keep enough in the jar to cover the ginger.

Pickling is another way to store ginger. It removes some of its bite, making it ideal for recipes that don't require cooking. Pickled ginger is also wonderful in dipping sauces.

Ginger is a strong spice. Cut it very fine so that the flavor will be evenly distributed throughout a dish. Here's the best way to cut ginger:

1. Slice ginger thinly on the diagonal (with the grain).

2. Place a few slices of ginger on top of each other. Cut them into narrow julienne strips, then mince.

PICKLED GINGER

Raw ginger is available at virtually all supermarkets; good-quality pickled ginger can be purchased at Asian food stores and many supermarkets.

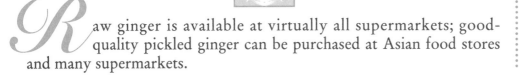

YIELDS 1 QUART

*Preparation time:
30 minutes*

*Cooking time:
1 minute*

I prefer to make my own pickled ginger because it's less expensive and has neither preservatives nor red dye.

1 pound fresh ginger   *1 cup rice vinegar*
4 cups water   *¼ cup sugar*

1. Peel the ginger. Using a food processor or sharp knife, slice the ginger as thin as possible.

2. Bring 3 cups of water to a rolling boil. Add the ginger for 1 minute. Drain. Set ginger aside.

3. While the water is coming to a boil, combine the vinegar, 1 cup remaining water, and sugar. Stir until the sugar is dissolved. While the ginger is still warm, add to the vinegar mixture and allow to cool. Store in a glass jar with a tight-fitting cover.

Pickled Ginger is ready to eat now. Store in the refrigerator for up to 6 months.

An olive-oil spray can be made at home by pouring olive oil into an atomizer bottle. Some supermarkets carry olive-oil sprays alongside the other vegetable cooking sprays.
   If you prefer, instead of spraying, use a pastry brush and brush sparingly with olive oil.

PARMESAN TOAST

My good friend Robert Sanford, the manager of E.A.T., one of my favorite Manhattan food stores, shared with me this method for making Parmesan Toast.

I don't include quantities with this recipe as you don't need them. Make as much or little as you require. Serve this toast with soup or salad for lunch or a light dinner.

Focaccia is a thick pizza bread available at Italian markets and gourmet shops. I also recently saw some for sale at my local supermarket. If you are unable to find focaccia, any bread will do.

Focaccia   *Hot red pepper flakes (see Note)*
Olive oil   *Grated Parmesan cheese*

1. Preheat the oven to 350°F.

2. Slice the focaccia thin, ¼ inch thick, with a serrated bread knife. Brush or spray slices with the olive oil.

3. Mix a small amount of pepper flakes into the grated cheese. Sprinkle on the oiled bread.

4. Bake until the toast is crusty, 15 to 20 minutes. Serve at room temperature.

The toast can be made 1 day ahead and stored at room temperature in an airtight container.

Note: *I use ¼ teaspoon of hot red pepper flakes for each ¼ cup of grated cheese.*

Toast Rounds

I like to keep a supply of these on hand to use instead of crackers with appetizers like Chino Caponata (page 53) and Curried Roasted Garlic Spread (page 59).

1 French baguette, cut into ¼-inch-thick slices

Olive oil, to brush or spray on bread

YIELDS APPROXIMATELY 50 SLICES

Preparation time: 5 to 10 minutes

Cooking time: 20 to 30 minutes

1. Preheat the oven to 250°F.

2. Lay the slices of bread on a cookie sheet. Spray or brush them sparingly with olive oil. Bake until the bread is light tan and crisp throughout, not just on the outside, 20 to 30 minutes. The easiest way to test these is to eat one. Serve immediately or store for future use.

The toast can be stored in an airtight container at room temperature for up to 5 days.

Variation: *To make Sourdough Croutons, cut a sourdough baguette into ½-inch cubes. Toss or spray with olive oil, then follow the directions for the rounds.*

In advance:
several days for bread
to harden

Preparation time:
5 minutes

DRIED BREAD CRUMBS

I never buy bread crumbs at the market. I prefer to use those left-over pieces of excellent bread I'd otherwise have to throw out.

Any size piece good-quality baguette

Leave the bread out for several days. It should become as hard as a base-ball bat (see Note). Break or cut the stale bread into chunks; put into the bowl of a food processor. Pulse on and off until the bread has been reduced to crumbs.

Bread crumbs can be refrigerated for up to 6 months.

Note: If you need bread crumbs and haven't got a few days to wait for the bread to get hard, cut the bread into cubes and bake at 250°F. for 45 minutes to 1 hour. Process as you would stale bread.

« *It has been said that frugality is a hallmark of a good cook. Some of the most talented prac-titioners I know are nearly fanatical about never wasting a morsel —chunks of stale bread are used for bread crumbs or bread pud-ding . . . and vegetable trimmings invariably find their way into stock. This does not re-flect a penurious bent so much as a love of and respect for food and its preparation. Cooking economically is part of the challenge of cooking well.* »

—Pierre Franey

HOUSE BALSAMIC VINAIGRETTE

This is my basic salad dressing. Over the past few years, I've re-duced the oil in it by one-third. The ratio is now two-to-one oil-to-vinegar, and I find the flavors perfectly balanced. I often double or triple this recipe to have enough for the week.

Yields about
½ cup

Preparation time:
10 to 15 minutes

1 teaspoon salt
2 tablespoons red wine vinegar
1 tablespoon balsamic vinegar
1½ teaspoons Dijon-style mustard
½ teaspoon freshly ground black
    pepper

6 tablespoons olive oil
1 small garlic clove, minced
1 scallion, white and green parts
    cut into ⅛-inch rounds
2 tablespoons chopped fresh parsley

1. Stir the salt into the wine and balsamic vinegars. Add the mustard, and stir. Add the pepper and olive oil. Whisk or shake in a tightly covered jar until blended.

Can be prepared to this point up to 1 week ahead and refrigerated.

2. Add the garlic, scallion, and parsley. Shake well and serve.

The vinaigrette can be prepared up to 1 hour ahead.

PORCINI VINAIGRETTE

I got this recipe for a terrific vinaigrette from Lynn Barnett, a friend, colleague, and excellent caterer. Whenever possible I save some of the soaking water from porcini mushrooms to make this dressing. It's good on any lettuce salad.

½ cup soaking water from porcini
   mushrooms
¼ teaspoon salt
2 tablespoons lemon juice
1 teaspoon Dijon-style mustard

2 tablespoons olive oil
¼ teaspoon freshly ground black
   pepper
1 tablespoon soy sauce

1. Strain the soaking liquid into a saucepan and reduce over low heat until only 2 tablespoons remain, about 15 minutes (see Note). Allow to cool.

2. Dissolve the salt in the lemon juice. Add 1 tablespoon of the reduced porcini water, the mustard, olive oil, pepper, and soy sauce. Whisk or shake in a tightly covered jar until blended.

The vinaigrette can be prepared several days ahead and refrigerated. Return to room temperature before using.

Note: Reserve the second tablespoon of reduced porcini water to make another batch of Porcini Vinaigrette or use in stocks or stews.

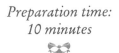

YIELDS ¼ CUP

*Preparation time:
10 minutes*

*Cooking time:
15 minutes*

When you reduce the soaking water for dried porcini, be careful not to let it boil away. It's a good idea to set a timer for 10 minutes and check the pot. However, if it does boil away, add ¼ cup of water to the saucepan and continue the reduction until 2 tablespoons remain. As long as it hasn't burned, it can be salvaged.

Chapter 4

FINGER FOODS AND APPETIZERS

A lthough the terms are often used interchangeably, I like to distinguish between hors d'oeuvres and appetizers. Hors d'oeuvres —also called finger food—are those bite-size, well-seasoned morsels we all love to eat.

At many of the large affairs I cater I serve only hors d'oeuvres. This solves the New York problem of a big guest list and a small space. Typically, guests wander about, stopping to chat in small groups, and nibble their way through the party.

Appetizers, on the other hand, are presented at the table before the rest of the meal. This is where I serve dishes such as year-round Bruschetta, Grilled Shiitake Mushrooms on Arugula, and Pepper Surprises—dishes that require a knife and fork, or at least a plate under them.

Most of the finger foods and appetizers in this section, as well as many of the recipes throughout this book, are perfect for an antipasto consisting of several of these recipes.

ROASTED BUTTERNUT SQUASH

T his is one of my fall favorites, when butternut squash is at its sweetest. I don't bother peeling the squash if it's organically grown. Serve this with toothpicks or on bamboo skewers for an informal appetizer with a warm, nutty flavor.

2½ cups peeled butternut squash, cut into 1-inch cubes (see Note)
1 tablespoon olive oil
2 teaspoons fresh thyme (optional)

½ teaspoon salt
¼ teaspoon freshly ground black pepper

1. Preheat the oven to 375°F.

2. Mix the squash, oil, thyme, salt, and pepper.

Can be prepared up to this point 1 hour ahead.

3. Place a 12-inch iron skillet over high heat for 2 minutes.

SERVES 4 TO 6 AS AN HORS D'OEUVRE OR SIDE DISH

Preparation time: 15 minutes

Cooking time: 45 minutes

❧ *Roasted Butternut Squash is an excellent accompaniment to roasted lamb or pork.*

4. Crumple a paper towel and moisten a small area of it with a little olive oil by turning the bottle upside-down while holding the paper against the opening. Being careful not to burn your fingers, wipe the bottom of the hot skillet with the oil.

5. Add the squash to the skillet and immediately place in the oven.

6. Turn the squash once and shake the skillet a couple of times during roasting. The squash is cooked when the pieces are soft and slightly browned to charred in places, about 45 minutes. Serve warm.

Note: Don't crowd the skillet or the pieces won't brown properly. A medium butternut squash will yield 4 cups of diced squash. If you want to cook the entire squash, be sure to use 2 skillets or cook in 2 batches. If not, you can use the rest of the squash in Roasted Winter Squash Soup (page 74).

CHINO CAPONATA

My Chino Caponata has been evolving for twenty years. It began as a Chinese eggplant with garlic sauce, took on the influence of a French ratatouille, and I finally named it Chino Caponata when it acquired Italian overtones. Lusty and unbelievably versatile, I use it as an appetizer with Toast Rounds (page 47), as a side dish, as part of a buffet, and as a topping for pasta.

    This recipe can easily be doubled, but be sure to fry the eggplant in two batches to ensure proper charring—the secret to its intense, smoky taste.

*1 medium eggplant
   (approximately 1 pound)*
1 teaspoon salt

SEASONING SAUCE
*½ cup tomato sauce, preferably
   homemade (see page 34)*
1 tablespoon soy sauce
*1 tablespoon sherry vinegar or
   other vinegar of your choice*
2 teaspoons sugar

2 tablespoons medium-dry sherry
1 teaspoon chili oil (see page 43)
*1 tablespoon plus 1 teaspoon
   peanut oil*
1 cup chopped Spanish onion
1 tablespoon minced garlic
*1 red bell pepper, roasted
   (see page 38)*
*1 tablespoon chopped fresh
   oregano*
1 tablespoon drained small capers

*YIELDS 3¼ CUPS;
SERVES 8 TO 12 AS AN
HORS D'OEUVRE OR AS
PART OF AN ANTIPASTO,
6 AS A SIDE DISH*

*Preparation time:
40 minutes, plus 1
hour to salt the
eggplant*

*Cooking time:
10 minutes*

1. Trim off the ends of the eggplant and discard. Cut the eggplant into ½-inch cubes. Toss with the salt and set aside for 1 hour.

2. Rinse the eggplant cubes under running water. Let them drain in a colander for 10 minutes; blot well between paper towels.

3. Prepare the seasoning sauce by combining the tomato sauce, soy sauce, vinegar, sugar, sherry, and chili oil. Set aside.

4. Place a 12-inch wok or iron skillet over high heat until it smokes, 2 to 3 minutes. Add 2 teaspoons of the peanut oil. Immediately add the eggplant cubes. Stir every couple of minutes and press down repeatedly on the eggplant with the back of a spatula to aid scorching. Cook for approximately 5 minutes over high heat until the eggplant is soft and well-charred. Remove the eggplant from the pan.

5. Return the wok to a high heat and add the remaining 2 teaspoons of oil. Add the onion and fry, stirring frequently, until it begins to brown, about 2 minutes. Add the garlic and stir-fry for 1 minute more. Add the charred eggplant and seasoning sauce and stir until the sauce has been absorbed, about 1 minute. Add the roasted pepper, oregano, and capers and stir for a few seconds before removing from the heat. Serve warm or at room temperature.

Can be prepared up to 5 days in advance. Keep refrigerated. Return to room temperature before serving.

STUFFED CHERRY TOMATOES

YIELDS APPROXIMATELY 20, PLUS 1 CUP EXTRA PUREE

Preparation time: 20 minutes

T often make more of this yogurt and chickpea puree than I need so I'll have some the next day with which to stuff endive leaves. I also use the puree as a dip with crudités and chips.

For a light, quick meal, I enjoy these tomatoes with a simple, green salad and whole-wheat toast.

YOGURT AND CHICKPEA PUREE
1 cup cooked chickpeas, homemade (see page 35) or canned (see page 153)

½ cup nonfat yogurt
1 tablespoon grated Parmesan cheese
1 small garlic clove, minced

¼ teaspoon salt
⅛ teaspoon freshly ground black
  pepper
⅛ teaspoon ground cumin,
  preferably roasted (see page 40)

20 cherry tomatoes
  (approximately 1 pint)
Salt

1. Combine the chickpeas, yogurt, cheese, garlic, salt, pepper, and cumin in a blender and puree until smooth.

Puree can be prepared several days ahead. Refrigerate.

2. Cut the stem ends off the cherry tomatoes. Using a grapefruit spoon or other small spoon, scoop out the seeds and pulp. Lightly salt the insides of the tomatoes and turn them upside down to drain on several layers of paper towels.

Tomatoes should be prepared at least 30 minutes, but no more than 3 hours, before stuffing.

3. Stuff the cherry tomatoes with the chickpea puree. Serve cold or at room temperature.

Stuffed tomatoes can be prepared up to 1 hour before serving.

Unless they are perfectly ripe when I buy them, I allow tomatoes to ripen at room temperature for a few days before I eat them or put them in the refrigerator.

STUFFED MUSHROOMS, ZUCCHINI, AND PEPPERS

The most unusual event I ever catered was a three-day June wedding at a rustic hotel in the woods near Lake Placid. My staff and I prepared elaborate breakfasts, lunches, and dinners for the bride and groom and their ninety guests.

During the days this happy crowd canoed, hiked, and played tennis. When they gathered for cocktails in the evening, they devoured plates of these savory hors d'oeuvres.

If you prefer, increase the mushrooms to two boxes and omit the pepper and zucchini. The entire recipe can be doubled for a large party.

SERVES 12 OR MORE AS AN HORS D'OEUVRE OR PART OF AN ANTIPASTO

Preparation time: 30 to 40 minutes

Cooking time: 15 to 20 minutes

1 box button mushrooms (10 to 12 ounces)
Olive oil, to brush the vegetables
1 red or yellow bell pepper
1 small zucchini

STUFFING
¼ cup coarsely chopped shallots
1 tablespoon chopped garlic
1 tablespoon olive oil
½ red or yellow bell pepper, roasted

and chopped, with juice (see page 38)
¼ cup chopped oil-cured black olives
½ cup dried bread crumbs (see page 48)
1 egg, beaten
1 cup coarsely grated Parmesan cheese
¼ cup chopped fresh parsley

1. Rinse the mushrooms under a light spray of cold water. Pop the stems off with your fingers. Cut a thin slice of mushroom off the tops of the caps so they won't fall over when you broil them. Brush the hollow bottoms lightly with olive oil. Roughly chop the stems and pieces and set them aside.

2. Cut the bell pepper lengthwise into quarters. Remove the seeds and ribs. Cut each quarter in half crosswise. Rub lightly with olive oil. Cut the zucchini into 1-inch pieces and scoop out half of the center, turning each piece into a small bowl.

3. To make the stuffing, sauté the shallots and garlic in the olive oil until they soften, 2 to 3 minutes. Add the reserved mushroom stems and pieces. Cook until the mushrooms give up their liquid, 3 to 5 minutes. Remove from the heat.

4. Combine the mushroom mixture with the roasted pepper and its juice, olives, bread crumbs, egg, cheese, and parsley.

5. Place the mushroom caps, pepper pieces, and zucchini on a lightly greased cookie sheet or shallow pan and stuff them with the above mixture.

Vegetables can be stuffed several hours ahead.

6. Preheat the broiler. Brush or spray the tops of the stuffing lightly with olive oil.

7. Broil 6 inches from the heat until well-browned, 7 to 10 minutes.

8. Remove the mushrooms and zucchini from the oven. Turn the oven to 450°F. and bake the peppers for 5 minutes. Serve warm or at room temperature.

HUMMUS WITH HERBS AND SPICES

his hummus is different. It has less tahini than most and additional herbs and scallions.

When I prepare Hummus with Herbs and Spices to use on a sandwich, I make it thicker than when I use it as a dip. I start with a slice of multigrain bread, then a layer each of hummus, alfalfa sprouts, watercress, and thinly sliced avocado, and finally the top slice of bread.

YIELDS 2 ½ CUPS

Preparation time:
15 minutes

2 cups cooked chickpeas, home-
made (see page 35) or canned
(see page 153) with ¼ cup liquid
(see Note)
½ cup tahini
¼ cup lemon juice

½ cup chopped scallions, green and
white parts
½ cup chopped fresh parsley
1 teaspoon ground cumin, prefer-
ably roasted (see page 40)

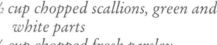

TAHINI

ahini is a paste made from ground sesame seeds. Joya and Sahadi, two of the better-known brands, are available at Middle Eastern groceries and most supermarkets.

If you expect to use the tahini within two months of opening the jar, it's not necessary to refrigerate (unless your kitchen is very hot).

When you first open the jar of tahini, you are likely to find the oil floating on top; the paste will have sunk to the bottom. Stir well with a chopstick or the handle of a wooden spoon to combine. The oil won't separate again.

Another way to blend the tahini is to empty the contents of the jar into a food processor or blender and then process until combined.

1. Combine the chickpeas, ¼ cup of the cooking liquid, tahini, and lemon juice in a blender or food processor. Process until completely smooth. It should have the consistency of thick mashed potatoes.

2. Add the scallions and parsley. Pulse on and off a few times until just combined. Add the cumin and stir. Add additional chickpea liquid, if you want a thinner mixture. Serve at room temperature.

Hummus can be prepared several days in advance. Refrigerate if you're keeping it overnight. Return to room temperature before serving.

Note: If you are using canned chickpeas, add water and lemon juice in place of the cooking liquid.

JÍCAMA WITH PICKLED GINGER DIPPING SAUCE

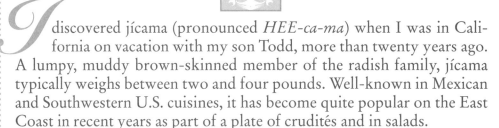

I discovered jícama (pronounced *HEE-ca-ma*) when I was in California on vacation with my son Todd, more than twenty years ago. A lumpy, muddy brown-skinned member of the radish family, jícama typically weighs between two and four pounds. Well-known in Mexican and Southwestern U.S. cuisines, it has become quite popular on the East Coast in recent years as part of a plate of crudités and in salads.

While they may not look promising, the interior of the jícama is delightfully crisp, white, and slightly sweet, a perfect foil for the sharp taste of the Pickled Ginger Dipping Sauce.

SERVES 8 OR MORE AS AN HORS D'OEUVRE

Preparation time: 15 to 20 minutes

PICKLED GINGER DIPPING SAUCE
½ cup rice vinegar
1 tablespoon plus 1 teaspoon sugar
¼ cup chopped pickled ginger (see page 45 or Note)
1 teaspoon chili oil (see page 43)
2 teaspoons Oriental sesame oil

2 tablespoons chopped scallions, green and white parts
¼ cup chopped fresh coriander (cilantro; optional)

1 small jícama (about 2 pounds)

1. To make the dipping sauce, combine the vinegar, sugar, pickled ginger, chili oil, and sesame oil in a bowl.

Sauce can be prepared to this point up to 1 week ahead. Keep refrigerated.

2. Add the scallions and coriander to the sauce the day you serve it.

3. Just before serving, peel the jícama and cut in julienne strips.

Note: Pickled ginger is also available at Oriental food stores and many supermarkets.

CURRIED ROASTED GARLIC SPREAD

YIELDS OVER 1 CUP

*Preparation time:
15 minutes, plus 1
hour to blend flavors*

*Cooking time:
40 minutes*

Roasted garlic has a soft, mellow taste. This spread can be served on Toast Rounds (page 47) or as a dip with crudités. It also makes a terrific low-fat topping for baked potatoes, grilled mushrooms, and steamed vegetables. I've even used it as a sandwich spread in place of mayonnaise. Leftover roasted garlic can be spread on bread in place of butter, tossed into pasta, added to a simple vinaigrette, or served as a condiment with beans, chicken, and grilled fish.

1 head garlic
½ teaspoon olive oil
2 tablespoons sour cream
1 cup plain nonfat yogurt
1 teaspoon ground cumin, preferably roasted (see page 40)

1 teaspoon curry powder
¼ teaspoon salt
¼ teaspoon freshly ground black
  pepper

Try this spread on a lamb sandwich for a nonvegetarian taste treat.

1. Preheat the oven to 375°F.

2. Leave the garlic whole. If there's a lot of papery skin near the top of the bulb, cut it off. Place the garlic in a small ovenproof dish. Drizzle the olive oil over the top, cover, and bake for 40 minutes. Uncover and let cool.

Garlic can be roasted up to 1 week ahead.

3. Combine the sour cream, yogurt, cumin, curry powder, salt, and pepper.

4. Remove the skins from 10 to 12 cloves of the roasted garlic by firmly pinching the root end of each clove until the soft garlic squeezes out.

Most garlic, except for purple spring garlic, has a green stem in the center of each clove. Remove this stem, as it adds a bitter taste.

Mash the cloves and add to the yogurt mixture. Let sit at room temperature for at least 1 hour to allow the flavors to combine.

The spread can be refrigerated for several days.

ARTICHOKES WITH MUSTARD VINAIGRETTE

I can think of nothing lovelier than a perfectly cooked artichoke. Rolande Circurel, a friend and talented artist, taught me this easy method. When cooked this way—with slivers of garlic tucked between the leaves and a bit of oil in the water—the taste of the artichoke needs no embellishment. I always make one or two extra to use the next day in Spring Artichoke Pasta (page 131).

I often serve this mustard vinaigrette alongside. The vinaigrette is also good with salads, steamed vegetables, and as a dipping sauce for crudités.

If possible, buy artichokes that are dark green with a slight tinge of purple and a minimal number of brown spots.

MUSTARD VINAIGRETTE
1 tablespoon Dijon-style mustard
½ teaspoon salt
4 teaspoons balsamic vinegar
2 tablespoons olive oil
2 tablespoons corn oil

¼ teaspoon freshly ground
    black pepper
4 large artichokes
2 garlic cloves, sliced
1 teaspoon salt
2 teaspoons olive oil

1. To prepare the vinaigrette, dissolve the mustard and salt in the balsamic vinegar. Add the olive oil, corn oil, and pepper and whisk until well blended.

Vinaigrette can be prepared several days ahead and refrigerated.

2. Using a serrated knife, cut 1 to 2 inches from the top of each artichoke. Cut off the remaining sharp-pointed tips of the leaves. (Scissors make the job easier.)

3. Insert the garlic slices between the leaves of each artichoke.

SERVES 4 AS A FIRST COURSE

Preparation time: 20 minutes

Cooking time: 25 to 30 minutes

4. Bring 4 inches of water to a boil. Add the salt and artichokes. Drizzle the olive oil over the artichokes, cover, and boil until the artichokes are cooked, 25 to 30 minutes depending on their size. They're done when you can pull out one of the leaves with only a bit of resistance. Artichokes can be served hot, at room temperature, or cold.

Pepper Surprises

SERVES 8 AS A FIRST COURSE, 12 TO 16 AS PART OF AN ANTIPASTO

Preparation time: 15 to 20 minutes

Cooking time: 25 minutes

I like these luscious little appetizers as a first course on a bed of arugula or watercress before a pasta entree, and as part of an antipasto of bite-size hors d'oeuvres.

3 red or yellow bell peppers
2 tablespoons oil-packed dried tomatoes, chopped, drained, with 1 tablespoon oil reserved
4 ounces mozzarella cheese, cut into small cubes or shredded (1 cup)
2 ounces cheddar cheese, cut into small cubes or shredded (½ cup)
Salt
¼ teaspoon freshly ground black pepper
⅓ cup chopped fresh basil

1. Preheat the oven to 400°F.

2. Cut the peppers vertically into quarters. Remove the seeds and ribs. Then cut each quarter in half crosswise.

3. Place a teaspoon of the tomato oil in the palms of your hands, and rub the peppers with the oil. Bake the peppers skin side down until they are fairly soft and scorched on the skin side, about 20 minutes.

4. While the peppers are roasting, place the mozzarella, cheddar, ½ teaspoon salt, pepper, basil, tomatoes, and the remaining 2 teaspoons of tomato oil in a bowl and toss well.

5. Remove the peppers from the oven and sprinkle them lightly with salt. Raise the oven temperature to 425°F.

6. When the peppers are cool enough to handle, place a tablespoon of the cheese mixture in the center of each piece of pepper.

Peppers can be prepared to this point several hours ahead. Refrigerate; return to room temperature before baking.

7. Bake the stuffed peppers until the cheese melts, 3 to 5 minutes. Serve hot or at room temperature.

Year-Round Bruschetta

This recipe is inspired by a bruschetta—a masterpiece of texture and flavor—I fell in love with at Sette Mezzo, a popular Manhattan restaurant. This version bears little resemblance to those served at most Italian restaurants or to the simple Bruschetta on page 63.

I used to make this bruschetta only in the late summer, when I could buy magnificent local beefsteak tomatoes. But these days I can generally find acceptable plum tomatoes all year. While certainly it's nice, it's not necessary to have excellent tomatoes with which to make this bruschetta.

Although usually served as an appetizer, I often make a lunch of it. If I have company, I might also serve the French Lentil Salad with Goat Cheese (page 113). Although traditionally made with Tuscan bread, any coarse-grained white bread with a good thick crust will do.

2 tablespoons olive oil
1 garlic clove

BRUSCHETTA MIXTURE
4 oil-packed dried tomatoes, drained
½ cup chopped tomato
1 roasted bell pepper (see page 38), chopped
12 oil-cured black olives, pitted and chopped
2 tablespoons drained capers

¼ cup finely diced blanched haricots verts (thin green beans) or asparagus
2 teaspoons balsamic vinegar
4 teaspoons olive oil
¼ teaspoon freshly ground black pepper
Salt to taste

16 pieces of bread, approximately 2 x 3 inches and ½ inch thick

1. Preheat the boiler.

2. Heat the olive oil in a small skillet. Crush the garlic and sauté lightly

for 2 minutes. Remove and discard the garlic and set the oil aside.

3. To make the bruschetta mixture, combine the dried and fresh tomatoes, roasted pepper, olives, capers, *haricots verts* or asparagus, vinegar, oil, pepper, and salt.

Garlic-infused oil and bruschetta mixture can be prepared up to 1 hour in advance.

4. Broil the bread quickly on one side, 30 seconds to 1 minute. Turn the bread over and paint the uncooked side lightly with a little of the garlic-steeped oil. Broil the second side for another 30 seconds.

5. Place the bruschetta mixture on top of the toasts and cut into bite-size pieces. Serve while still warm.

SIMPLE BRUSCHETTA

This bruschetta evokes memories for me of sunny skies and Italian cafes. While I make this bruschetta year-round, it's best in August or September, when local beefsteak and plum tomatoes are at their peak. When I'm in a hurry or I have unexpected company, I toss this together for an easy-to-make last-minute appetizer.

SERVES 8 AS AN APPE-TIZER, 12 OR MORE AS PART OF AN ANTIPASTO

Preparation time: 10 minutes

Cooking time: 5 minutes

2 tablespoons olive oil
1 garlic clove, cut in half

BRUSCHETTA MIXTURE
1 teaspoon balsamic vinegar
2 tablespoons olive oil
¾ teaspoon salt

Pinch of freshly ground black pepper
⅓ cup chopped fresh basil
3 cups chopped plum tomatoes

16 pieces of bread, approximately 2 x 3 inches and ½ inch thick

1. Heat the olive oil in a small skillet. Crush the garlic and sauté lightly for 2 minutes. Remove the garlic and set the oil aside.

2. To prepare the bruschetta mixture, combine the vinegar, oil, salt, pepper, basil, and tomatoes.

Garlic oil and bruschetta mixture can be prepared up to 1 hour in advance.

3. Broil the bread quickly on one side, 30 seconds to 1 minute. Turn the bread over and brush the uncooked side lightly with as much of the garlic-steeped oil as you need. Broil the second side for an additional 30 seconds.

4. Place the bruschetta mixture on top of the toasts and cut into bite-size pieces. Serve while the toast is still warm.

GRILLED SHIITAKE MUSHROOMS ON ARUGULA

*S*hiitake mushrooms have a rich, meaty flavor that contrasts well with the peppery arugula in this dish. The heat of the grilled mushrooms softens and mellows the arugula's bite; the marinade replaces salad dressing. No matter how much I make of this elegant appetizer, there never seems to be enough.

SEASONING SAUCE
2 tablespoons soy sauce
2 tablespoons Oriental sesame oil
2 tablespoons olive oil
2 teaspoons sugar
1 bunch arugula, stems removed

12 shiitake mushrooms, 1½ to 2½ inches across (approximately ½ pound)
4 teaspoons roasted sesame seeds (see page 40)

1. Prepare the seasoning sauce by combining the soy sauce, sesame oil, olive oil, and sugar.

Seasoning sauce can be prepared up to a week ahead.

2. Preheat the broiler.

3. Wash the arugula and spin dry. Place an equal amount on 6 salad plates.

4. Clean the mushrooms and remove the stems. Place them cup side up on a broiling rack.

5. Brush the seasoning sauce on the mushroom caps. Position the rack 4 to 6 inches from the heat and broil until the mushrooms look brown and crusty, 2 to 3 minutes. They cook very quickly, so keep an eye on them.

6. Immediately place the mushrooms on top of the arugula. Pour the small amount of seasoning sauce that's left in the pan over the arugula. Sprinkle with the roasted sesame seeds and serve.

Note: During the summer, I choose small shiitake mushrooms to grill. I leave the stems on, omit the arugula, and serve them at barbecues as finger food.

SHIITAKE MUSHROOMS

Several years ago, I visited a mushroom farm in Amityville, Virginia. What an extraordinary sight—thousands of huge mushrooms growing on logs. These farms provide a year-round supply of cultivated mushrooms with a wild mushroom flavor.

While available all year, shiitake mushrooms are most plentiful in spring and autumn. During the winter, the mushrooms are grown indoors on artificial logs. With parasollike caps that range in size from two to eight inches across, the most desirable are those with large tops, small stems, and a pronounced pleasant aroma. Avoid mushrooms that look shriveled or have no smell, as they'll also have no flavor.

To clean, simply brush them lightly with a dry pastry brush. These mushrooms are rarely dirty.

GRILLED EGGPLANT WITH MISO

SERVES 4 TO 6 AS A
FIRST COURSE

Preparation time:
10 minutes, plus 1
hour to salt the
eggplant; 30 minutes
to heat the grill

Cooking time:
5 minutes

I love this grilled eggplant no matter what the time of year it is. In the summer I prepare it on the grill; in the winter, in the oven.

The salty-sweet flavor of miso (page 72) makes this savory first course also a perfect side dish with any stir-fried vegetable and either white or brown rice. Although the nutritional value of miso is destroyed in the cooking, its characteristic taste is not harmed.

Salt
1 medium eggplant (about 1
    pound), cut into ½-inch-thick
    rounds

3 tablespoons light miso
¼ cup sake (Japanese rice wine)
Olive oil, for brushing

MENU FOR A PASTA DINNER SHOWCASING THE ANTIPASTO

BRAISED SPICED
LEEKS (PAGE 67)

ROASTED CHILE
PEPPERS (PAGE 38)

ANTIPASTO SALAD
(PAGE 111)

BRAISED ESCAROLE
WITH GARLIC
(PAGE 217)

PASTA CAPONATA
(PAGE 143)

BAKED EGG CUSTARD
(PAGE 250)

1. Salt the eggplant and set aside for 1 hour. Rinse, drain, and pat dry.

2. Meanwhile, make a fire in a covered barbecue and allow it to burn down so the coals are white-hot, about 30 minutes (see Note).

3. Combine the miso and sake in a small bowl and set aside.

4. Brush the eggplant slices lightly with oil. Lay them on the grill, cover, and cook until they are well-charred, about 3 minutes each side. Check after 2 minutes to make sure they aren't burning. If they seem to be cooking too fast, move them to the sides of the grill to finish at a lower heat.

5. Turn the eggplant slices over and spread with the miso and sake mixture. Cover the grill and cook for 3 minutes more. Serve hot.

Note: This eggplant can also be prepared in an oven. Broil the eggplant on both sides about 6 inches from the heat until well-charred, 2 to 4 minutes for each side. Remove from the oven. Turn the oven to 450°F., then spread miso on one side of the eggplant. Return the eggplant to the oven and bake until the miso is heated through, 1 to 2 minutes.

BRAISED SPICED LEEKS

SERVES 8 AS
PART OF AN ANTIPASTO
OR SIDE DISH

Preparation time:
10 minutes

Cooking time:
55 minutes

The sweet-salty flavor of soy sauce and honey highlights the mild onion taste of these leeks. The five-spice powder adds its pungent scent.

Not only are these aromatic leeks a regular item on my antipasto plate but I also enjoy them frequently as part of a vegetarian composed plate, as a side dish with any Chinese meal, and as an accompaniment to meat and chicken.

SEASONING SAUCE
¼ cup medium-dry sherry
2 tablespoons soy sauce
2 teaspoons honey
½ teaspoon five-spice powder

8 medium leeks
1½ cups vegetable stock (see page 30) or stock of your choice
1 tablespoon butter

1. Combine the sherry, soy sauce, honey, and five-spice powder. Set aside.

2. Trim the root ends of the leeks close, but not so close that the layers separate. Cut off the dark green part of the leeks and reserve for stock. Lay the leeks flat on a cutting surface and split them in half lengthwise almost all the way through to within an inch of the root end, making sure they don't separate. Rinse the leeks under warm running water, scrubbing lightly with a vegetable brush to remove all the sand.

3. Cook the leeks in the stock and butter over low heat in a partially covered ovenproof skillet until the liquid has almost evaporated, about 30 minutes.

4. Preheat the oven to 350°F.

5. Pour the seasoning sauce over the leeks and bake uncovered for 20 minutes. Remove the skillet from the oven and place over high heat. Baste the leeks several times, until the sauce has reduced and caramelized, 3 to 5 minutes. Serve hot or at room temperature.

Tomatoes Stuffed with Herbs and Cheese

While stuffed tomatoes are best in late summer or early fall, when succulent beefsteak tomatoes are available, I serve these any time of year that I find decent medium-size tomatoes.

*SERVES 8 AS PART OF
AN ANTIPASTO,
AS AN APPETIZER, AND
AS A SIDE DISH;
SERVES 4 AS A
FEATURED ENTREE*

*Preparation time:
15 to 20 minutes*

*Cooking time:
10 to 15 minutes*

2 tablespoons olive oil
4 medium tomatoes
*2 teaspoons chopped fresh oregano
  leaves, or ½ teaspoon dried*
*2 teaspoons chopped fresh thyme,
  or ½ teaspoon dried*
¼ cup chopped fresh parsley

½ cup dry bread crumbs (page 48)
*¼ cup shredded gruyère or cheddar
  cheese (1 ounce)*
½ teaspoon salt
*¼ teaspoon freshly ground black
  pepper*

1. Preheat the oven to 350°F. Lightly oil a lipped baking sheet with ½ teaspoon of olive oil.

2. Cut the tomatoes in half horizontally and gently squeeze out the seeds. Place them on the baking sheet cut side up.

3. Drizzle ½ teaspoon of olive oil into each hollow of the tomato halves.

4. Mix the oregano, thyme, parsley, bread crumbs, cheese, salt, and pepper and use to lightly fill the tomatoes. Sprinkle any remaining stuffing on the top.

5. Drizzle the remaining olive oil over the tops of the stuffed tomatoes. Bake until the tomatoes are soft and the cheese is melted, about 10 minutes. Run under a broiler until the bread crumbs and cheese begin to brown, 30 seconds to 1 minute. Watch carefully, as these can burn quickly. Serve hot or at room temperature.

I recommend using Italian flat-leaf parsley. The taste is superior to the curly variety.

Chapter 5

SOUPS, LIGHT AND SUBSTANTIAL

*W*ho doesn't love a steaming-hot bowl of soup on a cold winter night? Soup warms you inside and makes you feel that all is well with the world.

Soup can start a meal or be the meal. Some, like the Vegetable Soup with French Pesto, need only a warm loaf of crusty bread and an interesting dessert to make an informal winter dinner, whereas the Fresh Sweet Pea Soup could be the first course for a most elegant spring dinner party.

It takes ingenuity to make an outstanding vegetarian soup, but it can be done. You must compensate for the absence of cured pork, chicken stock, or veal glaze. I do this with strong, flavorful vegetable stocks, roasted peppers, dried mushrooms, roasted cumin, and numerous other spices and herbs.

Soup is often even better the day after you make it. Cook it a day or two ahead so it's waiting for you when you want it.

Asparagus Chowder

*W*hen spring arrives, long walks, beautiful flowers, and asparagus beckon to me. I welcome the season by making this soup with the first good asparagus I can find. I look for asparagus with tight tips and fresh-looking bottoms. New potatoes, red or white, should feel hard when you squeeze them.

This soup looks and tastes rich, but it has only a fraction of the fat of most chowders.

*SERVES 6
AS A FIRST COURSE,
4 AS A LIGHT ENTREE*

*Preparation time:
20 to 30 minutes*

*Cooking time:
30 to 35 minutes*

2 medium leeks, white part only, cleaned and chopped (about 2½ cups) (see page 32)
1 tablespoon butter
4 cups vegetable stock (see page 30) or stock of your choice
1 pound unpeeled new potatoes, cut into ¼- to ⅓-inch cubes
1 teaspoon salt

1 teaspoon fresh thyme leaves
2 pounds asparagus, cleaned, trimmed, and cut into ½-inch pieces
½ teaspoon freshly ground black pepper
¼ cup half-and-half
¼ cup finely chopped fresh parsley

1. In a heavy-bottom pot, sauté the leeks in butter over medium heat until they're soft but not brown, 6 to 7 minutes.

2. Add the stock, potatoes, salt, and thyme. Cover and bring to a boil. Lower the heat and simmer until the potatoes can be easily pierced with a fork, about 15 minutes.

3. Add the asparagus and pepper and simmer uncovered until the asparagus are cooked, about 10 minutes.

4. Transfer half the solids to a blender or food processor. Add the half-and-half and puree until smooth. Return this mixture to the pot and bring to a simmer over low heat. Serve hot, garnished with parsley.

This soup can be refrigerated for 2 days. Reheat gently before serving.

◀● I often make this chowder with chicken stock.

"Cream" of Carrot Soup

I can tell from their faces that some of my guests don't believe there is no cream in this rich, smooth soup. I've made it both with and without cream, and was surprised to find I like it even better without.

*Serves 6 to 8
as a first course*

*Preparation time:
20 minutes*

*Cooking time:
20 minutes*

2 cups chopped leeks, white and light green parts only (about 2 medium), cleaned before chopping
2 tablespoons olive oil
3 cups chopped unpeeled carrots
2 teaspoons sugar

2 tablespoons chopped fresh parsley
2 teaspoons salt
½ teaspoon freshly ground black pepper
6 cups vegetable stock (see page 30) or stock of your choice
2 tablespoons minced fresh dill

◀● This soup is also delicious when made with chicken stock.

1. In a large, heavy-bottom pot, sauté the leeks in the olive oil over medium-low heat until they're wilted, 3 to 4 minutes. Add the carrots, sugar, parsley, salt, and pepper. Stir.

2. Add the stock and turn the heat to high. Bring the soup to a boil, then turn the heat to low, cover, and simmer the soup until the carrots are soft, about 15 minutes.

3. Lift out the solids with a wire strainer or slotted spoon and put them in a food processor with a little of the liquid. Puree. Return the carrot puree to the pot, add the dill, and stir. Serve hot.

This soup can be refrigerated for 2 days. Reheat before serving.

MISO SOUP

Miso is a Japanese fermented soybean paste to which rice or barley is added; I prefer the rice miso.

Miso comes in an infinite number of shades from light tan, to reddish brown to deep, dark mahogany brown. The darker the miso, the longer the fermentation process and the stronger the flavor. To retain its full nutritional value, miso should not be cooked.

Stored in the refrigerator in a glass jar, miso will last for one year. Miso, udon noodles (Japanese wheat noodles), and tofu (also known as bean curd) can be purchased at health food stores and Asian markets.

1 teaspoon salt
2 ounces dry udon noodles
6 cups vegetable stock (see page 30) or water
2 unpeeled carrots, sliced on the diagonal
1 cup sugar-snap peas or snow peas, strings and ends removed
(about 3 ounces)
2 scallions, white and green parts cut into ¼-inch rounds
1 cup large-dice firm tofu
4 teaspoons light miso
4 teaspoons soy sauce
2 teaspoons Oriental sesame oil

1. Bring a medium to large pot of water to a boil. Add the salt and the noodles. Boil until the noodles are tender, 6 to 7 minutes.

2. Meanwhile, in a separate large pot, bring the stock to a rolling boil. Add the carrots and turn the heat to medium-low. Simmer until the carrots are cooked through, about 2 minutes. Add the peas and scallions and simmer 1 minute more. Add the tofu and cook for several seconds. Remove from the heat.

SERVES 4
AS A FIRST COURSE

Preparation time:
15 to 20 minutes

Cooking time:
10 minutes

To avoid a steam burn when removing the cover of a pot, slide it off horizontally.

3. Dissolve the miso in ¼ cup of the soup. (I use chopsticks to mix in the miso and help it dissolve.) Pour the miso mixture into the soup and add the soy sauce. Stir well.

4. Drain the noodles and add them to the soup. Serve piping hot with ½ teaspoon sesame oil added to each bowl.

FRESH SWEET PEA SOUP

I am a great fan of Jean-Georges Vongerichten, chef and owner of Jo-Jo, the well-known Manhattan restaurant in which he serves his distinctive rendition of light French food. He was generous enough to share this wonderful recipe with me.

This soup can be properly made only with fresh sweet peas, not frozen or dried. Ideally the water should be boiling as you pick the peas because the sugar in the peas begins to turn to starch soon after they're picked. Short of picking your own peas, go to the store and taste a pea from the pod. If it's sweet, buy the peas and make the soup immediately.

This wonderful soup is full of flavor, whether you make it with vegetable stock, chicken stock, or water. Most of the preparation time is spent shelling the peas. If you recruit a friend to help, the work goes quickly.

2 pounds fresh peas in the pod
2 cups chopped onions
1 medium leek, cleaned (page 32)
  and chopped (about 1¼ cups)
1 unpeeled carrot, chopped
2 tablespoons olive oil
3 cups vegetable stock (see page 30)
  or water
1 teaspoon salt
¼ teaspoon freshly ground black
  pepper

GARNISH
Sautéed leeks, celery, and carrots
Sourdough Croutons (page 47)

SERVES 4
AS A FIRST COURSE

Preparation time:
45 minutes to 1 hour

Cooking time:
50 minutes

1. Wash the pea pods, then shell the peas. Reserve the pods.

2. Sauté the onions, leek, and carrot in the olive oil until they wilt, about 5 minutes. Add the pea pods and the stock. Bring to a boil, reduce the heat to low, cover, and simmer for 40 minutes.

3. Strain the stock, discard the solids, and return the liquid to the saucepan. Add the peas and simmer until they're tender, about 5 minutes. Remove the peas and puree them in a little of the stock. Return the puree to the stock and simmer for 1 minute. Add the salt and pepper. Serve piping hot with a garnish of sautéed leeks, celery, carrots and croutons made from sourdough bread, if desired.

This soup is best served the same day, but will keep refrigerated for 1 day if necessary.

ROASTED WINTER SQUASH SOUP

*M*ost Thanksgivings I begin our traditional family dinner with a cup of this distinctive soup. For a light but satisfying autumn meal, I also serve a large bowl of it with a salad and a good coarse-grained bread.

To achieve its deep, rich flavor I roast the squash before adding it to the liquid.

SERVES 6 AS A FIRST COURSE, 4 AS A LIGHT ENTREE

Preparation time: 30 minutes

Cooking time: 1 hour

1 large acorn squash (about 2 pounds), or other winter squash
¼ cup shelled walnuts
1 teaspoon melted butter
1 medium leek, white and light green parts, cleaned (page 32) and chopped (about 1¼ cups)
1 tablespoon olive oil
1 tablespoon chopped fresh sage, or 1 teaspoon dried
⅛ teaspoon five-spice powder
4 cups vegetable stock (see page 30) or stock of your choice

½ teaspoon salt
¼ teaspoon freshly ground black pepper
1 small to medium apple

1. Preheat the oven to 375°F.

2. Halve and seed the squash. Turn the cut side down and bake on a cookie sheet or in a shallow roasting pan until the flesh is tender, 45 minutes to 1 hour.

3. Combine the walnuts with the melted butter and spread on a cookie sheet. Roast the walnuts alongside the squash until they turn deep brown, 7 to 8 minutes. Set aside.

4. Meanwhile, in a heavy-bottom pot, sauté the leek in the olive oil for 1 to 2 minutes. Add the sage and five-spice powder. Cover and cook until the leek is soft, about 10 minutes. Add the stock, salt, and pepper and bring to a simmer, then uncover.

5. Peel, core, and dice the apple. Add it to the simmering stock and cook until soft, about 15 minutes.

6. Remove the squash from its shell. Dice and add to the pot. Simmer for a few minutes, then puree the soup by passing it through a food mill or by pulsing in a blender or food processor.

Soup can be prepared several hours ahead.

7. When ready to serve, gently reheat the soup. Serve piping hot with the roasted walnuts sprinkled on top.

Summer Tomato Soup

A long time ago, I lived in Poplar Bluff, Missouri, for two years. Only synthetic-tasting supermarket tomatoes were available, so out of desperation I decided to grow my own.

After weeks of tending the seedlings, I found myself in an all-out battle with the blue jays and blackbirds over my budding tomatoes—and the birds were winning. I'd frighten them off by running at them, flapping my arms, and shouting, which was effective but exhausting. Besides, as soon as I left the house, they were back in attack waves.

I tried a scarecrow. The birds thought he made a great perch.

Finally I strung disposable aluminum pans—the kind supermarket

◄• *Chicken stock is good in this recipe.*

HOW TO PEEL TOMATOES QUICKLY AND EASILY

To make peeling tomatoes effortless, cut a one-inch-long cross on the side of each before you blanche them. Use a sharp knife—you want to slice through the skin without cutting deeply into the flesh.

Immerse the tomatoes in boiling water for thirty to sixty seconds. Quickly dunk them in ice water for several seconds, and the skins will slip off easily.

pies are baked in—along a cord. As the wind hit them they rattled and clattered and clashed together, creating a racket not even a blue jay could endure.

This was my favorite soup the summer of 1970, made from my own home-grown, bird-free tomatoes. Parmesan Toast (page 46) is the perfect crunchy accompaniment.

SERVES 4 TO 6

Preparation time: 30 minutes

Cooking time: 25 to 30 minutes

2 pounds tomatoes
2 tablespoons olive oil
1 medium red onion, chopped
2 tablespoons chopped garlic
1 teaspoon sugar
1⅓ teaspoons salt
½ teaspoon freshly ground black pepper
4 cups vegetable stock (see page 30) or stock of your choice
½ cup chopped fresh basil
¼ cup chopped fresh parsley

1. Blanch, peel, seed, and dice the tomatoes.

2. Heat a heavy-bottom saucepan over high heat for 1 minute. Add the olive oil and onion and lower the heat to medium. Sauté until the onion softens, 3 to 4 minutes. Add the garlic and sauté until light golden, 2 to 3 minutes.

3. Add the tomatoes, sugar, salt, and pepper. Simmer for 10 minutes.

4. Add the stock and simmer for 20 minutes. Add the basil and parsley; simmer for 5 minutes more. Serve piping hot.

This soup can be refrigerated for 2 days. Reheat before serving.

*SERVES 4
AS A FIRST COURSE*

Preparation time: 15 minutes

Cooking time: 10 minutes

WINTER TOMATO SOUP

To preserve the nutritional value of the yogurt, I prefer to serve this soup halfway between lukewarm and hot. I call this Winter Tomato Soup because I usually make it when the weather's cold and the only available tomatoes at the market send me racing for a can of good imported ones, but it's also good served cold in the summer.

Alicia Cajiao, a good friend and talented artist, helped me devise this soup one blustery winter afternoon.

1 quart vegetable stock (see page 30) or stock of your choice
1½ cups chopped onions
2 tablespoons olive oil
2 teaspoons minced garlic
1 tablespoon flour
Salt and lots of freshly ground

black pepper
1 teaspoon sugar
½ cup tomato sauce, preferably homemade (see page 34)
¼ cup chopped fresh basil
1 cup plain low-fat or nonfat yogurt

1. Heat the stock in a 1½- to 2-quart pot.

2. In a separate heavy-bottom saucepan, sautée the onions in 1 tablespoon of the olive oil over medium heat until the onions begin to soften, about 3 minutes. Add the garlic and sauté until golden, 3 minutes more.

3. Add the remaining tablespoon of olive oil. Heat for a few seconds, then add the flour. Stir for 2 minutes. Add the heated stock and stir well.

4. Add salt, pepper, and sugar. Stir for a few seconds. Add the tomato sauce and simmer for 30 minutes. Remove from the heat and whisk in the basil and the yogurt. Serve hot, at room temperature, or chilled.

This soup can be refrigerated for 2 days.

I *like to use Spanish onions—those large yellow onions that weigh in at about a pound apiece and are available year-round at the supermarket. They're a little milder than the small onions and a lot less trouble to peel.*

When available, I often substitute the increasingly popular mild onions like Walla Walla and Vidalia.

SERVES 8 TO 10 AS A
FIRST COURSE,
6 AS AN ENTREE

Preparation time:
20 to 30 minutes

Cooking time:
1½ to 2 hours

Garlic can burn in seconds, turn bitter, and ruin the dish you're cooking. Add other ingredients—such as onions, scallions, and ginger—to the pan first or along with the garlic; they add moisture, which keeps the garlic from burning.

BLACK BEAN SOUP WITH SHERRY

The flavor of this partially pureed black bean soup is based on a slow-cooked *sofrito*, which is a chopped vegetable mixture sautéed to form the base of a soup. This technique is used in many Latin American countries. It is said that an adequate *sofrito* can be made quickly, but a truly good one takes time and patience. Fortunately, other than an occasional stir, there is little work involved once the *sofrito* begins to cook.

SOFRITO
1 tablespoon olive oil
1 small onion, chopped
2 celery stalks, chopped
10 garlic cloves, chopped
8 shallots, finely chopped

6 cups Garden Salad Stock (see
    page 33) or stock of your choice
1 pound dried black beans, soaked

and drained (not canned)
½ teaspoon freshly ground black
    pepper
⅓ teaspoon Tabasco sauce
2 teaspoons ground cumin, prefer-
    ably roasted (see page 40)
1 teaspoon dried oregano
1 teaspoon dried thyme
1 to 2 teaspoons salt
⅓ cup medium-dry sherry

1. Heat the olive oil in a large, heavy-bottom saucepan over medium heat for 30 seconds. Reduce the heat to low, and add the onion, celery, garlic, and shallots. Sauté slowly, stirring occasionally, until the moisture evaporates and vegetables begin to turn golden, 30 to 40 minutes.

2. Add the stock, beans, ground pepper, Tabasco, cumin, oregano, and thyme and simmer until the beans are soft, 1 to 1½ hours. Stir once in a while to keep the beans from sticking to the bottom of the pot.

3. When the beans are soft, add 1 teaspoon of the salt. Taste and add more salt if needed. Puree one-third of the soup in a blender or food processor and return the pureed soup to the pot.

4. Add the sherry and cook for 5 minutes. Serve hot.

This soup can be refrigerated for 3 days. Reheat before serving.

MIDDLE-EASTERN CHICKPEA SOUP

This hearty soup is truly the proverbial meal-in-a-bowl. I eat it frequently, accompanied by good bread and followed by a salad. When flavorful fresh tomatoes are available, I use them. However, canned tomatoes work perfectly well here.

1 cup chopped onion
1 tablespoon olive oil
½ cup chopped unpeeled carrots
½ cup chopped celery
3 garlic cloves, minced
5 cups vegetable stock (see page 30)
   or stock of your choice
2 teaspoons salt
2 teaspoons ground cumin,
   preferably roasted (see page 40)
1 teaspoon freshly ground
   black pepper
1 bay leaf
⅓ cup white rice, washed and
   drained
2 tablespoons chopped fresh parsley
1 (16-ounce) can tomatoes

1 cup cooked chickpeas, homemade
   (see page 35) or canned (see
   page 153)

GARNISH
Lemon wedges
Chopped fresh coriander (cilantro)
Grated Parmesan cheese

SERVES 6 TO 8 AS A
FIRST COURSE

Preparation time:
20 minutes

Cooking time:
40 to 45 minutes

For optimal flavor, Parmesan cheese should be freshly grated. The best is *Parmigiano-Reggiano*. Its flavor is deep, rich, almost buttery, not sharp and salty like inferior Parmesan cheeses.

All *Parmigiano-Reggiano* comes from the region of Emilia-Romagna in Italy. Every process, from the diet of the cows to the exact time the cheese is aged, is regulated. Only cheese that conforms to these rigorous standards can bear this name.

1. In a large, heavy-bottom pot, sauté the onion in the olive oil until softened, 3 to 4 minutes. Add the carrots and celery, and cook until soft, another 3 to 4 minutes. Add the garlic and sauté until it begins to turn golden, 2 to 3 minutes.

2. Add the stock and turn the heat to high. Bring the soup to a simmer, then add the salt, cumin, pepper, bay leaf, rice, and parsley.

3. Empty the can of tomatoes with their liquid into a bowl. Squish the tomatoes thoroughly, then add the crushed tomatoes to the soup.

4. When the soup returns to a simmer, turn the heat to low. Cover and simmer for 30 minutes, stirring occasionally. Add the chickpeas and simmer an additional 30 minutes. Remove the bay leaf.

5. Serve piping hot. Garnish with lemon wedges, coriander, and a sprinkling of cheese.

This soup can be refrigerated for 3 days. Reheat before serving.

Escarole and White Bean Soup

Follow this peasant soup with a simple pasta like Spaghetti with Tomatoes, Basil, and Parsley (page 149) and a good store-bought bread for a tasty family dinner.

SERVES 8 TO 10 AS A SOUP COURSE, 6 AS A LIGHT ENTREE

Preparation time: 20 minutes

Cooking time: 15 minutes

2 bunches escarole, about 2 pounds (see Note)
1 Spanish onion, chopped
2 tablespoons olive oil
4 garlic cloves, minced
8 cups vegetable stock (see page 30) or stock of your choice
1 cup cooked white beans, home-made (see page 35) or canned (see page 153), with their liquid (see Note)

1 tablespoon salt
1 teaspoon freshly ground black pepper
⅔ cup grated Parmesan cheese

1. Wash the escarole and spin-dry. Cut into 1-inch pieces.

2. In a large, heavy-bottom pot, sauté the onion in the olive oil until it begins to brown, about 5 minutes. Add the garlic and sauté until it turns golden, 1 to 2 minutes. Add the escarole and sauté, stirring constantly for 2 to 3 minutes.

3. Add the stock and bring to a simmer over high heat. Add the white beans and bring to a simmer again, then turn the heat to low, cover, and simmer for 5 minutes. Add the salt and pepper, remove from the heat, and sprinkle the Parmesan on top. Serve hot.

The soup can be prepared a day ahead and refrigerated. Reheat gently.

Note: Swiss chard can be subtituted for the escarole. Or, to turn this soup into Escarole and Pasta Soup, substitute ⅓ cup orzo for the beans and simmer until the orzo is cooked through, about 8 minutes.

This soup is particularly good when prepared with chicken stock.

French Green Lentil Soup

*T*his soup is sophisticated enough for a fancy dinner party. I prefer to make it with the high-class French green lentils that can be purchased at many health-food stores. They're smaller than the common brown lentil and hold their shape better when cooked.

SERVES 6 AS A SOUP COURSE, 4 AS AN ENTREE

Preparation time: 20 to 30 minutes

Cooking time: about 1 hour

You can substitute water for stock when cooking any of the soup or bean recipes in this book.

1 tablespoon olive oil
1 large onion, diced
1 tablespoon minced garlic
1 tablespoon minced fresh ginger
6 cups vegetable stock (see page 30) or water
1 bay leaf
1 tablespoon ground cumin, preferably roasted (see page 40)
1½ cups lentils, washed and drained

1 teaspoon salt
½ teaspoon freshly ground black pepper
½ cup diced unpeeled carrots
½ cup diced celery
1 cup tomato sauce, preferably homemade (see page 34)
1 tablespoon Porcini Powder (page 42; see Note)
Fresh coriander (cilantro), for garnish (optional)

SERVES 8 TO 10 AS A FIRST COURSE, 6 AS AN ENTREE

Preparation time: 1 hour

Cooking time: 1½ to 2 hours

1. Heat the olive oil in a large, heavy-bottom saucepan. Add the onion, and sauté over medium heat until it begins to brown, 3 to 4 minutes. Add the garlic and sauté for 1 minute. Add the ginger and sauté for a few seconds.

2. Add the stock and bring to a simmer. Add the bay leaf, cumin, and lentils. If using mushrooms instead of the Porcini Powder, mince and add them to the soup now. Cover and simmer for 30 minutes.

3. Add salt, pepper, carrots, celery, tomato sauce, and Porcini Powder, if using. Cook over low heat for 30 to 45 minutes. Remove the bay leaf. Serve hot.

This soup can be refrigerated for 2 days. Reheat before serving.

Note: You can substitute 2 dried mushrooms for the Porcini Powder. Soak the mushrooms in 1 cup water for 30 minutes. Lift them from the soaking water and squeeze over the water to return any liquid to the cup, then dice. Strain the soaking water through a fine-mesh sieve and use it in place of 1 cup stock.

MINESTRONE

This Italian soup is one of my all-time favorites.

When my son Todd—now a grown man and a talented caterer and glass blower—was a little boy, I couldn't get him to eat vegetables. No matter what I did, he turned his nose up at them.

Then I discovered that he loved vegetable soup. Every day he came home from school starving, and I fed him this soup for his snack. I don't think he ever realized he was eating dreaded vegetables, and I certainly didn't tell him.

4 cups chopped leeks, white and dark green parts (about 3 medium; see Note)
¼ cup olive oil
1⅓ cups sliced unpeeled carrots
1⅓ cups sliced celery

1½ cups cooked kidney beans, homemade (see page 35), plus liquid
1½ cups diced unpeeled potatoes
2 cups canned tomatoes

1 cup peeled, seeded and diced
  fresh tomato
½ cup chopped fresh parsley
4 thyme sprigs
2 teaspoons dried oregano
2 teaspoons salt
½ teaspoon freshly ground
  black pepper

2 cups sliced button mushrooms
8 cups mushroom stock (see page
  32) or water
⅔ cup short pasta, such as
  orecchietti or small shells
Grated Parmesan cheese

When adding a new ingredient to soup, turn the heat to high. When the liquid returns to simmer, reduce the heat.

1. In a large, heavy-bottom pot, sauté the leeks in the olive oil until they soften, 4 to 5 minutes. Add the carrots and sauté 30 seconds. Add the celery, kidney beans, potatoes, canned and fresh tomatoes, parsley, thyme, oregano, salt, pepper, mushrooms, and stock. Simmer for 1 hour.

2. Add the pasta and cook for 30 minutes to 1 hour more, or until the soup is very thick. Remove the thyme sprigs. Sprinkle with grated cheese and serve hot.

The soup can be prepared several days ahead and refrigerated. Reheat gently.

Note: Use the whole leek except for the last 3 inches of the dark green. Reserve those ends for stock or discard.

SPLIT PEA AND LENTIL SOUP

Whenever I have my friend Joan Lewisohn over for dinner, she selects wines to match my menu—wines she has matured in her cellar that are no longer on the market. I serve her dishes prepared from my unpublished recipes. We have a great time, with each of us thinking she's gotten the better end of the deal. This tasty soup is her inspiration.

*SERVES 6 TO 8 AS A
FIRST COURSE*

*Preparation time:
20 minutes, plus 1
hour to soak the peas*

*Cooking time:
1 hour and 15 minutes*

**MENU FOR AN INFORMAL
EARLY SPRING DINNER**

....

*Vegetable Soup
with French Pesto
(page 84)*

*Braised Fava Beans
with Fresh Herbs
(page 163)*

*Grilled Polenta
(page 178)*

*Swiss Chard with
Shallots (page 216)*

*Slow-Cooked Rice
Pudding (page 253)*

1¼ cups yellow split peas (½ pound)
2 cups water
1 tablespoon olive oil
½ cup chopped onion
½ cup chopped celery
½ cup chopped unpeeled carrots
½ cup chopped parsnips
4 cups vegetable stock (see page 30)
   or water
1 bay leaf

2 cups peeled, seeded, and diced
   fresh tomatoes
1¼ cups lentils (½ pound),
   preferably French green lentils
¼ teaspoon freshly ground
   black pepper
2 teaspoons salt
1 teaspoon ground cumin,
   preferably roasted (see page 40)

1. Soak the split peas in the water for 1 hour.

2. Heat a large, heavy-bottom saucepan for 1 minute. Add the olive oil and then the onion. Sauté until the onion begins to color, about 5 minutes. Add the celery, carrots, and parsnips, and sauté until they soften, about 5 minutes.

3. Add the stock, bay leaf, tomatoes, lentils, and split peas and their soaking water (see Note). Bring to a simmer over high heat, add the pepper, and stir. Turn the heat to low, cover, and simmer until the beans are tender, about 1 hour. Add the salt and cumin. Remove the bay leaf. Serve piping hot.

This soup can be refrigerated for 2 days. Reheat before serving.

Note: Split peas are soaked to shorten the cooking time, not to remove oligosaccharides that can cause intestinal gas. Therefore, it's okay to use the soaking water, which has acquired some flavor from the peas.

*Serves 8 to 10 as a
first course,
6 as an entree*

✦

*Preparation time:
30 minutes*

✦

*Cooking time:
30 minutes*

Vegetable Soup with French Pesto

*T*his soul-satisfying soup is one of a handful of my recipes that have evolved over many years. French country women first created this impressive soup to celebrate the start of the fresh basil and *haricots* season. When fresh cranberry beans are available, I substitute them for the dried white beans.

FRENCH PESTO
3 garlic cloves, minced
¼ cup chopped fresh parsley
3 tablespoons olive oil
3 cups chopped fresh basil
½ cup freshly grated Parmesan
    cheese

1 tablespoon olive oil
1 cup diced unpeeled carrots
1 cup diced celery
2 medium leeks, white and light
    green parts, cleaned (page 32)
    and chopped

8 cups vegetable stock (see page 30)
    or water
2 cups diced tomatoes
2 teaspoons salt
½ teaspoon freshly ground black
    pepper
¼ teaspoon saffron threads
1½ cups cooked small white beans,
    homemade (see page 35) or
    canned (see page 153)
2 cups green beans, cut into 2-inch-
    long pieces (about ½ pound)
2 cups diced zucchini (2 small)

1. To prepare the pesto, combine the garlic, parsley, olive oil, basil, and cheese in a blender or food processor and puree briefly. Set aside.

2. In a large, heavy-bottom pot, heat the olive oil. Add the carrots, celery, and leeks; sauté over low heat until the vegetables are soft but not brown, 5 to 10 minutes.

3. Add the stock and with the pot uncovered, bring to a simmer over high heat. Lower the heat, add the tomatoes, and simmer for 15 minutes. Add the salt, pepper, and saffron and simmer for a few minutes more.

4. Add the white beans and cook for a few minutes, then add the string beans and cook for 5 minutes. Add the zucchini and simmer 3 minutes more.

5. Place the pesto in a soup tureen. Add 1 cup of the simmering soup and mix well. Add the remaining soup and stir. Serve immediately.

This soup can be refrigerated for 2 days. Reheat gently before serving.

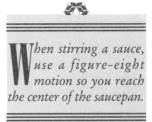

When stirring a sauce, use a figure-eight motion so you reach the center of the saucepan.

Chapter 6

VEGETABLE SALADS

Instead of using a bowl, I often combine the ingredients for my salad dressings in a glass jar with a tight-fitting cover. I shake the ingredients instead of whisking them. Any leftover dressing is ready to be stored in the refrigerator, with no bowl to wash. Allow the dressing to return to room temperature and shake vigorously just before using.

The dressing is the one part of the salad that's usually high in fat. Add it sparingly; it takes surprisingly little to coat vegetables. Remember, you want to moisten, not drown them.

At the age of forty-eight, I find it increasingly easy to gain weight and more difficult to keep my cholesterol low. I have to be conscious of what I eat to keep myself in good health. As a result, I've come to rely more on vegetable salads. I try to eat at least one every day.

At home I frequently have a leafy-green salad for lunch with a piece of cheese, a couple of olives, and a slice of good bread. One of my favorite lunches is a mixture of bitter and mild greens tossed with a light vinaigrette and topped with a warmed piece of goat cheese, on which I've sprinkled roasted sesame seeds.

Many evenings I have a salad at dinner as well. When given a choice, I eat the salad first. It fills me up so I eat less of the main course—a trick I learned from the late Adele Davis, one of the first authors to influence my health and eating habits. Large vegetable salads, moderate portions of everything else, and a couple quarts of water a day have been the key to keeping my waistline over the years—along with my daily hour of exercise.

While I love salad greens, they can't be counted on to stay fresh for more than two or three days. Every once in a while I crave a salad and think there is nothing appropriate in the refrigerator. Finally I've come to realize I don't need leafy greens to make a marvelous salad.

I always have some of the following around: carrots, celery, avocados, cucumbers, tomatoes, parsley, coriander, red onions, scallions, and red cabbage; also cauliflower, broccoli, and string beans, which can quickly be blanched. These vegetables keep at least a week and tend to be in most kitchens.

Invent your own salad. Chop a few vegetables that seem appealing together and add any dressing from this chapter. It's hard to go wrong.

ASPARAGUS AND CARROT VINAIGRETTE

SERVES 4 AS A
FIRST COURSE

Preparation time:
20 minutes

Cooking time:
5 minutes

In my quest for "perfect health," I visited a French doctor, Dominique Richard, a homeopathic practitioner at Bio-Essentials in New York City. Dominique's own radiant good health and *joie de vivre* inspired immediate confidence in me. He prescribed homeopathic drops to take thirty minutes before eating to increase my energy. And it worked—the drops made me feel better than ever.

In addition to improving my health, Dominique shared several of his wonderful recipes. This dish was inspired by one of those recipes.

TAHINI VINAIGRETTE
¼ cup lemon juice
¼ cup olive oil
2 tablespoons tahini
1 tablespoon mirin (see Note)
1 teaspoon Dijon-style mustard

2 tablespoons soy sauce

1 pound asparagus
2 scallions, white and green parts
1 cup coarsely grated unpeeled carrots

1. To prepare the vinaigrette, combine the lemon juice, olive oil, tahini, mirin, mustard, and soy sauce and whisk until blended. Set aside.

The vinaigrette can be prepared several hours ahead.

2. Cut the tender part of the asparagus into 2-inch pieces. Blanch for 3 to 4 minutes, then submerge in ice water; drain.

3. Cut the scallions in half lengthwise, then cut into ½-inch pieces.

4. Combine the asparagus, scallions, and carrots. Toss with as much of the dressing as you need to coat the vegetables.

The salad can be prepared up to 1 hour ahead.

Note: Mirin is a low-alcohol sweet wine used frequently in Japanese cooking. It's available in Oriental food stores and most supermarkets.

For the asparagus, you can substitute broccoli, snow peas, sugar-snap peas, cauliflower, or string beans.

Remove the tough part of the asparagus by holding the bottom of one spear at a time in a gently closed fist. With your dominant hand, slap the spear firmly. The asparagus spear will break cleanly right at the place where it changes from tender to tough.

GREEN BEANS WITH DOUBLE SESAME DRESSING

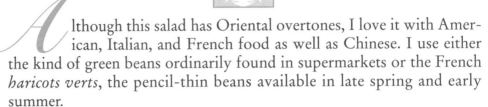

lthough this salad has Oriental overtones, I love it with American, Italian, and French food as well as Chinese. I use either the kind of green beans ordinarily found in supermarkets or the French *haricots verts*, the pencil-thin beans available in late spring and early summer.

When I cook green beans I remove only the stem end of the bean; the tip contains lots of vitamins.

DOUBLE SESAME DRESSING
2 tablespoons sherry vinegar
2 tablespoons soy sauce
1½ tablespoons peanut oil
½ tablespoon Oriental sesame oil
1 tablespoon ground roasted

sesame seeds (see page 40)
*¼ teaspoon freshly ground black
   pepper*

1 pound green beans, trimmed

1. To prepare the dressing, combine the vinegar, soy sauce, peanut oil, sesame oil, sesame seeds, and pepper. Whisk or shake in a tightly covered jar until blended.

Dressing can be prepared several hours in advance.

2. Steam the beans for 3 to 4 minutes, then plunge them in ice water. Drain well.

3. Put the beans in a serving bowl, then toss with as much of the dressing as you need to coat the string beans. Serve.

The salad can be prepared up to 3 hours ahead.

TO CLEAN GREENS: SUBMERGE, LIFT, AND SPIN

Fill a bowl with cold water, then add the greens. It's important to put the water in the bowl first, otherwise the greens can be bruised by the running water.

If the greens come tied together, as do arugula, spinach, and watercress, leave them bunched and cut through the stems with a single knife stroke. Discard the stems and submerge the greens.

Lift the greens out of the water, allowing the dirt and grit to settle to the bottom of the bowl. Empty the bowl and refill it with fresh water. Repeat this process until the water is clean and no dirt or grit is left when you remove the greens. Spin the greens dry. Wrap the vegetables in cotton dish towels and refrigerate until ready to use. Radicchio and endives should be submerged whole and dried with a towel. Organically grown mesclun needs no washing, drying, or cutting.

FRESH BEET SALAD WITH ORANGES AND FRIED ONIONS

This unusual and intensely flavorful beet salad was inspired by Rich Faron, a well-known chef in East Hampton, New York.
Although more time-consuming to make than other salads in this book, the complex flavors of sweet beets, tangy oranges, and deep, dark fried onions make it well worth the effort.

SERVES 6 TO 8 AS A
FIRST COURSE, OR AS
PART OF A BUFFET;
4 AS AN ENTREE FOR
LUNCH

Preparation time:
30 minutes

Cooking time:
40 minutes

4 medium or 6 to 8 small beets
1 rosemary sprig
¼ cup rice vinegar
¼ cup orange juice
½ teaspoon salt
2 medium oranges
½ tablespoon olive oil
1½ cups thinly sliced onions

BEET DRESSING
1 tablespoon olive oil
1 teaspoon balsamic vinegar

1 to 2 ounces Roquefort cheese
(optional)

1. Remove the stems and leaves from the beets, leaving an inch or two of stem attached to keep the beets from bleeding (see Note). Scrub the beets with a vegetable brush to clean them. Steam until almost soft, 15 to 20 minutes. To test, pierce a beet with a poultry skewer; the skewer should go through with only a trace of resistance. Remove the beets from the steamer and set them aside to cool.

2. Reduce the liquid remaining in the pot to 1 cup. If you should end up with less than 1 cup of liquid, add enough water to make 1 cup.

3. Place the beet liquid, rosemary, rice vinegar, orange juice, and salt in a saucepan and reduce over a low heat until ¼ cup remains, about 10 minutes. Remove from the heat and allow to cool. Peel and set aside.

4. Meanwhile, peel and section the orange, removing the white membrane. Set aside.

5. Heat a cast-iron skillet over high heat for 2 minutes. Add the olive oil and then the onions, lower the heat to medium, and sauté the onions until they're almost black, 10 to 15 minutes. Allow to cool.

6. When the beets have cooled, cut them into thin strips.

Can be prepared to this point 1 day ahead. Cover and refrigerate until ready to serve.

7. To make the beet dressing, add the olive oil and balsamic vinegar to the reserved ¼ cup of reduced beet mixture and stir until blended.

8. Place the dressing in a bowl. Add the orange sections, sautéed onions, and julienned beets. Gently fold together. I serve this on a white platter with small chunks of cheese around the edges of the beets.

Note: Save the young, tender beet greens. When blanched, they can substitute for Swiss chard.

Fresh Beets with Yogurt Dressing

SERVES 6 AS A
FIRST COURSE

Preparation time:
20 minutes

Cooking time:
20 minutes

Years ago I made this salad dressing with only sour cream. Now I use a mixture of yogurt and sour cream. I prefer the lighter taste. The dressing can also be used on cucumbers, coleslaw, and blanched cauliflower.

1 bunch medium beets (about
1½ pounds)

YOGURT DRESSING
6 tablespoons plain low-fat yogurt
2 tablespoons sour cream
2 tablespoons lemon juice
2 teaspoons Dijon-style mustard
1 teaspoon salt

½ teaspoon freshly ground black
pepper
¼ cup minced fresh chives
¼ cup minced fresh dill
1 teaspoon sugar

1 head leafy lettuce, such as ro-
maine, Boston, or loose-leaf

1. Remove the stems from the beets, leaving an inch attached to keep the beets from bleeding. Scrub the beets, but do not peel them.

2. Steam the beets until they are cooked through, about 20 minutes. Test to see if the beets are cooked by piercing one with a poultry skewer until it passes through the beets easily. Drain the beets. Allow them to cool, then peel.

3. While the beets are cooling, prepare the dressing by combining the yogurt, sour cream, lemon juice, mustard, salt, pepper, chives, dill, and sugar. Whisk until blended.

Beets and dressing can be prepared up to 1 day in advance. Keep them refrigerated in separate containers.

4. Place the lettuce around the edges of a platter, leaving the center clear. Slice the beets and toss gently with the dressing. Place the beets in the center. Serve cold or at room temperature.

Fennel and Orange Salad with Herb-Lime Vinaigrette

SERVES 6 AS A FIRST COURSE, 8 TO 12 AS PART OF A BUFFET

Preparation time: 15 minutes

*T*particularly like this salad in December, when clementines, those wonderfully sweet-tart seedless tangerines, are around. The clean, sharp flavor of this salad goes particularly well before beans or a robust pasta.

HERB-LIME VINAIGRETTE
1 tablespoon olive oil
1 tablespoon lime juice
1 teaspoon fresh thyme or oregano
¼ teaspoon salt
⅛ teaspoon freshly ground black pepper

1 medium to large fennel bulb
2 to 3 clementines, or 1 large navel orange
1 bunch arugula or watercress

To cut fennel, first slice off its feathery top. Then remove a thin slice off the bottom, but don't remove the core. Next cut the bulb lengthwise down the center. Cut each half lengthwise in half again. The fennel will be in quarters, the layers held together by the edible center core.

The fennel is now ready to be cut according to the recipe's instructions.

1. To prepare the vinaigrette, combine the oil, lime juice, thyme or oregano, salt, and pepper and whisk until blended or shake in a covered jar.

The vinaigrette can be prepared several hours ahead.

2. Remove the stalks and fronds of the fennel and discard, saving only the bulb. Cut away any brown or dry-looking spots from the top layer of the bulb. Julienne the fennel bulb into thin strips.

3. Peel and divide the clementines into segments. Wash and dry the arugula and divide equally on 4 plates.

4. Toss the fennel and orange with the vinaigrette and place on top of the arugula. Serve.

Bitter Greens with Tomato-Olive Dressing

SERVES 6 AS A FIRST COURSE,
4 AS A LIGHT LUNCH

Preparation time: 20 minutes, plus 1 hour to blend flavors

Before she married, my mother was a vaudeville dancer. In her act she wrapped her body around her partner, slithering to the sensuous notes of a clarinet and a softly played drum, pretending to be a snake. Needless to say, she had to be slender and agile.

All her life my mother worked hard at staying thin. Most days lunch was half a grapefruit and a hard-boiled egg—with a cracker or two thrown in if she was really hungry. However, she loved this salad and happily ate it in place of her regular lunch whenever I prepared it.

TOMATO DRESSING
1 plum tomato, chopped
1 scallion, white and green parts chopped
2 tablespoons chopped black or green olives
3 tablespoons olive oil
1½ teaspoons balsamic vinegar

1 teaspoon salt
⅛ teaspoon freshly ground black pepper

1 small head radicchio
1 bunch arugula
2 Belgian endives

1. To make the dressing, combine the tomato, scallion, olives, olive oil, vinegar, salt, and pepper. Set aside for 1 hour.

2. Just before serving, toss the radicchio, arugula, and endives with the dressing.

Guacamole Salad

SERVES 8 AS A FIRST COURSE

Preparation time: 20 to 30 minutes

I invented this spicy salad quite by accident. I wanted a salad, but there were no greens in the house—only an avocado, a tomato, and a few other odds and ends in the refrigerator. When I tossed together the few vegetables I did have, I was delighted with the results. It was then I realized I didn't need lettuce to make a great salad. However, if I have greens, I use them as a bed for this Guacamole Salad.

LIME VINAIGRETTE
¼ *teaspoon salt*
1 *teaspoon lime juice*
¼ *teaspoon freshly ground black*
  pepper
2 *tablespoons olive oil*

1 *medium avocado, peeled and diced*
2 *kirby cucumbers, seeded and*
  diced (about 1 cup)

2 *medium tomatoes, seeded and*
  diced
2 *scallions, white and green parts,*
  cut into ⅛*-inch rounds*
1 *cup diced celery*
8 *cups chopped romaine lettuce, in*
  2-inch pieces (if available)
1 *bunch watercress, stems removed*
  and cut into quarters (if
  available)

1. To make the vinaigrette, stir the salt into the lime juice. Add the pepper and olive oil. Beat with a wire whisk, or shake in a tightly covered jar, until blended.

2. Combine the avocado, cucumbers, tomatoes, scallions, and celery in a bowl. Add only as much vinaigrette as you need to coat the vegetables.

3. Wash and dry the lettuce and watercress. Make a bed of them and top with the avocado mixture. Serve.

MESCLUN, BLUE CHEESE, AND PEARS

SERVES 6 TO 8 AS A
FIRST COURSE, 4 AS A
LIGHT LUNCH

Preparation time:
15 minutes

This is one of my personal favorites for lunch.

Bleu d'auvergne is my first choice for this salad, but any good blue cheese can be substituted. Make sure to buy the pears a few days in advance and allow them to ripen at room temperature to their full sweetness.

For the mesclun, which is a combination of seven or more baby field lettuces, you can substitute your own combination. Any two or three of the following together will work: Belgian endives, arugula, radicchio, oak leaf, and frisée.

I also use Basic Balsamic Vinaigrette frequently on this salad.

RED WINE VINAIGRETTE
2 tablespoons red wine vinegar
1 teaspoon Dijon-style mustard
⅓ teaspoon salt
⅛ teaspoon freshly ground black
*   pepper*
¼ cup olive oil

1 garlic clove, crushed
6 cups mesclun, or a combination
*   of radicchio, arugula, and*
*   Belgian endives*
2 ripe pears, peeled and sliced
4 ounces blue cheese (see Note)
2 tablespoons ground roasted
*   sesame seeds (see page 40)*

1. To make the vinaigrette, combine the vinegar, mustard, salt, pepper, and oil and whisk or shake in a tightly covered jar until blended.

The vinaigrette can be prepared several days ahead and refrigerated. Return to room temperature before using.

2. Add the garlic to the salad dressing.

3. In a large bowl, toss the mesclun with enough of the salad dressing to coat the leaves. Place the dressed leaves on a light-colored serving plate. Surround the leaves with the sliced pears.

4. Crumble the cheese and sprinkle across the top of the mesclun. Scatter the ground sesame over the cheese.

Note: I also serve this salad without the blue cheese, especially when the entree is rich or has cheese in it.

Orange, Avocado, and Radish Salad

Preparation time: 30 minutes

*P*retty and colorful, this is one of my favorite winter salads. The dressing is also good on a simple salad of greens, sliced orange or grapefruit, and a bit of chopped red onion or toasted almonds on top.

Citrus Dressing
1 teaspoon salt
3 tablespoons lemon juice
1 tablespoon orange juice
1 teaspoon Dijon-style mustard
¼ teaspoon freshly ground black pepper
¼ cup olive oil

6 cups chopped romaine, red leaf, or oak leaf lettuce, in 2-inch pieces
2 or 3 navel oranges
1 medium avocado, halved and pitted
1 cup sliced red radishes or icicle radish (daikon)
1 garlic clove, crushed

1. Make the dressing by combining the salt, lemon juice, orange juice, and mustard in a jar with a tight-fitting lid. Add the pepper and oil.

Dressing can be prepared several hours ahead.

2. Make a base of the lettuce on a flat serving platter or individual plates.

3. Peel and slice the oranges in half lengthwise, then cut into ¼-inch-thick slices.

4. Cut the avocado in half lengthwise. Twist the two halves to separate them and remove the pit. Peel the avocado and cut into ¼-inch-thick slices.

5. Arrange the orange and avocado slices alternately over the lettuce. Scatter the radish slices over the top.

6. Add garlic to the dressing, cover, and shake. Pour the dressing over the salad and serve.

*W*hen you open a bottle of red wine vinegar, add a tablespoon of red wine. It will deepen and enhance the flavor of the vinegar.

Salad Niçoise

In the spring I make this salad with tender *haricots verts*, the thin green beans the French adore that have recently become popular in this country.

Then in early fall, when I'm out at the far end of Long Island, I search for the freshly dug new potatoes that are a specialty of the area.

Even in February you can now find excellent new red potatoes at the supermarket. Fingerlings and Creamers—small new potatoes with creamy textures—are available from California all year long.

The vinaigrette can be used with any bean salad.

Fresh Thyme Vinaigrette
1 tablespoon Dijon-style mustard
2½ tablespoons red or white wine
*   vinegar*
3 tablespoons olive oil
2 tablespoons corn oil
2 teaspoons chopped fresh thyme
1 teaspoon salt

½ teaspoon freshly ground black
*   pepper*

1½ pounds new potatoes
1 pound green beans
¼ cup snipped chives or chopped
*   red onion*
2 tablespoons chopped fresh parsley

1. To make the vinaigrette, combine the mustard, vinegar, olive oil, corn oil, thyme, salt, and pepper and whisk or shake in a tightly covered jar until blended.

The vinaigrette can be prepared several hours ahead.

2. Scrub the new potatoes, but do not peel. Steam until they can be easily pierced, 15 to 20 minutes. Allow the potatoes to cool slightly, about 10 minutes.

3. While the potatoes are cooling, steam the beans until they are cooked through, 4 to 6 minutes depending on their size. Submerge in ice water to stop the cooking. Cut large beans into 1-inch pieces; leave small ones whole.

4. When the potatoes are cool enough to handle but still warm, cut them into quarters or sixths, depending on their size. Remove 2 tablespoons of

SERVES 4 AS AN ENTREE, 6 TO 8 AS A FIRST COURSE

Preparation time: 20 to 25 minutes

Cooking time: 20 to 25 minutes

MENU FOR A LUNCH WITH GUESTS

SALAD NIÇOISE (PAGE 99)

BASIC WHITE BEANS (PAGE 35)

RED-COOKED CABBAGE (PAGE 214)

CHOCOLATE ANGEL FOOD CAKE (PAGE 247)

the dressing and set aside. Mix the potatoes with the remaining dressing. Gently fold in the chives and parsley with a wooden spoon or rubber spatula. Spread the potatoes on a flat plate.

5. Mix the beans with the 2 tablespoons of dressing. Place on top of the potatoes, leaving a 2-inch rim of potatoes showing all around. This is best served while the potatoes are still warm, but can also be served at room temperature.

BAKED TOMATO SLICES WITH GOAT CHEESE

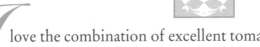

I love the combination of excellent tomatoes with fresh goat cheese. Once at the end of August, on a pre-autumnal day when I was tired of my usual summer salads, I invented this dish. The goat cheese softens as it warms, changing both its flavor and consistency, so that even when the cheese returns to room temperature it has a new taste and texture.

These are best made in the late summer, when tomatoes are at their peak. I also serve these hot from the oven as part of a composed plate.

SERVES 6 AS A FIRST COURSE, SIDE DISH, OR AS PART OF A BUFFET

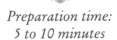

Preparation time: 5 to 10 minutes

Cooking time: 5 minutes

1 teaspoon olive oil
2 large or 3 medium tomatoes
¼ cup fresh goat cheese (1 ounce)
1 to 2 tablespoons skim milk
1 tablespoon shredded fresh basil

⅛ teaspoon freshly ground black
   pepper
Salt to taste
2 bunches watercress or arugula
1 to 2 teaspoons roasted sesame
   seeds (see page 40)

1. Preheat the oven to 450°F.

2. Spray or lightly coat a baking pan with olive oil.

3. Remove a thin slice from the top of the tomatoes and reserve for another use or discard. Slice each tomato into 3 thick slices, and place them on the pan.

4. Mash the goat cheese with enough of the skim milk to moisten and make it creamy. Mix in the basil and pepper. Add salt, if needed.

5. Top the tomato slices with the goat cheese mixture. Bake until the cheese begins to turn golden, 3 to 5 minutes.

6. Place the watercress or arugula on the individual salad plates. Top with the baked tomato slices. Sprinkle with the roasted sesame seeds. Serve warm or at room temperature.

CHERRY TOMATO AND ONION SALAD

SERVES 6 TO 8 AS A FIRST COURSE

Preparation time: 10 minutes

The jewellike combination of red and yellow cherry tomatoes makes this a beautiful salad, especially during the dreary days of winter. But don't worry if you can't find yellow cherry tomatoes—the salad tastes just as good when made with all red ones.

2 cups (1 pint) red cherry tomatoes
2 cups (1 pint) yellow cherry toma-
    toes, or 2 additional cups of red
    cherry tomatoes
½ cup diced red onion

HERB VINAIGRETTE
2 tablespoons rice vinegar or white
    wine vinegar

2 tablespoons olive oil
2 tablespoons chopped fresh
    oregano, basil, coriander, or
    parsley, or a combination
Salt and freshly ground black
    pepper to taste

2 bunches watercress

1. Cut the tomatoes in halves or quarters, depending on their size. Mix with the onion.

2. In a separate bowl, combine the vinegar, oil, and oregano and whisk until blended. Add salt and pepper to taste. Pour over the tomatoes and onion and toss.

Can be prepared to this point up to 2 hours ahead.

3. Wash and dry the watercress. Divide equally on the individual serving plates. Top with the tomatoes and onions. Serve.

CHOPPED SALAD

SERVES 6 AS A FIRST COURSE, 8 OR MORE AS PART OF A BUFFET

Preparation time: 20 minutes, plus 1 hour for chilling greens

This is my version of an Italian salad served at many fine restaurants. Since the leafy-greens are shredded, it's an ideal salad to serve as part of a buffet: no big pieces of lettuce that are hard to transfer from the serving plate to your plate.

Sometimes I substitute the Porcini Vinaigrette (page 49) for this balsamic dressing.

BALSAMIC MUSTARD VINAIGRETTE
1½ teaspoons Dijon-style
 mustard
½ teaspoon salt
⅛ teaspoon freshly ground black
 pepper
½ tablespoon red wine vinegar
1 tablespoon balsamic vinegar
¼ cup olive oil

1 head bibb lettuce or ½ head
 Boston lettuce
1 bunch arugula
1 head radicchio
2 Belgian endives
¼ cup chopped fresh coriander
 (cilantro)
½ cup chopped fresh dill
1 grated unpeeled carrot
1 bunch chives, snipped

When you're going to serve red onions raw, soak them in ice water for 30 minutes, then drain. This will make the onions milder and more digestible.

1. To make the vinaigrette, dissolve the mustard, salt, and pepper in the red wine and balsamic vinegars. Using a wire whisk, beat the olive oil in slowly.

Dressing can be prepared up to 1 week ahead and refrigerated. Return to room temperature before serving.

2. Wash the lettuce, arugula, radicchio, endives, coriander, and dill. Spin-dry. Wrap the lettuce and herbs in a cotton towel.

Refrigerate the greens for at least 1 hour, but not overnight.

3. Shred the lettuce, arugula, radicchio, and endives; toss with the carrot and chives.

4. Add the dressing a little at a time until all the vegetables are just coated. You won't need all the dressing. Serve on a large platter.

Summer Salad

*I*t's worth searching for those small baby vegetables that appear during the summer. Use your favorites. The following is a combination I particularly like.

The House Balsamic Vinaigrette on page 48 is my choice of dressing for this salad, but I like the Porcini Vinaigrette on page 49 and the Tahini Vinaigrette on page 89 with it as well.

2 unpeeled carrots, sliced
2 cups haricots verts, *or thin green*
beans, stem ends removed
2 cups whole baby patty pan
squash (about 20)

½ medium red onion, chopped
House Balsamic Vinaigrette
(page 48)

1. Steam the carrots for 4 minutes; remove them from the steamer and immediately submerge in ice water for several seconds. Drain and dry well on paper towels.

2. Steam the beans for 3 to 4 minutes, then submerge in ice water. Steam the squash for 2 to 3 minutes, then cool in ice water.

Salad can be prepared several hours ahead.

3. Combine the carrots, beans, and squash in a bowl. Mix in the onion. Add as much vinaigrette as you need to coat the vegetables and toss. Serve at room temperature.

SERVES 6 TO 8 AS A
FIRST COURSE, 12 AS
PART OF A BUFFET

Preparation time:
10 minutes

Cooking time:
15 minutes

*T*o dissolve salt in a simple stir-fried or sautéed vegetable dish, add it to the hot oil before adding the other ingredients.

To dissolve salt in salad dressings, add it to the vinegar. Shake or stir until the salt dissolves.

Watercress, Endive, Snow Pea, and Pear Salad

SERVES 6 TO 8 AS A
FIRST COURSE, 12 AS
PART OF A BUFFET

Preparation time:
20 minutes

This salad has appeared on my catering and class menus more frequently than any other salad. The sweetness of the pears contrasts delightfully with the bitterness of the greens, creating a strikingly new taste. It's different and everyone loves it.

2 cups snow peas, strings and stem ends removed
1 bunch watercress, washed and stems removed
2 cups Belgian endives, julienned

1 Bartlett or Comice pear, cut into thin wedges and sprinkled with lemon juice
House Balsamic Vinaigrette (page 48)
1 tablespoon roasted sesame seeds (see page 40)

1. Blanch the snow peas for 30 seconds in boiling water. Plunge into ice water to stop the cooking. Drain well and dry with paper towels.

2. Wash and dry the watercress. Put the watercress, endives, snow peas, and pears in a large bowl. Add as much vinaigrette as you need to coat the vegetables and toss. Sprinkle with sesame seeds and serve.

Chapter 7

BEAN, GRAIN, AND PASTA SALADS

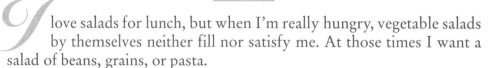

love salads for lunch, but when I'm really hungry, vegetable salads by themselves neither fill nor satisfy me. At those times I want a salad of beans, grains, or pasta.

About five years ago I increased the amount of beans I eat. Most days now I eat a half a cup of them, along with an apple a day and salmon once or twice a week, to lower my cholesterol. In the summer I prefer beans cold instead of hot. Salads like Black Bean, Corn, and Red Pepper Salad; White Bean, Arugula, and Onion Salad; and Antipasto Salad delight my taste buds while being, literally, just what the doctor ordered.

Grain dishes are popular choices for today's buffet. Roasted Barley Salad and Couscous Salad with Mint are two of my favorites. Either also makes an appetizing and filling lunch when accompanied by a green salad and a piece of cheese.

Interestingly, pasta salads were not served in Italy when I was last there in 1986, and friends who visited this past year tell me this hasn't changed. The Italians consider it improper to eat their pasta cold.

Since I like to break the barriers of tradition, I began to experiment with cold pasta. I found that I adore pasta salads like Bowtie Pasta with Oriental Vinaigrette and Orzo Salad with Stir-Fried Vegetables, and I eat them frequently.

I serve bean, grain, and pasta salads year-round. While I emphasize them when the weather's warm, even in winter I present these hearty salads on my buffets and as the first courses for both vegetarian and non-vegetarian meals.

THE BEST WAY TO COOK CORN

prefer to steam rather than boil corn. An average ear steams in 5 to 8 minutes. Use a steamer or pasta pot and don't crowd the pot. The lid should close easily, and the corn should have plenty of wiggle room.

BLACK BEAN, CORN, AND RED PEPPER SALAD

SERVES 6 AS A FIRST
COURSE, 8 OR MORE AS
PART OF A BUFFET

*Preparation time:
30 minutes*

*Cooking time:
45 minutes to 1 hour*

Come the month of August, I can usually be found in Amagansett, at the eastern end of Long Island, where the corn is picked and sold the same day at the farm stands along the main road.

I buy just one ear of corn, strip the silks back partway, and bite into it. If it tastes sweet, I buy as much corn as I plan to cook that day.

1 cup dried black beans, soaked
    and drained (see Note)
2 cups water
2 teaspoons salt
4 ears corn, cooked
1 bunch chives, chopped
1 red bell pepper, chopped
½ cup chopped red onion
3 tablespoons rice vinegar

3 tablespoons olive oil
¼ teaspoon freshly ground black
    pepper
¼ cup chopped fresh parsley
¼ cup chopped fresh coriander
    (cilantro)
¼ cup chopped fresh dill
½ teaspoon ground cumin, prefer-
    ably roasted (see page 40)

1. Simmer the beans gently in the water until they are soft, 45 minutes to 1 hour. Add 1 teaspoon of salt during the last few minutes of cooking.

2. Remove the beans from the pot and reduce the liquid to 3 tablespoons. Pour this glaze over the beans.

3. Cut the kernels from the corn.

4. Combine the corn with the beans and its liquid. Add the chives, red pepper, onion, vinegar, olive oil, 1 teaspoon salt, black pepper, parsley, coriander, dill, and cumin. Toss. Serve at room temperature.

This salad can be made several hours ahead. Can be kept for 1 day in the refrigerator; return to room temperature before serving.

Note: If using canned beans, substitute 2½ cups of canned beans (see page 153) for the 1 cup of uncooked beans and eliminate steps 1 and 2.

FIERY BLACK-EYED PEA SALAD

*I*n the South, black-eyed peas are found in soups, salads, and entrees. While in Georgia on a tour to promote one of my earlier books, I developed a great liking for this small, thin-skinned, mild-tasting, creamy white bean with its single black dot.

It is unnecessary to refrigerate bean, pasta, and grain salads if you're serving them within two hours. Cover lightly and leave at room temperature until ready to serve.

VINAIGRETTE
1 tablespoon olive oil
1 tablespoon sherry vinegar
Salt and pepper to taste
1¼ cups cooked black-eyed peas, homemade (see page 36) or canned (see page 153)
⅓ cup chopped red onion

⅓ cup chopped red bell pepper
1 to 2 teaspoons finely minced raw or roasted jalapeño pepper
¼ cup chopped fresh coriander (cilantro)
1 bunch arugula, watercress, or other greens

1. To make the vinaigrette, combine the oil, vinegar, salt, and pepper.

Vinaigrette can be prepared several days ahead and refrigerated. Bring to room temperature before serving.

2. Warm the black-eyed peas for a couple of minutes over low heat. Remove from the heat and mix with the onion, red pepper, jalapeño, and coriander. Toss gently with the vinaigrette. Serve at room temperature on a bed of arugula, watercress, or other leafy green.

CANNELLINI SALAD WITH RED WINE VINAIGRETTE

I found the people in Italy friendlier than anywhere else I've traveled. Waiters and shopkeepers would applaud my feeble attempts to speak a few words of their language, never impatient as I haltingly stumbled over the simplest phrases.

These white beans served in a simple vinaigrette remind me of the food I ate in the small villages that surround Rome; the dish is unpretentious and delicious.

VINAIGRETTE
½ teaspoon salt
2 teaspoons red wine vinegar
¼ teaspoon freshly ground black
   pepper
1 tablespoon olive oil

1 cup cooked cannellini or other
   white beans, homemade (see
   page 35) or canned (see page 153),
   with 1 tablespoon cooking
   liquid or stock
1 scallion, white and green parts
   finely chopped, or ½ cup
   chopped red onion

SERVES 2 AS A FIRST
COURSE OR AS A LIGHT
LUNCH, 4 OR MORE
WHEN PART OF AN
ANTIPASTO

Preparation time:
10 minutes

1. To make the vinaigrette, dissolve the salt in the vinegar. Add the pepper and oil. Whisk or shake in a tightly covered jar until blended.

Vinaigrette can be prepared several days ahead and refrigerated. Return to room temperature before serving.

2. Add the beans along with cooking liquid or vegetable stock, and scallion. Toss well. Serve at room temperature.

The salad can be prepared up to 1 hour ahead.

White Bean, Arugula, and Onion Salad

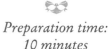

On one of my many visits to Barefoot Contessa, a fabulous food emporium in East Hampton, New York, I tasted an outstanding salad made with white beans, sautéed onions, and arugula. When I got home, I set about inventing my own rendition. My first try, while delicious, was loaded with oil. Then I discovered that by incorporating the flavorful liquid from the cooked beans I was able to cut way back on the amount of dressing—and therefore fat—the salad needed.

SERVES 4 AS AN
ENTREE, 6 AS A FIRST
COURSE, 8 OR MORE AS
PART OF A BUFFET

Preparation time:
15 to 20 minutes

Cooking time:
5 minutes

DRESSING
1 tablespoon sherry vinegar
1 teaspoon salt
1 tablespoon olive oil
⅓ teaspoon freshly ground black
   pepper

1 Spanish onion, sliced (2 to 2½ cups)

1 tablespoon olive oil
2 bunches arugula, stems removed
   and leaves cut in half
2½ cups cooked white beans,
   homemade (see page 35) or
   canned (see page 153), with 3
   tablespoons cooking liquid or
   vegetable stock

MENU FOR AN OUTDOOR SUMMER BUFFET

....

NOODLES WITH SPICY SESAME SAUCE (PAGE 118)

WHITE BEAN, ARUGULA, AND ONION SALAD (PAGE 109)

GRILLED EGGPLANT WITH MISO (PAGE 66)

CHARRED BEAN SPROUTS WITH SCALLIONS AND CARROTS (PAGE 226)

CHOCOLATE ANGEL FOOD CAKE (PAGE 247) WITH FRESH FRUIT

SERVES 4 AS A FIRST COURSE OR PART OF A LIGHT LUNCH

Preparation time: 15 minutes

Cooking time: 5 minutes, plus 10 minutes to cool

1. Make the dressing by first mixing the salt with the sherry vinegar, then adding the olive oil and the pepper. Whisk, or shake in a tightly covered jar, until blended.

The dressing can be prepared several days ahead and refrigerated. Return to room temperature before serving.

2. Sauté the sliced onion in the oil until it is golden brown, about 5 minutes. Remove the pan from the heat and add the arugula. Using 2 wooden spoons, toss the arugula and onion together.

3. Add the beans and their liquid or stock and toss again. Add the dressing and toss. Serve at room temperature.

This salad can be made several hours ahead. Can be kept for 1 day in the refrigerator. Return to room temperature before serving.

WHITE BEAN SALAD WITH TOMATOES AND HERBS

E.A.T., one of Manhattan's finest food emporiums, has some of the best takeout food in the city. I was motivated to invent this salad after eating one of their excellent bean salads.

Over and over in creating and modifying recipes for this book, I found I needed far less oil to turn out dishes that I loved—and I'm not easy to please—than I had previously thought. You might want to experiment with some of your own recipes. I think you'll be surprised at how much less oil you can use without giving up any of the original flavor.

Serve White Bean Salad with Tomatoes and Herbs with a green salad and whole wheat toast for an excellent all-season lunch.

1 tablespoon plus 1 teaspoon olive oil
2 garlic cloves, chopped
1 cup tomato sauce, preferably homemade (see page 34)
½ teaspoon minced fresh thyme
½ teaspoon minced fresh marjoram
1 teaspoon salt

¼ teaspoon freshly ground black pepper
2 cups cooked white beans, homemade (see page 35) or canned (see page 153)
¼ cup chopped fresh parsley
1 tablespoon sherry vinegar

1. Heat 1 teaspoon of the olive oil. Add the garlic and sauté over low heat until it softens and begins to color, about 2 minutes.

2. Stir in the tomato sauce and simmer gently, 2 to 3 minutes. Add the thyme, marjoram, salt, pepper, and beans. Simmer gently until the beans are hot, 2 to 3 minutes. Remove from the heat and stir in the parsley.

3. Allow to cool for 5 to 10 minutes; add the remaining tablespoon of olive oil and the vinegar. Serve at room temperature.

This salad can be made several hours ahead. Can be kept for 1 day in the refrigerator. Return to room temperature before serving.

ANTIPASTO SALAD

My favorite cheeses for this versatile salad are: *ricotta salata* (ricotta that's been salted and aged to remove most of its moisture), gruyère, and St. Nectaire. If you can't find any of these cheeses, use a good imported Swiss cheese.

I like to stuff this salad into endive leaves, arrange attractively with other appetizers, and then serve as an appetizer or as part of an antipasto or buffet.

ANISE VINAIGRETTE
2 tablespoons olive oil
1 tablespoon red wine vinegar
1 tablespoon balsamic vinegar
½ teaspoon freshly ground black pepper
½ teaspoon salt
½ teaspoon ground anise seed
1 cup cooked chickpeas, homemade (see page 35) or canned (see page 153)
1 cup diced ricotta salata (in ⅓-inch cubes)

¼ cup oil-cured black olives, pitted and cut in half
2 tablespoons chopped fresh parsley
½ cup diced roasted red bell peppers (see page 38)
½ cup diced yellow bell peppers
½ cup sliced scallions, white and light green parts (in ⅛-inch rounds)

GARNISH
Arugula, Belgian endives, and radicchio

MENU FOR AN ITALIAN BUFFET

ANTIPASTO SALAD (PAGE 111)

BRAISED MUSHROOMS (PAGE 219)

STUFFED ZUCCHINI (STUFFED MUSHROOMS, ZUCCHINI, AND PEPPERS RECIPE ON PAGE 55, BUT WITH ADDITIONAL ZUCCHINI INSTEAD OF THE MUSHROOMS AND PEPPERS)

ROASTED SHALLOTS (PAGE 39)

CLASSIC ROASTED PEPPERS (PAGE 38)

ORZO PRIMAVERA (PAGE 141)

RICOTTA TORTE (PAGE 248)

SERVES 4 TO 6 AS A MAIN COURSE, 8 AS A FIRST COURSE, 12 OR MORE WHEN PART OF AN ANTIPASTO OR A BUFFET

Preparation time: 30 minutes, plus 1 hour to marinate

1. To make the vinaigrette, mix the oil, vinegars, pepper, salt, and anise seed in a bowl or jar. Whisk, or shake in a tightly covered jar, until blended.

Vinaigrette can be prepared several days ahead and refrigerated. Return to room temperature before serving.

2. Combine the chickpeas, *ricotta salata*, olives, parsley, red and yellow peppers, and scallions.

3. Toss the chickpea mixture with the dressing and allow to sit for at least 1 hour.

The chickpea salad can be prepared up to 3 hours in advance. Best served at room temperature the day it's made, but can be refrigerated for 1 day. Return to room temperature before serving.

4. Place the arugula leaves in the center of a serving platter. Place the chickpeas on top and alternate the endive and radicchio leaves around the perimeter of the chickpeas. Serve.

CHICKPEA AND CELERY SALAD WITH CORIANDER

Coriander is one of those tastes you either love or hate. Those like me who love it swear they can't cook without it. Those who hate it say it tastes like soap. For the latter group, replace the coriander with an equal amount of parsley.

SERVES 4 AS A FIRST COURSE OR AS PART OF A LIGHT LUNCH, 6 TO 8 AS PART OF A BUFFET OR ANTIPASTO

Preparation time: 20 minutes

2 cups cooked chickpeas, home-made (see page 35) or canned (see page 153)
1 cup chopped celery
½ cup chopped celery leaves
⅓ cup chopped fresh coriander (cilantro)
¼ cup chopped red onion or scallion

½ teaspoon salt
1 tablespoon rice vinegar
2 tablespoons olive oil

Combine the chickpeas, celery, celery leaves, coriander, onion, salt, pepper, vinegar, and oil. Toss well.

This salad can be prepared several hours ahead and left at room temperature. Can be kept for 1 day in the refrigerator. Return to room temperature before serving.

FRENCH LENTIL SALAD WITH GOAT CHEESE

This salad is one of my all-time favorites and a staple in my catering business. I prefer *Boucheron*, but any goat cheese with a little bite is good.

Stuff this lentil salad into Belgian endive leaves for an hors d'oeuvre, or serve on lettuce with a few olives on the side for an appetizer.

SHERRY VINEGAR DRESSING
3 tablespoons sherry vinegar
3 tablespoons olive oil
Salt and pepper to taste

1 cup lentils, washed and drained, preferably French green lentils

1½ cups vegetable stock (see page 30) or water
⅓ cup snipped fresh chives
¼ cup chopped fresh coriander (cilantro)
½ teaspoon minced garlic
½ cup diced goat cheese (2 ounces)

SERVES 4 AS A MAIN COURSE LUNCH, 8 AS AN APPETIZER, 12 OR MORE WHEN SERVED AS PART OF AN ANTIPASTO

Preparation time: 20 minutes, plus 30 minutes for the lentils to relax

Cooking time: 45 minutes

For a nonvegetarian variation, sauté ⅓ cup diced prosciutto in 1 tablespoon olive oil until it's crispy; sprinkle on top of the salad.

1. To prepare the dressing, combine the vinegar, oil, salt, and pepper. Whisk, or shake in a tightly covered jar, until blended.

Dressing can be prepared several days ahead and refrigerated.

2. Place the lentils in a saucepan and add the stock or water. Cover and bring to a boil. Lower the heat and simmer until the lentils absorb the stock, about 45 minutes. Remove from the heat, leave the cover on, and let the lentils relax for 30 minutes.

3. Mix the lentils with the chives and coriander.

4. Add the garlic to the dressing.

5. Add the dressing to the lentil mixture. Fold in the cheese gently. Serve.

This salad can be made several hours ahead. Can be kept for 2 or 3 days in the refrigerator. Return to room temperature before serving.

Sprouted Mixed Peas with Herbs

*M*ixed sprouted peas (lentils, adzukis, and green peas) can be found in the fresh produce section at most large supermarkets. I prepare enough to have some left for the next day for lunch on top of bibb lettuce with a piece of cheese. Other times I make Sprouted Peas with Cottage Cheese and Avocado (page 115).

*Serves 4 as a light entree,
6 as a first course*

*Preparation time:
15 to 20 minutes*

*Cooking time:
15 to 20 minutes*

For a nonvegetarian variation, scatter sautéed chopped prosciutto on top.

1 cup chopped leeks, white and green parts (about 1 small leek)
1 tablespoon olive oil
1 tablespoon minced garlic
1 (4-ounce) package mixed sprouted peas
2 tablespoons vegetable stock (see page 30) or water
⅓ cup tomato sauce, preferably homemade (see page 34)

2 tablespoons chopped fresh coriander (cilantro) or parsley
1 tablespoon minced fresh oregano
1 tablespoon fresh thyme
½ teaspoon salt
¼ teaspoon freshly ground black pepper

1. Sauté the leeks in the olive oil until they're wilted, 3 to 4 minutes. Add the garlic and sauté for 1 minute.

2. Add the sprouted peas and stock or water. Cover and simmer for 10 to 15 minutes. Add the tomato sauce and simmer for 1 minute. Add the coriander or parsley, oregano, and thyme. Remove from the heat. Add the salt and pepper. Serve at room temperature.

This salad can be made several hours ahead. Can be kept for 1 day in the refrigerator. Return to room temperature before serving.

Sprouted Peas with Cottage Cheese and Avocado

*Y*ou added mayonnaise to the cottage cheese!" exclaims everyone I give the recipe for this salad. Yes, I do. A small amount of mayonnaise adds richness and flavor to the cottage cheese.

SERVES 2 FOR A LIGHT
LUNCH

*Preparation time:
10 minutes*

*¼ avocado, pitted, peeled, and
   sliced in wedges
Lemon juice
1 cup Sprouted Mixed Peas with
   Herbs (page 114)
⅔ cup cottage cheese, regular or
   low-fat*

*1 teaspoon mayonnaise
1 tablespoon chopped fresh chives
⅛ teaspoon freshly ground black
   pepper*

1. Mist the avocado slices with lemon juice and put them in the center of the plate. Surround them with the sprouted peas or place the sprouts next to them.

2. In a separate bowl, mix the cottage cheese, mayonnaise, chives, and pepper. Place this mixture on top of the avocado.

Orzo Salad with Stir-Fried Vegetables

*T*his salad, made with orzo (pasta in the shape of rice) and stir-fried vegetables, is a colorful addition to a buffet or barbecue. You can add or substitute vegetables such as snow peas, sweet peas, fennel, asparagus, green beans, and mushrooms for an endless variety of tastes.

SERVES 6 TO 8 AS A
FIRST COURSE,
12 OR MORE AS PART
OF A BUFFET

*Preparation time:
30 minutes*

*Cooking time:
10 minutes*

*2 tablespoons olive oil
1 cup chopped red bell pepper
1 cup chopped red onion
1 cup chopped celery
½ cup chopped unpeeled carrots
1 cup cooked corn kernels*

*2 tablespoons chopped fresh thyme
½ cup chopped fresh parsley
2 teaspoons salt
½ teaspoon freshly ground black
   pepper
1½ cups orzo (see Note)*

1. Heat the oil in a wok or iron skillet until smoking. Add the red pepper, onion, celery, and carrots. Sauté for 2 minutes. Add the corn and stir-fry for 1 minute more. Add the thyme, parsley, 1 teaspoon of the salt, and pepper. Remove from the heat.

2. Bring a medium pot of water to a rolling boil. Add the remaining teaspoon of salt and the orzo. Cover until the water returns to boiling. Cook the orzo for 7 to 9 minutes, or until tender but firm. Drain.

3. Add the orzo to the stir-fried vegetables. Toss well. Serve at room temperature.

This salad can be made several hours ahead. Can be kept for 1 day in the refrigerator. Return to room temperature before serving.

Note: To make Rice Salad with Stir-Fried Vegetables, substitute 3 cups of cooked basmati rice for the orzo.

WARM PASTA SALAD WITH ARUGULA AND GOAT CHEESE

I first had the combination of pasta with arugula and goat cheese in California. We were at an outdoor cafe; the waves of the Pacific were crashing on the rocks below. As I dipped into my salad, it was love at first bite. Serve this with a few slices of locally grown tomatoes and a whole-grain bread for a perfect lunch any season.

SERVES 4 AS A LIGHT MEAL, 6 AS A FIRST COURSE, AND 6 TO 8 AS PART OF A BUFFET

Cooking time: 15 to 20 minutes

•➤ *Add a bit of sautéed, diced pancetta—a salt-cured unsmoked Italian bacon.*

½ cup chopped shallots
4 garlic cloves, chopped
1 tablespoon olive oil
1 bunch arugula or watercress, stems removed
2½ teaspoons salt
½ pound small pasta shells
⅓ cup soft mild goat cheese (1½ ounces)

⅓ cup grated Parmesan cheese
¼ teaspoon freshly ground black pepper
2 tablespoons chopped fresh parsley

1. Sauté the shallots and garlic in the olive oil until crispy, 5 to 10 minutes.

2. Wash and spin-dry the arugula.

3. Bring a large pot of water to a rolling boil. Add 2 teaspoons of salt and pasta. Cover until the water returns to a boil. Cook the shells 7 to 9 minutes, or until tender but firm. Drain the pasta and reserve 2 tablespoons of the pasta water.

4. Immediately add the goat and Parmesan cheeses to the pasta so that the heat of the pasta will melt the cheese.

5. Add the remaining ½ teaspoon salt, pepper, cooked shallots and garlic, parsley, arugula or watercress and the 2 tablespoons of pasta water. Toss. I prefer to serve this salad while it's still warm.

Salad can also be prepared several hours in advance and served at room temperature.

BOWTIE PASTA WITH ORIENTAL VINAIGRETTE

This spicy pasta salad is becoming one of the new stars of my catering business. At a recent corporate dinner for thirty, I served this as a first course followed by grilled salmon and Sichuan Green Beans (page 228).

(page 228)

ORIENTAL VINAIGRETTE
2 tablespoons sherry vinegar
2 tablespoons soy sauce
1½ tablespoons peanut oil
½ tablespoon Oriental sesame oil
¼ teaspoon freshly ground
   black pepper

1 unpeeled carrot, cut on a diagonal
2½ cups snow peas
½ pound bowties or other short
   dried pasta
1 teaspoon salt
½ tablespoon Oriental sesame oil

½ tablespoon peanut oil
1 garlic clove, chopped
1 tablespoon pickled or fresh ginger, cut into thin strips
½ cup red or yellow bell pepper, diced or triangle-cut
2 scallions, white and green parts cut into ¼-inch rounds

GARNISH
1 tablespoon roasted sesame seeds (see page 40)
2 tablespoons oven-roasted pine nuts (see page 41)

MENU FOR AN EAST-WEST BUFFET

BOWTIE PASTA WITH ORIENTAL VINAIGRETTE (PAGE 117)

BRAISED FAVA BEANS WITH FRESH HERBS (PAGE 163)

CHINESE CHARRED PEPPERS AND ZUCCHINI (PAGE 220)

SICHUAN ASPARAGUS (PAGE 228)

MOROCCAN ORANGES (PAGE 258) AND GINGER COOKIES (PAGE 262)

SERVES 6 FOR A FIRST COURSE OR LIGHT LUNCH, 8 TO 12 AS PART OF A BUFFET

Preparation time: 30 minutes

Cooking time: 15 minutes

MENU FOR A CHINESE BUFFET

Noodles with Spicy Sesame Sauce (page 118)

Stir-Fried Vegetables with Peppers (page 231)

Red-Cooked Cabbage (page 214)

Whole-Grain Fried Rice (page 182)

Fresh Fruit

1. To prepare the vinaigrette, combine the vinegar, soy sauce, peanut oil, sesame oil, and black pepper. Whisk, or shake in a covered jar, until blended.

Vinaigrette can be prepared several days ahead and refrigerated.

2. Use a pasta pot (see page 126), if you have one, to blanch the carrots for 3 minutes; add the snow peas and cook for 2 minutes more. Remove the vegetables from the steamer and immerse them in a bowl of ice water for 1 to 2 minutes. Drain.

3. Add water sufficient for cooking pasta to the steaming water from the vegetables and bring it to a rolling boil. Add the bowties and salt and cook 8 to 9 minutes. Drain the pasta, submerge in cold water to stop the cooking, and drain again. Toss with the sesame oil.

4. Heat a wok or iron skillet over high heat for 1 minute. Add the peanut oil, turn the heat to low, and add the garlic; let the garlic sizzle for a few seconds. Add the ginger and stir with chopsticks or a wooden spoon for 1 minute. Add the red pepper, turn the heat to high, and stir-fry for 2 minutes.

Can be prepared up to this point several hours ahead, but do not combine until shortly before serving.

5. Combine the pasta, carrots, snow peas, garlic, ginger, red pepper mixture, and the scallions; toss. Add the vinaigrette and toss again. Scatter the sesame seeds and pine nuts over the top. Serve within the hour.

Serves 4 as a first course

❧

Preparation time: 15 minutes

❧

Cooking time: 5 to 10 minutes

NOODLES WITH SPICY SESAME SAUCE

*I*f you're wondering why I've included a recipe for Noodles with Spicy Sesame Sauce when you can order it in any Chinese restaurant, it's because my clients and students swear this version is better than any other. Most other recipes call for peanut butter, but I find that tahini produces tastier results.

SPICY SESAME SAUCE
⅓ *cup tahini*
½ *cup steeped Chinese or other*
  black tea
2½ *tablespoons soy sauce*
1 *teaspoon chili oil (see page 43)*
1 *tablespoon Oriental sesame oil*
1 *tablespoon sugar*

1 *tablespoon red wine vinegar*

½ *pound fresh or dried linguini or*
  any other long pasta
1 *teaspoon Oriental sesame oil*
½ *cup shredded peeled cucumber*
¼ *cup sliced scallions, white and*
  green parts, in ⅛-inch rounds

1. To make the sauce, combine the tahini, tea, soy sauce, chili oil, sesame oil, sugar, and vinegar in the bowl of a food processor and pulse on and off until blended.

Sauce can be prepared up to 3 days ahead and refrigerated.

2. Bring a large pot of water to a rolling boil. Add the pasta. Cover until the water returns to a boil. Cook fresh pasta 2 to 3 minutes; dried pasta until tender but firm, 8 to 10 minutes. Drain. Submerge the pasta, whether you're using fresh or dried, in ice water. Drain again. Toss with the sesame oil, then mix with the sauce.

3. Just before serving, add the cucumber and scallions. Serve at room temperature.

ROASTED BARLEY SALAD

*U*se organic barley from the health food store; it's coarser and less processed than the barley sold in supermarkets. Roasting the barley before cooking it brings out its rich, nutty flavor.

DRESSING
½ *teaspoon salt*
¼ *teaspoon pepper*
2 *tablespoons olive oil*
2 *tablespoons rice vinegar*

1 *cup raw barley*
2 *cups vegetable stock (see page 30)*
  or water
1 *cup diced red or yellow bell*
  pepper
1 *cup thinly sliced unpeeled carrots*
½ *cup chopped red onion*

SERVES 6 AS A FIRST
COURSE, 8 OR MORE AS
PART OF A BUFFET

Preparation time:
20 to 30 minutes, plus
10 minutes to drain
and 30 minutes for the
barley to relax

Cooking time:
1 hour and 30 minutes

**MENU FOR A LIGHT
SUMMER LUNCH**

· · · · · · · · · ·

*Couscous Salad
with Mint (page 120)*

*Bitter Greens with
Tomato-Olive
Dressing (page 95)*

*Hummus with Herbs
and Spices (page 57)
on whole-wheat
bread*

· · · · · · · · · ·

Fresh fruit

*Serves 6 as a first
course, 8 or more as
part of a buffet*

❧

*Preparation time:
20 minutes*

1. To make the dressing, combine the salt, pepper, oil, and vinegar. Whisk, or shake in a covered jar, until blended.

Dressing can be prepared several days ahead and refrigerated.

2. Wash the barley; drain for at least 10 minutes.

3. Place a wok or iron skillet over high heat for 1 minute.

4. Add the barley and turn the heat to low. Dry-roast the barley for 30 minutes, stirring the grains occasionally with a wooden spoon. The barley develops a rich, roasted aroma.

5. In a separate pot with a tight-fitting lid, bring the stock or water to a boil. Add the roasted barley and stir. Cover and turn the heat to low. Simmer until the stock is absorbed, 45 minutes to 1 hour. Remove from the heat. Leaving the lid on the pot, allow the barley to relax for 30 minutes.

6. Place the barley in a bowl and add the red pepper, carrots, and onion. Stir the dressing and add it to the barley. Toss well. Serve at room temperature.

This salad can be prepared several hours in advance. Best served at room temperature the day it's made, but can be refrigerated for 2 days. Return to room temperature before serving.

Couscous Salad with Mint

This recipe was the result of one of my frequent marathon cooking sessions with my friend Sigun Coyle. We make up the recipes as we go and cook until one of us drops.

*1½ cups water
1 cup couscous*

*DRESSING
3 tablespoons olive oil
3 tablespoons lemon juice
1 teaspoon salt
¼ teaspoon freshly ground*

black pepper

*½ cup chopped red bell pepper
½ cup snipped chives, or ¼ cup
    chopped scallion
1 cup chopped peeled cucumber
¼ cup chopped fresh mint
2 tablespoons chopped fresh parsley*

1. Bring the water to a boil in a saucepan with a tight-fitting lid. Add the couscous. With a wooden spoon or chopsticks, stir using a figure-8 motion, for a few seconds. Remove from the heat, cover, and set aside for 10 minutes.

2. Meanwhile, prepare the dressing by combining the olive oil, lemon juice, salt, and pepper. Whisk, or shake in a covered jar, until blended.

3. Fluff the couscous with a fork. Add the dressing and the red pepper, chives, cucumber, mint, and parsley. Toss well. Allow to cool to room temperature before serving.

This salad can be prepared several hours in advance. Best served at room temperature the day it's made, but can be refrigerated for up to 3 days. Return to room temperature before serving.

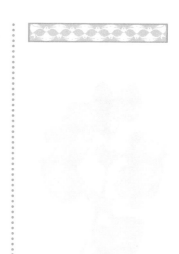

VEGETABLE RICE SALAD WITH TARRAGON VINAIGRETTE

This rice salad is tasty without being either sophisticated or exotic. I always make it when my Uncle Morris comes to visit. I'm sad to say I have never been able to convince him to try any of the dishes I'm known for. Uncle Morris only wants "good old-fashioned American food."

This is perfect with a summer barbecue.

SERVES 4 TO 6 AS A FIRST COURSE OR PART OF A LIGHT ENTREE, 8 OR MORE AS PART OF A BUFFET

Preparation time: 20 minutes, plus 15 minutes for rice to relax

Cooking time: 15 minutes

TARRAGON VINAIGRETTE
1 teaspoon salt
¼ teaspoon freshly ground black pepper
3 tablespoons tarragon vinegar
3 tablespoons olive oil

1½ cups water
1 cup basmati rice

1 cup frozen peas, thawed
1 bunch watercress
1 cup sliced cremini or button mushrooms
2 scallions, white and green parts chopped
1 unpeeled carrot, sliced in thin rounds or chopped

1. To make the vinaigrette, combine the salt, pepper, vinegar, and oil. Whisk, or shake in a covered jar, until blended.

Vinaigrette can be prepared several days ahead and refrigerated. Return to room temperature before serving.

2. Bring the water to a rolling boil. Wash and drain the rice; stir into the boiling water. Turn the heat to low and cook 15 minutes. With the cover on, let the rice relax for 15 minutes.

3. While the rice is still hot, add the peas, watercress, mushrooms, scallions, and carrot and toss for a couple of minutes. (The heat of the rice will wilt the vegetables.)

4. Add the dressing and toss again. Serve warm or at room temperature.

CURRIED WILD RICE SALAD

*M*y friend Joan Green is a great lady as well as a fabulous Chinese cook and teacher. Whenever we have a chance to visit—all too infrequently since she lives in upstate New York—we love to exchange ideas and recipes.

Joan has a wonderful way with grains, and together we created this dish while searching for the perfect accompaniment to a duck and chutney salad. Stuff this savory rice salad into a hollowed-out raw tomato, surround it with mesclun, and add a few chunks of gruyère or your favorite cheese for a summer lunch. This salad is ideal for both vegetarian and nonvegetarian buffets for festive and informal occasions.

3 cups vegetable stock (see page 30), or stock of your choice
½ cup wild rice, washed and drained
1 tablespoon olive oil
½ cup chopped shallots
1 tablespoon curry powder
1 cup basmati rice, washed and drained
1 teaspoon salt
¼ teaspoon freshly ground black pepper

½ cup white raisins
½ cup chopped carrots
1 cup chopped red bell pepper
½ cup sliced black olives
¼ cup chopped fresh parsley

LEMON VINAIGRETTE
2 tablespoons lemon juice
1 teaspoon salt
½ teaspoon freshly ground black pepper
2 teaspoons Dijon mustard

MENU FOR A LIGHT SUMMER DINNER

....

VEGETABLE RICE SALAD WITH TARRAGON VINAIGRETTE (PAGE 121)

SICHUAN GREEN BEANS (PAGE 228)

BAKED TOMATO SLICES WITH GOAT CHEESE (PAGE 100)

PEACH AND CHERRY COBBLER (PAGE 260)

SERVES 8 TO 10 AS PART OF A COMPOSED SALAD PLATE, 12 OR MORE AS PART OF A BUFFET

Preparation time: 30 minutes

Cooking time: 1 hour, plus 30 minutes for wild rice to relax

4 tablespoons olive oil

Lettuce or 1 bunch watercress

¼ cup roasted pine nuts
(see page 41)

1. In a 2-quart saucepan with a tight-fitting lid, bring 1½ cups of the stock to a rolling boil. Add the wild rice and stir. Cover, turn the heat to low, and simmer until all the liquid has been absorbed, about 1 hour. Turn the heat off and let wild rice relax, covered, for about 30 minutes.

2. In a separate saucepan with a tight-fitting lid, heat the olive oil. Add the shallots and sauté until they begin to color, 2 to 3 minutes. Add the curry powder and sauté for another minute.

3. Add the basmati rice and stir until the rice is coated with the oil. Add the remaining 1½ cups of stock, salt, and black pepper. Turn the heat to high until the liquid reaches a rolling boil. Turn the heat to low, cover, and simmer. After 15 minutes, check to make sure that the stock has been absorbed. Turn the off heat.

4. Add the raisins, carrots, and bell pepper to the basmati rice. Stir, cover, and let rice relax for 15 minutes.

5. Combine the cooked wild rice and basmati rice, gently tossing the grains together as you would a leafy-green salad. Add the olives and 2 tablespoons of the parsley and toss again.

6. To prepare the vinaigrette, combine the lemon juice, salt, pepper, mustard, and oil in a jar with a tight-fittting lid and shake until blended.

7. Add the vinaigrette to the rice and toss gently, but thoroughly.

Can be prepared to this point up to 2 hours ahead and left at room temperature. Do not refrigerate.

8. Just before serving, spread the lettuce or watercress around the outer edges of a large plate. Pile the rice in the center. Sprinkle the remaining tablespoons of parsley and the roasted pine nuts on top of the rice. Serve at room temperature.

Variations: Add blanched snow peas or sugar snap peas when they are available. Cooked corn is another delicious and colorful addition.

Chapter 8

PASTA

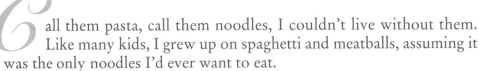

*C*all them pasta, call them noodles, I couldn't live without them. Like many kids, I grew up on spaghetti and meatballs, assuming it was the only noodles I'd ever want to eat.

In fact, it was not through Italian food but my pursuit of Chinese cooking that I first began to explore the possibilities of cooking with noodles. I discovered noodles that were deep-fried, noodles with curry sauces, noodles with delectable bits of vegetables and meat. While many of my pasta dishes today reveal Italian influences, my early Chinese training often creeps in.

Most weeks I eat hot or cold pasta at least four times. There are so many ways to make pasta dishes, I can't imagine ever getting bored. And others must feel as I do, because pasta is the darling of the 1990s. What was long thought of as peasant food, we now find on the finest tables. We flock to fancy restaurants and pay outrageous prices for dishes that are bargains when we make them at home.

To cook pasta, I use a large kettle at least as tall as the length of the pasta. I love the Italian pasta pots with the two-handled colander inserts that can be lifted out. With these pots I can remove the first pound of pasta while the cooking water's still boiling and cook a second pound in the same still-boiling water. Also, it's easier and safer to lift just the pasta from the pot, rather than having to hoist a heavy pot of boiling water. While it's hardly essential equipment, I find an Italian pasta pot is a godsend.

I fill the pot with water to between two-thirds and three-quarters of capacity. Using the highest heat possible, I bring the water to a *rolling* boil. I add the salt—two teaspoons for a half-pound of pasta, one table-spoon for a pound—and the pasta.

If you have a home range, the heat won't be hot enough to quickly return the water to a boil unless you cover the pot. This probably isn't necessary if you have a professional range. Anytime you have trouble maintaining a rolling boil, keep the pot partially or completely covered while the pasta cooks. The object here is the same as when blanching veg-etables: you want the pasta out of the boiling water without delay so the flavor stays in the pasta and not in the water.

I don't add oil to the water to keep the pasta from sticking together. Instead, I stir the pasta every two or three minutes.

Dried pasta should be cooked until it's tender but firm. Orzo cooks in eight minutes; most short tubular pastas, in eight to ten; long thin pastas, in seven to nine. Check the package for the manufacturer's suggested cooking time—usually a range of two or three minutes is given. I start to test the pasta a minute before the shortest cooking time.

Fresh pasta requires less cooking and, unlike dried pasta, cannot be cooked firm. Cook until just tender, two to four minutes after the water returns to a boil. *Never overcook.* Start to taste when you think the pasta's almost cooked.

I drain pasta without delay. Then I stir it at once into the heated sauce to keep it from sticking together. (Don't rinse the pasta or add oil. After you rinse pasta, the sauce won't adhere to it.) I always reserve the "pasta water." If the sauce seems dry, I add a little pasta water to bring it back to its original consistency.

Don't kill the sauce! If you've made the sauce ahead of time, turn off the heat as soon as it's done. I reheat it on low heat during the last few minutes that the pasta is cooking. As soon as the pasta is cooked, I add it to the still-simmering sauce. Then I remove the skillet with the sauce and pasta from the heat and immediately add the Parmesan cheese, if I'm using it. While I want the cheese to melt, I don't want to cook it.

When I'm serving pasta hot, I bring it to the table at once in a heated bowl. To heat the bowl, I use the bowl as a cover for the cooking pasta. Or you could add a few cups of boiling pasta water to the bowl, swish it around, and pour it out. If the pasta is to be served cold, I submerge it in ice water for a few seconds to stop the cooking and drain it immediately.

I prefer a short pasta such as bowties or shells for a buffet. Guests have an easier time serving themselves and the line moves faster.

Some cookbooks call for a pound of pasta to serve four people. I find a pound to be enough for six and occasionally more. Many of my sauces are richly flavored, and when I add vegetables to a pasta dish, I usually add a lot. I prefer to serve a moderate portion of pasta along with a salad, a side vegetable, maybe a soup to start, and a good bread. However, if you are serving pasta with only a small salad on the side, a pound will serve four amply and will be skimpy for six.

Roasted Vegetable Pasta

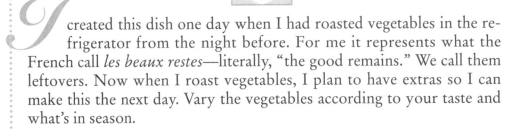

SERVES 4 AS AN ENTREE, 6 AS A FIRST COURSE

Preparation time: 30 minutes

Cooking time: 45 minutes to 1 hour

I created this dish one day when I had roasted vegetables in the refrigerator from the night before. For me it represents what the French call *les beaux restes*—literally, "the good remains." We call them leftovers. Now when I roast vegetables, I plan to have extras so I can make this the next day. Vary the vegetables according to your taste and what's in season.

1 cup sliced leeks, white parts only (split in half lengthwise and cut into 1-inch pieces)
1 medium red onion, cut into eighths
1 red bell pepper, cut into 1-inch strips
½ medium fennel bulb, cut lengthwise into ½-inch strips
2 tablespoons olive oil
2 fresh thyme sprigs

Vegetable stock (see page 30) or water
4 garlic cloves, chopped
1½ cups tomato sauce, preferably homemade (see page 34)
½ cup chopped fresh basil
¼ cup white wine
1 tablespoon salt
¾ pound dried penne
⅓ cup grated Parmesan cheese
3 ounces mozzarella or goat cheese (optional)

1. Preheat the oven to 425°F.

2. Place the leeks, onion, red pepper, and fennel in a shallow roasting pan. Toss the vegetables with 1 tablespoon of the olive oil to coat them. (I use my hands.) Add the thyme. Roast until the vegetables are cooked through and have started to brown, 30 to 45 minutes. Check midway to make sure the vegetables aren't burning; a little charring is good. Add a little stock or water to the pan if the juices are evaporating.

3. While the vegetables are roasting, in a 12-inch skillet sauté the garlic in the remaining tablespoon of oil until it begins to color. Add the tomato sauce and simmer 1 minute. Turn off the heat, then add the basil. Stir the roasted vegetables into the sauce.

4. Turn the oven to 375°F. Add the wine to the roasting pan and stir, scraping up any bits and pieces that are stuck to the pan. Add these deglazed juices to the sauce.

5. Bring a large pot of water to a rolling boil. Add the salt and the penne. Cover until the water returns to a boil. Cook the pasta only 6 to 8 minutes (undercook), as it will continue to cook when it is baked later on.

6. Drain the pasta and add it to the sauce. Add the cheese and toss again. Grease a 2- to 2½ quart casserole. Pour in the pasta and add the optional layer of mozzarella on top or dot with goat cheese, if desired. Bake for 15 minutes. Serve immediately.

Vegetable Lo Mein

SERVES 6 AS AN ENTREE, 8 OR MORE AS PART OF A BUFFET

Preparation time: 45 minutes

Cooking time: 30 minutes

For a festive party dish that makes a spectacular presentation, nothing beats this lo mein with its crusty noodles and colorful stir-fried vegetables. Baking the noodles after frying them makes the noodles crunchy and unbelievably delicious. The only other way to achieve this effect is to deep-fry the noodles in an inch of oil—not something I'm inclined to do.

You can simplify this dish and eliminate three of the four tablespoons of peanut oil by not frying or baking the noodles. However, you give up what makes this dish unique—the wonderful crustiness of the noodles.

1 tablespoon cornstarch
2 tablespoons dry sherry
1 tablespoon salt
1 pound fresh lo mein noodles or Italian pasta
2 teaspoons Oriental sesame oil
4 tablespoons peanut oil
1 large Spanish onion, sliced
1 tablespoon chopped garlic
1 tablespoon minced fresh ginger
1 unpeeled carrot, julienned

8 cups shredded or julienned bok choy, white and green parts (1 medium bunch)
1 red or yellow bell pepper, julienned
2 cups snow peas, whole or slant-cut in half (6 ounces)
¾ cup vegetable stock (see page 30) or stock of your choice
⅓ cup soy sauce

1. Preheat the oven to 350°F.

2. Stir the cornstarch and sherry together. Set aside.

3. Bring a large pot of water to a rolling boil. Add the salt and the pasta, then cover until the water returns to a boil. Cook until the pasta is just done. Fresh pasta cooks quickly, 2 to 4 minutes. Drain and submerge in ice water. Drain again. Toss with the sesame oil (see Note).

Noodles can be prepared up to 1 day ahead and refrigerated.

4. Place a wok or cast-iron skillet over high heat for 3 to 4 minutes. By getting the wok really hot, you eliminate the problem of the noodles sticking to the wok. Add 1½ tablespoons of the peanut oil. Immediately add half the pasta. After 30 seconds, loosen the noodles with a spatula or shake the wok to prevent the noodles from sticking. Let the noodles brown until dark with a few scorched spots, 2 to 3 minutes, but make sure they don't burn.

5. Flip the noodles using 2 spatulas. Or, if you know how, shake the pan with a sharp movement of your wrists to flip the noodles. Brown the noodles on the other side, 2 to 3 minutes. Remove the noodles to a shallow roasting pan. Add 1½ tablespoons of the peanut oil and repeat the procedure with the remaining noodles.

6. Place the roasting pan with the noodles in it into the oven to bake for 20 to 30 minutes.

7. While noodles are baking, add the remaining 1 tablespoon of peanut oil to the wok in which the noodles were fried and heat for 1 minute. Add the sliced onion and stir-fry over high heat until it begins to char, 2 minutes. Add the garlic and ginger and stir-fry for 1 minute. Add the carrot for 30 seconds. Add the bok choy and pepper and stir-fry for 1 minute. Add the snow-peas and stir-fry for a few seconds.

8. Add the vegetable stock and bring to a simmer. Stir in the soy sauce; toss for a few seconds. Restir the cornstarch mixture and add it all at once to the wok. Toss the vegetables with the sauce until the sauce has thickened, a few seconds more. Remove from the heat. Place the crunchy noodles on a large, flat platter. Place the vegetables on top. Serve immediately.

Note: If you're not going to fry the noodles, after they're cooked, drain them, toss with the sesame oil, and place the vegetables on top.

Spring Artichoke Pasta

Serves 2 as an entree, 4 as a first course

Preparation time: 20 to 30 minutes

Cooking time: 10 minutes

One day I found myself staring at a day-old cooked artichoke in my refrigerator. Not being one to waste food, I wanted to be sure to put it to good use.

This pasta recipe is the result of that leftover artichoke. With no sauce to drip and the ability to linger at room temperature for hours, this pasta appears frequently as part of my buffets.

3 teaspoons salt
¼ pound artichoke pasta or regular linguni
½ cup chopped shallots (4 to 6 shallots)
1 tablespoon olive oil
1 tablespoon chopped garlic
¼ teaspoon freshly ground black pepper
¼ cup vegetable stock (see page 30) or water

¼ cup grated Parmesan cheese
2 tablespoons pitted and chopped oil-cured black olives
1 steamed large artichoke heart, cut into large dice, or 4 frozen artichoke hearts, quartered and thawed
2 cups torn fresh basil leaves
2 tablespoons oven-roasted pine nuts (see page 41)

1. Bring a large pot of water to a rolling boil. Add 2 teaspoons of the salt and the pasta. Cover until the water returns to a boil. Cook the pasta until tender but firm, 6 to 7 minutes. Drain.

2. Meanwhile, in a medium skillet, sauté the shallots in the olive oil until they soften, 3 to 4 minutes. Add the garlic and sauté until golden, about 2 minutes. Add the remaining teaspoon salt, pepper, and stock or water. Simmer until the liquid is reduced by half, about 1 minute. Remove from the heat.

3. Add the cooked pasta and cheese and toss. Add the olives, artichoke heart, basil, and pine nuts. Toss well. Serve warm or at room temperature.

SPAGHETTI WITH BROCCOLI DI RAPE AND ROASTED PINE NUTS

The easiest way to cook broccoli di rape is to steam it in a pasta pot. After you lift out the broccoli di rape, leave the water in the pot. Add sufficient boiling water to cook the pasta, and the flavor of the vegetable will infuse the pasta.

2 pounds broccoli di rape
   (see Note)
3 teaspoons salt
¾ pound spaghetti
2 tablespoons olive oil
3 tablespoons minced garlic
¼ cup chopped shallots (2 to 3 shallots)
1 cup vegetable stock (see page 30)
   or stock of your choice

½ teaspoon freshly ground black
   pepper
⅓ cup grated Parmesan cheese
2 tablespoons oven-roasted pine
   nuts (see page 41)

1. Bring a kettle of water to a boil in order to have more hot water to add to water left from steaming the broccoli di rape.

2. Trim the broccoli di rape, discarding 3 to 4 inches of the stem. Cut the leaves in half. Steam the leaves for 1 minute in a pot large enough to later cook the pasta. Remove the broccoli di rape, leaving the still-simmering water in the pot. Drain the broccoli di rape well in a colander.

3. Add the boiling water from the kettle to the simmering water left from the broccoli di rape. Add 2 teaspoons of salt; cook the spaghetti until tender but firm, 7 to 9 minutes.

4. While the spaghetti is cooking, heat the olive oil in a large skillet. Add the garlic and shallots and sauté over medium heat until the garlic begins to color, about 2 minutes. Add the stock and reduce by half, 3 to 4 minutes. Add the broccoli di rape and toss. Cook over high heat for 1 minute. Add remaining teaspoon of salt and pepper.

---

*SERVES 4 AS AN
ENTREE,
6 AS A FIRST COURSE*

*Preparation time:
20 to 30 minutes*

*Cooking time:
10 minutes*

•→ *I also make this dish with chicken stock, sprinkle it with hot pepper flakes, and serve it alongside broiled sweet Italian sausages.*

MENU FOR A WINTER NIGHT

*WINTER TOMATO
SOUP (PAGE 76)*

*CANNELLINI SALAD
WITH RED WINE
VINAIGRETTE
(PAGE 108)*

*SPAGHETTI WITH
BROCCOLI DI RAPE
AND ROASTED PINE
NUTS (PAGE 132)*

*BAKED EGG CUSTARD
(PAGE 250)*

5. When the spaghetti is done, drain and toss with the broccoli di rape. Remove from the heat and add the cheese. Toss again. Put in a serving bowl and sprinkle with the roasted pine nuts. Serve hot.

Note: Substitute Swiss chard for the broccoli di rape. The only change is that I cut the chard into smaller pieces.

Linguini with Spring Vegetables

This pasta is a variation on the classic pasta primavera. Use this recipe as a guideline—play with it, put in your favorite vegetables that are in season. I prepare it differently every time I make it.

3 teaspoons salt
½ pound linguini
1 tablespoon olive oil
1 shallot, sliced
1 cup sliced Spanish onion
1 medium leek, white and light green parts, cleaned (page 32) and cut into thin strips (about ¼ cup)
1 unpeeled carrot, cut into thin strips
2 garlic cloves, chopped
2 cups green beans that have been cut in half lengthwise, with

stem ends removed (½ pound)
1 cup peeled, seeded, and chopped tomato
1 cup vegetable stock (see page 30) or stock of your choice
¼ cup white wine
¼ teaspoon freshly ground black pepper
1 cup sugar-snap peas, strings removed (about 3 ounces)
¼ cup chopped fresh parsley
½ cup chopped fresh basil
½ cup freshly grated Parmesan cheese

SERVES 2 OR 3 AS AN ENTREE, 4 TO 6 AS A FIRST COURSE

Preparation time: 45 minutes

Cooking time: 10 minutes

1. Bring a large pot of water to a rolling boil. Add 2 teaspoons of salt and the pasta. Cover until the water returns to a boil. Cook until the linguini is tender but firm, 8 to 10 minutes.

2. Meanwhile, place a 12-inch skillet over high heat for 1 minute. Add the olive oil and the shallot, onion, and leek. Reduce the heat to medium and sauté until the onion has cooked through and begun to brown, 3 to 4 minutes. Add the carrot and garlic and sauté until limp and the garlic has begun to color, 2 minutes.

Dried porcini mushrooms should be measured before soaking. Pack them loosely into the measuring cup.

SERVES 2 AS ENTREE,
4 AS A FIRST COURSE

Preparation time:
30 minutes, plus
30 minutes to soak
mushrooms

Cooking time:
15 minutes

MENU FOR A SOPHISTICATED DINNER

FRESH SWEET PEA
SOUP (PAGE 73)

PASTA WITH MARSALA
AND WILD
MUSHROOMS
(PAGE 134)

MESCLUN AND PEAR
SALAD (PAGE 97,
RECIPE MADE WITH-
OUT THE CHEESE)

PUMPKIN CRÈME
BRÛLÉE (PAGE 252)

3. Add the beans, tomato, stock, wine, remaining 1 teaspoon salt, and pepper. Bring to a simmer over high heat. Lower the heat to medium-low and simmer until the beans are almost done, 3 to 4 minutes. Add the peas and toss for a few seconds. Add the parsley and basil.

4. Drain the pasta and add it to the sauce. Toss well. Place the pasta in a heated bowl. Add three-fourths of the cheese and toss again. Sprinkle the remaining cheese on top. Serve hot.

PASTA WITH MARSALA AND WILD MUSHROOMS

*M*arsala wine and wild mushrooms have a fortuitous affinity for each other. They combine to create an intense and memorable flavor.

½ cup dried porcini mushrooms
1 cup cold water
½ tablespoon olive oil
½ tablespoon butter
¼ cup chopped shallots (2 to 3 shallots)
1 tablespoon minced garlic
¼ pound fresh wild mushrooms, such as portobellos, cremini, or black chanterelles, sliced

3 teaspoons salt
¼ teaspoon freshly ground black pepper
½ cup marsala wine
2 tablespoons half-and-half
½ pound fresh or dried fettuccine or other long pasta
⅓ cup freshly grated Parmesan cheese

1. Soak the porcini in the water for 30 minutes. Lift the mushrooms from the soaking water, squeezing them over the water to return any liquid to the cup, and dice. Strain the porcini water through a fine-mesh sieve and reserve.

2. In a medium skillet, heat the olive oil and butter until the butter foams. Add the shallots and sauté until softened, 3 to 4 minutes. Add the garlic and sauté over low heat until the garlic begins to turn golden, 2 minutes.

3. Add the porcini and other mushrooms and sauté for 2 to 3 minutes.

Add 1 teaspoon salt, pepper, and porcini water. Simmer until the liquid is reduced by two-thirds, about 5 minutes. Add the marsala, and simmer until the liquid is further reduced by half, about 2 to 3 minutes. Add the half-and-half; simmer for a few seconds. Remove from the heat.

Sauce can be prepared up to 1 hour ahead. Reheat before using.

4. Bring a large pot of water to a rolling boil. Add the remaining 2 teaspoons salt and the pasta. Cover until the water returns to a boil, then cook until tender. Fresh pasta cooks in 2 to 3 minutes, dried, 6 to 10 minutes.

5. Drain the pasta and add it to the sauce. Remove the sauce from the heat. Add the cheese and toss. Serve hot.

FRESH PASTA WITH BLACK CHANTERELLES

Black chanterelles are scarce and expensive. Luscious, aromatic, and hard to come by, they're a taste you won't forget. Most of the time, I make this dish with shiitake, portobello, or blond chanterelles (also expensive, but more available than the black), or a combination of wild mushrooms.

¼ cup dried porcini mushrooms
1 cup cold water
¼ cup minced shallots (2 to 3 shallots)
1 tablespoon olive oil
1 teaspoon minced garlic
¼ pound fresh black chanterelles or other wild mushrooms, sliced
¼ cup white wine
¼ cup mushroom stock (see page 32) or stock of your choice
3 teaspoons salt
¼ teaspoon freshly ground black pepper
2 tablespoons half-and-half
½ pound fresh pasta
¼ cup grated Parmesan cheese
2 tablespoons chopped fresh parsley

1. Soak the porcini in the water for 30 minutes. Lift the mushrooms from the soaking water, squeezing them over the water to return any liquid to the cup, and dice. Strain the porcini water through a fine-mesh sieve and set it aside.

MENU FOR AN ELEGANT DINNER

ARTICHOKES WITH MUSTARD VINAIGRETTE (PAGE 60)

FRESH PASTA WITH BLACK CHANTERELLES (PAGE 135)

CHOPPED SALAD (PAGE 102)

CHOCOLATE SOUFFLÉ (PAGE 249)

SERVES 2 TO 3 AS AN ENTREE, 4 OR 5 AS A FIRST COURSE

Preparation time: 20 minutes, plus 30 minutes to soak mushrooms

Cooking time: 15 minutes

econstituted dried
mushrooms retain
more of their fla-
vor when soaked in
cold—rather than hot
or warm—water.

2. While the mushrooms are soaking, bring a large pot of water to a rolling boil.

3. In a medium skillet sauté the shallots in the olive oil until they begin to color, 3 to 5 minutes. Add the garlic and sauté 1 to 2 minutes.

4. Add the porcini and sauté for 2 minutes more. Stir in the fresh mushrooms, porcini water, wine, stock, 1 teaspoon salt, and pepper. Simmer for 4 to 6 minutes. Add the half-and-half and stir briefly.

Sauce can be prepared 1 hour ahead. Gently reheat before using.

5. Add the remaining 2 teaspoons salt and the pasta to the boiling water. Cover until the water returns to a boil. Boil the pasta for 2 minutes.

6. Drain and add the pasta to the sauce. Add a little of the pasta water if the sauce is too dry. Remove from the heat. Add the Parmesan cheese; mix well. Sprinkle with the parsley. Serve immediately.

CLEANING MUSHROOMS

ome French chefs would consider it heresy to wash mushrooms, but as I hate grit in mushrooms as much as I do in greens, I—*with great care*—wash certain mushrooms.

Cremini, portobello (with their sandy roots cut off), blond chanterelles, *pieds de moutons*, and button mushrooms should be immersed in cold water for a couple of seconds as you hold the stem between your index and middle fingers and gently massage each mushroom with your thumb to loosen any dirt. Alternatively, you can rinse them under a delicate spray as you lightly brush them with a soft mushroom brush or pastry brush.

Black chanterelles should merely be dipped into a bowl filled with cold water. Do not massage these as they're too delicate.

Don't wash shiitaki mushrooms; just lightly brush them with a pastry or mushroom brush.

CHINESE CHARRED VEGETABLE PASTA

This is a combination of Chinese and Italian ingredients and techniques. When I make Chinese Charred Peppers and Zucchini, I prepare extra to make this dish the next day.

1 tablespoon peanut oil
1 tablespoon minced garlic
⅓ cup sliced scallions, white and green parts
1 cup Chinese Charred Peppers and Zucchini, with liquid (page 220)
½ teaspoon chili oil (see page 43)
1 teaspoon Oriental sesame oil
2 teaspoons salt
½ pound short pasta (bowties are particularly good)
¼ cup grated Parmesan cheese
2 tablespoons chopped fresh coriander (cilantro)

1. Place a wok or 12-inch skillet over high heat for 1 minute. Add the peanut oil. Turn the heat to low and add the garlic and scallions. Sauté until the garlic begins to brown, 1 minute. Remove the skillet from the heat.

2. Add the Chinese Charred Peppers and Zucchini and its liquid. Stir. Add the chili oil and sesame oil.

Can be prepared up to 1 hour ahead. Reheat before using.

3. Bring a large pot of water to a rolling boil. Add the salt and pasta. Cover until the water returns to a boil. Cook until the pasta is tender but firm; most short pastas cook in 9 to 11 minutes.

4. Drain the pasta and add it to the sauce. Add a little of the pasta water if the sauce is too dry. Stir. Remove from the heat. Add the Parmesan cheese and coriander and toss. Serve hot or at room temperature.

Can be prepared up to 3 hours ahead.

SERVES 4 AS AN ENTREE, 6 AS A FIRST COURSE

Preparation time: 15 minutes

Cooking time: 10 minutes

MENU FOR AN EAST-WEST DINNER

JÍCAMA WITH PICKLED GINGER DIPPING SAUCE (PAGE 58)

GRILLED EGGPLANT WITH MISO (PAGE 66)

CHINESE CHARRED VEGETABLE PASTA (PAGE 137)

STIR-FRIED BOK CHOY WITH SEARED ONIONS (PAGE 229)

APPLE CRISP (PAGE 254)

FUSILLI WITH CHINESE CORIANDER SAUCE

SERVES 2 AS A FIRST COURSE,
4 AS A SIDE DISH

Preparation time:
20 minutes, plus
30 minutes to soak
mushrooms

Cooking time:
10 minutes

◆▶ *Add sautéed scallops for a nonvegetarian variation.*

This spicy pasta dish is just right for coriander lovers. I serve it as a side dish with stir-fried vegetables or Braised Mushrooms (page 219).

2 dried Chinese mushrooms
1 cup cold water
1½ teaspoons cornstarch
1 tablespoon white wine
2 teaspoons salt
⅓ pound fusilli
1 tablespoon olive oil
⅓ cup sliced scallions, white and
　green parts in ⅛-inch rounds
1 teaspoon minced fresh ginger

1 teaspoon minced garlic
⅔ cup vegetable stock (see page 30)
　or stock of your choice
1 tablespoon soy sauce
½ teaspoon sugar
¼ cup chopped fresh coriander
　(cilantro)
¼ teaspoon chili oil (see page 43)
1 teaspoon Oriental sesame oil

1. Soak the mushrooms in the water for 30 minutes. Lift the mushrooms from the soaking water and squeeze out as much water as possible. Cut into thin strips.

2. Dissolve the cornstarch in the white wine. Set aside.

3. Bring a large pot of water to a rolling boil. Add the salt and the pasta. Cover until the water returns to a boil. Cook the fusilli until tender but firm, 8 to 10 minutes. Drain.

4. While the fusilli is cooking, place a cast-iron skillet over high heat for 1 minute. Add the olive oil. Turn the heat to low and add the scallions, ginger, and garlic. Sauté until they begin to wilt, 2 minutes. Add the mushrooms, stock, soy sauce, and sugar.

5. Restir the cornstarch mixture. In a steady stream, add it to the skillet, stirring constantly to avoid lumps. Add the coriander and simmer for a few seconds. Remove from the heat. Stir in the chili oil and sesame oil. Add the fusilli and toss well to coat. Serve immediately.

Water chestnut powder, arrowroot, cornstarch, and kudzu share the same cooking properties: they thicken immediately and break down if cooked for too long. Add them just before you remove the food from the heat and then cook only long enough to thicken, not more than fifteen to twenty seconds.

I call for cornstarch in these recipes because it's the most familiar of the four thickening agents. Water chestnut powder is hard to find outside of Chinese communities. Kudzu and arrowroot are available at health food stores.

FUSILLI WITH ROASTED PEPPERS AND SHALLOTS

Many of my pasta dishes are entrees or first courses, but a few, such as this recipe, are accompanying dishes that I use as I do rice or potatoes.

Fusilli with Roasted Peppers and Shallots, when served with Asparagus with Brown Butter and Lemon (page 211) and Tomatoes Stuffed with Herbs and Cheese (page 68), would make a composed plate fit for any gathering.

⅓ cup vegetable stock (see page 30) or stock of your choice
¼ cup white wine
1 cup chopped roasted shallots (see page 39)
1 roasted bell pepper (see page 38), diced
2 tablespoons oil-packed dried tomatoes, drained and cut into strips
2½ teaspoons salt
¼ teaspoon freshly ground black pepper

½ pound fusilli or other short pasta
½ cup grated Parmesan cheese
1 cup whole fresh basil leaves, for garnish

SERVES 6 AS A SIDE DISH OR AS PART OF A COMPOSED PLATE

Preparation time: 15 minutes

Cooking time: 10 minutes

◀● *Try it as a side dish alongside roasted chicken or a veal chop. This dish can be made with chicken stock.*

MENU FOR A SUMMER LUNCH

GREEN BEANS WITH DOUBLE SESAME DRESSING (PAGE 90)

BOWTIES WITH WALNUTS AND RED PEPPERS (PAGE 140)

SLICED TOMATOES

A GOOD-QUALITY, STORE-BOUGHT COUNTRY BREAD

FRESH FRUIT

SERVES 3 TO 4 AS AN ENTREE, 4 TO 5 AS A FIRST COURSE

Preparation time: 20 minutes

Cooking time: 25 minutes

1. In a medium skillet, combine the stock and wine. Reduce for 1 minute. Add the shallots, bell pepper, and dried tomatoes. Simmer for a few seconds. Add salt and pepper to taste, then remove from the heat.

Can be prepared up to 1 hour ahead. Reheat before using.

2. Bring a large pot of water to a rolling boil. Add about 2 teaspoons salt and the pasta. Cover until the water returns to a boil. Cook the fusilli until tender but firm, 7 to 9 minutes.

3. Drain the pasta and add it to the pot. Remove from the heat. Add the grated cheese and stir. Garnish with basil leaves. Serve immediately.

BOWTIES WITH WALNUTS AND RED PEPPERS

*I*nspired by a recipe by Jacques Pepin, this unusually pretty pasta salad, with its range of contrasting colors against a background of bowtie pasta, makes a marvelous simple summer lunch.

1 teaspoon melted butter
¼ cup chopped walnuts
3 teaspoons salt
½ pound bowties or other short pasta
1½ cups chopped onions
1 tablespoon olive oil
1 tablespoon sliced garlic

½ teaspoon freshly ground black pepper
2 tablespoons fresh oregano, or ½ teaspoon dried
¼ cup chopped fresh parsley
2 roasted red bell peppers (see page 38), diced, juice reserved
⅓ cup grated Parmesan cheese

1. Preheat the oven to 325°F.

2. Mix the butter and chopped walnuts in a bowl, then transfer to a roasting pan. Roast until the walnuts have darkened in color, 5 to 10 minutes. Set aside.

3. Bring a large pot of water to a rolling boil. Add 2 teaspoons salt and the pasta. Cover until the water returns to a boil. Cook until tender but firm, 7 to 9 minutes. Before draining pasta, reserve ¼ cup of the pasta water.

4. In a medium skillet, sauté the onions over medium heat in the olive oil until they begin to brown, 8 to 10 minutes.

5. Add the garlic and sauté for 2 to 3 minutes. Add the reserved pasta water and simmer for 1 minute. Add the remaining 1 teaspoon salt, pepper, oregano, parsley, and roasted peppers and their juice, and remove from the heat.

6. Drain the pasta and add to the sauce. Toss. Add the walnuts and Parmesan cheese, and mix again. Serve hot or at room temperature.

ORZO PRIMAVERA

Orzo is pasta in the shape of rice. Colorful, creamy, and luscious, Orzo Primavera has been a staple on the buffet tables in my catering business for the past ten years.

4 teaspoons salt
½ pound orzo
1 tablespoon olive oil
1 red bell pepper, seeded, cored, and diced
4 shallots, minced; or 1 medium leek, cleaned (page 32) and chopped; or 1 medium onion, chopped
1 tablespoon minced garlic
1 unpeeled carrot, cut into thin circles

1 medium zucchini, diced
1 medium yellow summer squash, diced
½ cup vegetable stock (see page 30) or stock of your choice
½ cup tomato sauce, preferably homemade (see page 34)
¼ teaspoon freshly ground black pepper
2 tablespoons half-and-half
½ cup grated Parmesan cheese

1. Bring a pot of water to a rolling boil. Add 2 teaspoons of salt and the orzo. Cover until the water returns to a boil. Cook until just tender, 6 to 8 minutes.

2. Heat the oil in a medium skillet. Add the red pepper and sauté over very low heat for 10 minutes. Raise the heat to medium; add the shallots, leek, or onion, the garlic, and the carrot, and sauté until the carrot begins

MENU FOR A BUFFET

ORZO PRIMAVERA (PAGE 141)

CANNELLINI SALAD WITH RED WINE VINAIGRETTE (PAGE 108)

TOMATOES STUFFED WITH HERBS AND CHEESE (PAGE 68)

CLASSIC ROASTED PEPPERS (PAGE 38)

GREEN SALAD WITH HOUSE BALSAMIC VINAIGRETTE (PAGE 48)

CHOCOLATE ANGEL FOOD CAKE (PAGE 247) AND STRAWBERRIES WITH RASPBERRY SAUCE (PAGE 261)

SERVES 6 AS A FIRST COURSE, 8 AS A SIDE DISH, 8 TO 12 AS PART OF A BUFFET

Preparation time: 20 minutes

Cooking time: 15 minutes

to soften, 2 to 3 minutes. Add the zucchini and summer squash and cook for 1 minute more.

3. Turn the heat to high. Add the stock, tomato sauce, remaining 2 teaspoons salt, and pepper. When the sauce comes to a simmer, turn the heat to low. Stir well.

4. Drain the orzo in a colander and add to the sauce. Stir for several seconds until all the sauce is absorbed. Add the half-and-half and stir. Remove from the heat and add the grated cheese; stir again. Serve hot or at room temperature.

Orzo Primavera is best the day it's made, but can be refrigerated for 2 days. Return to room temperature, or gently reheat before serving.

PASTA RISOTTO

I first ate a risotto made with pasta during a pretheater dinner at Cafe Luxembourg, the well-known Manhattan Upper West Side restaurant. It came alongside a succulent veal chop, and I thought it was divine. The first thing I did the next morning was concoct my own version.

I frequently substitute this simple pasta for rice or potatoes on a vegetarian composed plate. It makes a great side dish for a vegetarian featured entree, such as Roasted Portobello Mushrooms (page 198) or Mixed Vegetables al Forno (page 206).

SERVES 4 TO 6 AS A SIDE DISH OR PART OF A COMPOSED PLATE

Preparation time:
15 minutes

Cooking time:
10 minutes

➼ *Try this with a simple nonvegetarian entree, such as grilled fish or roasted chicken. Chicken stock is terrific in this risotto.*

2½ teaspoons salt
1 cup orzo
¼ cup finely chopped shallots
   (about 2 shallots)
1 tablespoon olive oil
½ cup vegetable stock (see page 30)
   or stock of your choice

2 tablespoons half-and-half
½ cup frozen peas or sugar-snap
   peas, strings removed (see Note)
¼ teaspoon freshly ground
   black pepper
⅓ cup grated Parmesan cheese

1. Bring a large pot of water to a rolling boil. Add 2 teaspoons of salt and the orzo. Cover until the water returns to a boil. Cook until not quite

tender, 5 to 6 minutes. The orzo should be slightly underdone to allow for further cooking. Drain.

2. While the orzo is cooking, in a medium skillet sauté the shallots in the olive oil until they are golden brown, 4 to 5 minutes.

3. Add the stock to the skillet and bring to a simmer. Add the drained orzo and stir. Turn the heat to low. Cook until most of the stock has been absorbed by the orzo.

4. Add the half-and-half, peas, remaining ½ teaspoon salt, and pepper. Cook until heated through, stirring several times, 1 to 2 minutes. Remove from the heat and add the cheese. Stir. Serve immediately.

Note: If using fresh peas, add them with the stock.

Pasta Caponata

Whenever I make Chino Caponata, I prepare more than I need so I can also make this savory pasta. Particularly good as an entree for a special dinner party, I often feature this dish at dinners I cater.

1 tablespoon olive oil
1 garlic clove, minced
2 cups tomato sauce, preferably homemade (see page 34)
1 cup Chino Caponata (see page 53)

1 tablespoon mascarpone or heavy cream
2 teaspoons salt
½ pound bowties
½ cup grated Parmesan cheese

1. Heat the olive oil in a medium skillet. Add the garlic, and sauté until golden, 2 to 3 minutes.

2. Add the tomato sauce and bring to a simmer. Stir in the Chino Caponata and bring to a simmer again. Add the mascarpone or cream and stir. Remove from the heat.

Sauce can be prepared up to 1 day ahead and refrigerated. Reheat before using.

SERVES 2 TO 3 AS AN ENTREE,
4 AS A FIRST COURSE

Preparation time:
10 to 15 minutes

Cooking time:
10 minutes

MENU FOR AN INFORMAL
DINNER PARTY

ROASTED BUTTERNUT
SQUASH (PAGE 52)

WHITE BEANS WITH
PAN-ROASTED GARLIC
(PAGE 157) ON
GRILLED BREAD

ROASTED PEPPERS
AND ROASTED
SHALLOTS
(PAGES 38, 39)

RADIATORE WITH
PIZZIOLA SAUCE
(PAGE 144)

APPLES STEWED IN
CALVADOS (PAGE 255)

SERVES 2 TO 3
AS AN ENTREE,
4 AS A FIRST COURSE

Preparation time:
20 minutes

Cooking time:
15 to 20 minutes

3. Bring a large pot of water to a rolling boil. Add the salt and pasta. Cover until the water returns to a boil. Cook until the pasta is tender but firm, 6 to 10 minutes.

4. Drain the pasta and add it to the sauce. Stir and remove from the heat. Add the grated cheese and mix. Serve immediately.

RADIATORE WITH PIZZIOLA SAUCE

*T*his hearty, piquant tomato sauce is mellowed by the addition of goat cheese. I like to use radiatore—an American pasta that resembles miniature accordions—because they hold the sauce well.

1 cup chopped Vidalia or Spanish
   onion
1 tablespoon olive oil
1 tablespoon minced garlic
1 (14-ounce) can whole tomatoes
1 tablespoon fresh oregano, or 1
   teaspoon dried
2½ teaspoons salt
¼ teaspoon freshly ground black
   pepper
1 teaspoon sugar

½ pound radiatore or any other
   short pasta
¼ cup pitted and chopped oil-cured
   black olives
1 tablespoon capers, rinsed and
   drained
¼ teaspoon hot red pepper flakes
2 tablespoons chopped fresh parsley
2½ ounces fresh goat cheese, crumbled (about ½ cup)

1. In a medium skillet, sauté the onion in the olive oil until soft, 3 to 4 minutes. Add the garlic and sauté until golden, 1 to 2 minutes.

2. Empty the can of tomatoes, including the juice, into a bowl. Crush them (I use my hands; this gives the sauce a desirable rough texture), then add to the onion mixture. If using dried oregano, add it now. Simmer until the sauce is thick, about 15 minutes. While the sauce is simmering, add ½ teaspoon salt, pepper, and sugar.

3. Meanwhile, bring a large pot of water to a rolling boil. Add the remaining 2 teaspoons salt and the pasta. Cover until the water returns to a boil. Cook until tender but firm, 6 to 8 minutes.

4. Stir in the olives, capers, red pepper flakes, fresh oregano if using, and parsley into the sauce and simmer 1 minute longer.

5. Drain the pasta and add it to the sauce; toss. Add the goat cheese, remove from the heat, and toss again. Serve hot.

I prefer to make this sauce the same day, but it can be made a day ahead, refrigerated, and gently reheated. Omit the fresh oregano and the parsley, and add them when you reheat the sauce.

PENNE WITH CREAMY BASIL TOMATO SAUCE

*I*talians call this a pasta with pink sauce. The half-and-half softens the acidity of the tomatoes, creating a smoother flavor with less bite. Rich and creamy, it's ideal for a company meal as well as a family dinner.

1 tablespoon chopped garlic
1 tablespoon olive oil
2 cups tomato sauce, preferably homemade (see page 34)
2 tablespoons white wine
¼ cup half-and-half
¼ cup drained oil-packed dried tomatoes

2 teaspoons salt
½ pound penne or other short tubular pasta
½ cup torn fresh basil leaves
¼ cup grated Parmesan cheese

1. In a medium skillet, sauté the garlic in the olive oil over low heat until the garlic is light brown, 1 to 2 minutes. Add the tomato sauce and simmer for 1 minute. Add the wine and simmer for a few seconds. Stir in the half-and-half and simmer for a few seconds more. Add the dried tomatoes and stir.

Sauce can be prepared up to 1 day ahead and refrigerated. Reheat before using.

2. Bring a large pot of water to a rolling boil. Add the salt and the pasta. Cover until the water returns to a boil. Cook the penne until tender but firm, 8 to 10 minutes.

*T*wo rough equivalents for half-and-half are: 3 tablespoons of whole milk mixed with 1 tablespoon of heavy cream and 2 tablespoons of low-fat milk mixed with 1 tablespoon of heavy cream.

SERVES 2 TO 3 AS AN ENTREE, 4 AS A PASTA COURSE

Preparation time: 20 minutes

Cooking time: 10 minutes

*E*xcept when I'm cooking in a wok or stir-frying, I use wooden spoons to stir most dishes. Wooden spoons don't bruise or tear the pasta, nor do they scrape and scratch the bottom of my pots.

3. Add the basil and simmer sauce for a few seconds. Drain the pasta and add it to the sauce. Toss well to coat.

4. Remove the pasta and sauce from the heat. Add the cheese. Mix half of cheese in with the sauce; sprinkle the other half on top. Serve immediately.

PENNE WITH ROASTED TOMATO AND LEEK SAUCE

The roasting of the tomatoes before they are sautéed sets this sauce apart from other tomato sauces.

If you have leftovers, the next day oil a small heatproof dish and place the pasta in it. Dot the top with bits of fresh goat cheese and bake at 425°F. until the cheese softens and begins to melt, 6 to 7 minutes.

Serves 6 as an entree, 8 as a pasta course

Preparation time: 15 minutes

Cooking time: 1 hour and 20 minutes

1 tablespoon plus 1 teaspoon olive oil
3 pounds plum tomatoes
5 cups chopped leeks, white and light green parts (about 4 medium)
4 garlic cloves, chopped
3½ teaspoons salt
½ teaspoon freshly ground black pepper
1 teaspoon sugar
½ cup white wine
⅓ cup dried tomatoes
1 pound penne
2 cups torn fresh basil leaves
½ cup grated Parmesan cheese

1. Preheat the oven to 450°F.

2. Place 1 teaspoon of oil in the palms of your hands and rub each tomato with the oil. Place the tomatoes in a shallow roasting pan and roast for 30 minutes or until they begin to scorch. Remove the tomatoes from the oven.

3. Heat a large skillet for 1 minute. Add the remaining tablespoon of oil and sauté the leeks over medium-low heat until they begin to wilt, about 2 minutes. Add the garlic and sauté for 1 to 2 minutes.

4. Add the roasted tomatoes, 1½ teaspoons of salt, pepper, sugar, and wine. Break up the tomatoes with a wooden spoon as the sauce cooks. Simmer the sauce for 20 minutes. Add the dried tomatoes and cook for 2 minutes longer. The sauce will be thick with a coarse, rough texture.

Sauce can be prepared 1 day ahead, but do not add the basil or cheese. Refrigerate. Reheat before using.

5. Bring a large pot of water to a rolling boil. Add the remaining 2 teaspoons of salt and the penne. Cover until the water returns to a boil. Cook the penne until tender but still firm, 8 to 10 minutes.

lways add the Parmesan cheese after the sauce has been removed from the heat or the cheese will stick to the bottom of the pan.

6. Add the basil to the sauce.

7. Drain the penne and add it to the sauce. Remove from the heat. Toss the pasta and sauce using 2 wooden spoons. Add half the cheese and toss again. Sprinkle the remaining cheese on top of the pasta. Serve immediately.

LINGUINI WITH TOMATO SAUCE AND ROASTED POBLANO PEPPER

A hearty, piquant pasta that's perfect for a cool evening. I like to serve this with Braised Escarole with Garlic (page 217) or with a salad of bitter greens with Porcini Vinaigrette (page 49).

SERVES 2 AS AN ENTREE, 4 AS A SIDE DISH

Preparation time: 20 minutes

Cooking time: 10 minutes

¼ cup chopped shallots (2 to 3 shallots)
1 tablespoon olive oil
1 tablespoon minced garlic
1½ cups tomato sauce, preferably homemade (see page 34)
2 tablespoons white wine
½ roasted poblano pepper (see page 38), diced

1 teaspoon salt
⅓ pound linguini
⅓ cup grated Parmesan cheese

◄• For a nonvegetarian delight, add some diced sautéed prosciutto to the sauce.

Serves 2 as an entree, 4 as a side dish

❧

Preparation time: 20 minutes

❧

Cooking time: 15 minutes

1. In a medium skillet, sauté the shallots in the oil until they are soft, about 3 minutes. Add the garlic and sauté until lightly golden, 1 minute more. Add the tomato sauce and wine and bring to a simmer. Add the roasted pepper.

Sauce can be prepared up to 1 day ahead and refrigerated. Reheat before using.

2. Bring a large pot of water to a rolling boil. Add the salt and the pasta. Cover until the water returns to a boil. Cook the linguini until tender but firm, 7 to 9 minutes.

3. Drain the pasta and reserve some of the pasta water. Add the pasta and as much reserved water as you need to the simmering sauce, 2 to 3 tablespoons. Toss well to coat.

4. Remove the pot from the heat. Mix in half the Parmesan cheese, then sprinkle with the remaining half. Serve immediately.

Pasta Shells with Spicy Tomato Sauce

This is an easy-to-make last-minute dish with a South-of-the border taste.

4 garlic cloves, chopped
1 tablespoon olive oil
1 jalapeño pepper, seeded and chopped fine
8 plum tomatoes, each cut in sixths
3 teaspoons salt

¼ teaspoon freshly ground black pepper
⅓ pound shells or other short pasta
½ cup coarsely chopped fresh coriander (cilantro)

1. In a medium skillet, sauté the garlic over low heat in the olive oil until it begins to turn golden, 2 to 3 minutes. Add the jalapeño pepper and sauté for 1 to 2 minutes.

2. Add the tomatoes, 1 teaspoon salt and the pepper and cook, partially covered, until the tomatoes soften and begin to fall apart, 10 to 12 minutes. Stir every few minutes.

3. Meanwhile, bring a large pot of water to a rolling boil. Add the remaining 2 teaspoons of salt and the pasta. Cover until the water returns to a boil. Cook until the pasta is tender but firm, 7 to 9 minutes.

4. Drain the pasta and add it to the simmering sauce. Toss to combine. Add the coriander and toss lightly again. Serve hot.

Spaghetti with Tomatoes, Basil, and Parsley

Except for my Chinese cooking classes, I teach almost all of my students how to make this pasta dish. I discovered years ago that few cooks know how to make a really good, simple tomato sauce. I use this sauce with either long or short pasta.

SERVES 2 TO 3 AS AN ENTREE

Preparation time: 30 minutes

Cooking time: 40 minutes

¼ cup minced shallots (2 to 3 shallots)
1 cup chopped onion
2 tablespoons olive oil
3 garlic cloves, minced
4 cups diced plum tomatoes
3 teaspoons salt
1 teaspoon sugar
½ teaspoon freshly ground black pepper

¼ cup chopped fresh parsley
1 cup chopped fresh basil
½ pound spaghetti
Grated Parmesan cheese

1. In a medium skillet, sauté the shallots and onion in the olive oil over low heat until they begin to soften, about 2 minutes. Add the garlic and sauté until it begins to brown, 1 to 2 minutes.

2. Add the tomatoes, 1 teaspoon salt, sugar, and pepper. Simmer for 30 minutes. Add the parsley and basil; simmer 1 minute. Remove from the heat.

Sauce can be prepared to this point up to 1 day ahead and refrigerated. Reheat before using.

3. Bring a large pot of water to a rolling boil. Add the remaining 2 tea-

spoons of salt and the pasta. Cover until the water returns to a boil. Cook until the pasta is tender but firm, 7 to 9 minutes.

4. Drain the pasta and add it to the sauce. Stir well. Serve hot, sprinkled with grated cheese.

Chapter 9

BEANS

As a child in Manhattan, the only beans I remember were the canned baked beans our neighbors served with frankfurters at their Fourth of July barbecues. However, as an adult I periodically came across zesty bean mixtures at restaurants served as accompaniments to fish and meat and I was surprised how much I liked them. Eventually I included beans in my own cooking. Years ago I developed a luscious high-fat version of White Beans with Pan-Roasted Garlic to serve with roasted leg of lamb. Today, of course, I give beans the star billing they deserve without the fat.

Every region of the world has bean dishes it cherishes: Brazil has *feijoada,* spicy black beans with lots of meat and sausage; France, the incredibly rich *cassoulet;* the Middle East, the familiar chickpea and tahini dip *hummus;* New Orleans, red beans and rice. Throughout the world beans are relied on as an inexpensive source of protein. However, in this country beans have mostly been a staple of vegetarians looking for alternate sources of protein.

It's only in the last few years that the rest of us have caught on to what a nutritious and valuable food beans are: well balanced in protein and carbohydrates, low in fat, and high in fiber. More recently, American chefs and home cooks have also discovered how tasty beans can be.

Unfortunately, many bean dishes rely on fat for flavoring, sabotaging the very reason so many of us turn to beans in the first place. While it's true that beans by themselves are pretty boring, it's not necessary to load them with fat to make them taste wonderful. Small amounts of fat; creative combinations of leeks, shallots, garlic, scallions, and onions; an abundance of herbs and spices; and roasted hot and mild peppers can give you more flavor and eating satisfaction than absurd quantities of fat.

Dried beans should *always* be picked over and washed before being soaked. Spread them on a large pan. A cookie sheet with sides (often called a jelly-roll pan) is ideal for the job. Remove any small stones and bits of dirt. Put the beans in a bowl and cover them with water. Swish the water around with your hand. Discard this water.

Other than lentils, I soak all beans before cooking them. Soaking not only speeds the cooking time but makes beans more digestible. Split peas and black-eyed peas, while they can be cooked without soaking, will cook in shorter time if soaked for one to two hours.

There are two methods for soaking beans: overnight and quick-soak. No matter which method you choose, discard the soaking water to eliminate the oligosaccharides that can cause intestinal gas.

With the *quick-soak method*, cover the beans with three to four inches of water and bring to a boil for a minute or two. Cover the pot and remove from the heat, leaving the beans to soak for an hour.

For the *overnight method*, cover the beans with three to four inches of water and let them soak for six to eight hours or overnight.

Generally, one cup of dried beans yields two to three cups of cooked beans; for chickpeas, 1 cup dried makes about two cups cooked; white beans, about two and a half cups; lentils, about three cups.

The older the beans, the longer they take to cook. Unfortunately, there's no dependable way to know the age of beans. Therefore, never mix beans from two different batches, as each might cook in a different amount of time.

The best way to know if beans are done is to taste them. I start ten minutes before I expect them to be cooked through, and taste one bean every five or ten minutes until they're done. Use cooking times for beans only as a guide.

Add salt after the beans are soft. Salt toughens the outer skin of the bean if added too early.

The easiest way to seed a plum tomato is to cut it in half lengthwise, then use a small spoon—I like a grapefruit spoon with its serrated edge—to scoop out the seeds.

Larger tomatoes, like beefsteak tomatoes, are best seeded by cutting them in half horizontally, squeezing each half lightly to loosen the seeds, and then scooping the seeds out with a spoon.

CANNED BEANS

In every class, at least one student will ask if canned beans can be substituted for cooked beans. I sigh, roll my eyes toward heaven, and admit that, yes, in a pinch, they can.

I don't use canned beans. I find the taste and consistency of beans cooked from their dried state far superior to canned beans, which are often mushy and too salty. Besides, as you may have realized by now, other than the occasional tomato, canned food is not part of my pantry.

Having said this, if you do use canned beans, drain and rinse them well to remove the canned taste and some of the sodium.

In my supermarket, canned beans come in 10½-ounce, 15-ounce, and 16-ounce sizes. Depending on the size of the bean, there's about 1⅓ cups of beans in a 10½-ounce, 1⅔ cups in the 15- and 16-ounce cans.

Some canned beans are firmer than others. Try different brands until you find one you like.

WHITE BEANS WITH A LIGHT TOUCH OF TOMATO

Beans prepared this simple way, with fresh tomatoes and basil, are served in Italy as a side dish alongside a grilled steak or lamb chops. I like them as part of a composed plate with a couple of vegetables and a good coarse-grained bread, as an appetizer before a vegetable entree, or as part of a buffet.

1½ cups chopped seeded tomatoes
1 cup water
1 cup cooked white beans, home-
* made (see page 35) or canned*
* (see page 153), with ¼ cup cook-*
* ing liquid or stock*
½ cup torn fresh basil

1 tablespoon olive oil
Salt and freshly ground black pep-
* per to taste*

1. Heat the tomatoes with the water in a medium saucepan. Bring to a simmer and continue to simmer uncovered for 15 to 20 minutes.

2. Add the bean liquid and simmer for 1 minute. Then add the beans and cook until heated through, about 2 minutes. Add the basil and simmer for a few seconds.

3. Add the olive oil. Taste and add salt and pepper, if desired. Serve hot.

MEDITERRANEAN WHITE BEANS

I especially like this light bean dish at the end of summer, when the choicest beefsteak tomatoes appear. As the celery and garlic are coarsely chopped and the tomatoes only lightly cooked, each vegetable retains its texture and separate flavors.

1 tablespoon olive oil
4 celery stalks, coarsely chopped
8 garlic cloves, coarsely chopped
6 medium round tomatoes, or 10
   plum tomatoes, peeled, seeded,
   and coarsely diced
1 tablespoon chopped fresh
   oregano, or 1 teaspoon dried
1 tablespoon chopped fresh sage, or
   1 teaspoon dried
1 tablespoon chopped fresh thyme,
   or 1 teaspoon dried
1 cup chopped fresh parsley
½ teaspoon sugar
½ teaspoon salt
¼ teaspoon freshly ground black
   pepper
2½ cups cooked white beans,
   homemade (see page 35) or
   canned (see page 153)

1. Heat the oil in a heavy-bottom saucepan. Add the celery and sauté over low heat for 10 minutes. Add the garlic and sauté until the celery is cooked through but still firm, and the garlic is beginning to color, about 5 minutes more.

2. Add the tomatoes and cook until they no longer look raw, 5 to 10 minutes.

3. Add the oregano, sage, thyme, parsley, sugar, salt, pepper, and beans. Cook for 5 minutes. If there's a lot of liquid in the pan, raise the heat a bit until most has evaporated. Serve hot or warm.

Can be prepared up to 1 day ahead and refrigerated.

LEEKS AND BEANS

The key to the subtle flavors of this dish is the slow cooking, which allows the rich flavors of the leeks and beans to fuse in a deeply satisfying way.

3 cups chopped leeks, white part
   only (about 3 medium)
1 tablespoon olive oil
2 garlic cloves, chopped
2½ cups cooked white beans (see page
   35) or canned (see page 153)
½ teaspoon salt
½ teaspoon freshly ground black
   pepper
1 to 2 tablespoons chopped fresh
   sage (see Note)

MENU FOR A WINTER DINNER

WINTER TOMATO SOUP (PAGE 76)

LEEKS AND BEANS (PAGE 155)

BRAISED ESCAROLE WITH GARLIC (PAGE 217)

FRENCH BAGUETTE OR A COARSE-GRAIN TUSCAN BREAD

RICOTTA TORTE (PAGE 248)

SERVES 4 AS AN ENTREE

Preparation time: 20 minutes

Cooking time: 45 minutes

*SERVES 4 AS AN
ENTREE*

*Preparation time:
20 minutes*

*Cooking time:
20 minutes*

1. In a large, heavy-bottom saucepan, sauté the leeks in the olive oil over medium-low heat until they are soft and just beginning to brown, about 20 minutes.

2. Add the garlic and cook for 1 to 2 minutes. Then add the beans, salt, and pepper. Bring to a simmer and cook over low heat for 20 minutes.

3. Add the sage and cook for 2 minutes. Serve hot.

Note: If sage isn't available, you can substitute fresh thyme or equal parts of basil, coriander (cilantro), and parsley. If using dried herbs, add them when you add the beans.

CANNELLINI WITH MUSTARD CREAM SAUCE

I invented this dish one rainy day when I was puttering around the kitchen. I've always liked mustard cream sauces, and I thought how well the flavors would go with white beans. Using half-and-half instead of heavy cream keeps this dish low in fat while adding creaminess and softening the bite of the mustard.

*1 medium leek, white and light
    green parts, cleaned
    (see page 32) and chopped
    (about 1¼ cups)
1 tablespoon olive oil
4 garlic cloves, chopped
½ cup chopped fresh parsley
½ cup white wine
2 cups cooked cannellini, or other
    white beans, homemade (see*

*page 35) or canned
    (see page 153)
2 teaspoons coarse-grain mustard
    (see Note)
3 tablespoons half-and-half*

1. In a heavy-bottom saucepan, sauté the leek in the olive oil until it begins to brown, about 5 minutes. Add the garlic, and sauté for 1 minute.

2. Add the parsley and wine; simmer for 10 to 15 minutes. Add the beans and heat for 1 to 2 minutes.

3. Mix the mustard and half-and-half and add to the beans. Stir and remove from the heat.

Note: I use Grey Poupon's Country Dijon Mustard, available at supermarkets. Try different kinds of mustard—each will lend its own unique flavor.

White Beans with Pan-Roasted Garlic

SERVES 4 TO 6 AS PART OF A COMPOSED PLATE OR AS AN APPETIZER, 8 TO 10 AS PART OF A BUFFET

Preparation time: 10 minutes

Cooking time: 20 to 30 minutes

I teach by having the students work alongside me to prepare a dish. As we cut and chop, I discuss nutrition, ingredients, and the dishes we're preparing. Then we cook, and finally we eat what we've prepared. In the dozens of times I've taught this recipe, I've never had a single bean left on anyone's plate.

The distinctiveness of this dish is due to the pan-roasted garlic, an unconventional but highly effective way to produce roasted garlic that is meltingly soft and moist.

1 tablespoon olive oil
5 garlic cloves, lightly crushed
2½ cups cooked white beans, homemade (see page 35) or canned (see page 153), warmed
1 tablespoon heavy cream

1 teaspoon butter
Salt and freshly ground black pepper to taste
Roasted peppers and roasted shallots (see pages 37, 39) for garnish

1. Place a cast-iron skillet over high heat for 1 minute. Then transfer the skillet to the lowest heat possible. (I pile 4 burner grates for a gas stove on top of one another, turn the heat as low as possible, and then set the skillet on top. With an electric stove, turn the heat to the lowest possible setting and watch the garlic carefully to make sure it doesn't burn.) Add the olive oil and then the garlic. Sauté the garlic *very* slowly, stirring every 5 or 10 minutes, until golden brown, 20 to 30 minutes. Remove the garlic from the pan and mash it with a fork.

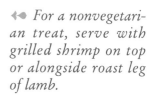

◆ *For a nonvegetarian treat, serve with grilled shrimp on top or alongside roast leg of lamb.*

2. Mash one-third of the beans (see Note). Add the cream and butter, then stir in the garlic. Season with salt and pepper. Gently reheat.

3. Garnish with roasted peppers and roasted shallots and serve.

Note: You can mash all the beans, none of the beans, or some of the beans; it's a matter of taste.

ROASTED VEGETABLE CASSOULET

This is a favorite of mine. I served it to my friend, Jan Buckaloo, who once lived with a French chef and was used to "the real thing"—cassoulet loaded with lamb and duck. Even she loved this flavorful version. It's more time-consuming than most recipes in this book, but well worth the effort. And it is an exceptional entree for a formal or informal dinner party.

SERVES 6 AS AN ENTREE

Preparation time: 30 minutes

Cooking time: 1 hour and 15 minutes

½ medium fennel bulb, cut vertically into ½-inch-thick pieces
2 medium leeks, white and light green parts, cleaned (see page 32) and cut into 1-inch pieces (about 2½ cups)
1 large portobello mushroom or 3 shiitake mushrooms, cut into 1-inch slices
1 unpeeled carrot, cut into 1-inch pieces
1½ teaspoons salt
¾ teaspoon freshly ground black pepper
2 tablespoons olive oil
1 tablespoon fresh thyme, or 1 teaspoon dried

6 shallots, peeled
6 garlic cloves, split, with buds removed
1 cup mushroom stock (page 32) or stock of your choice
2½ cups cooked great northern or other white beans, homemade (see page 35) or canned (see page 153)
½ cup chopped fresh parsley
2 tablespoons butter
⅓ cup grated Parmesan cheese
½ cup dried bread crumbs

MENU FOR A DINNER PARTY

PEPPER SURPRISES (PAGE 61)

ASPARAGUS AND CARROT VINAIGRETTE (PAGE 89)

ROASTED VEGETABLE CASSOULET (PAGE 158)

PEACHES IN RED WINE (PAGE 259)

1. Preheat the oven to 350°F.

2. Toss the fennel, leeks, mushrooms, and carrot with ½ teaspoon salt,

¼ teaspoon pepper, and 1 tablespoon olive oil. Put the vegetables in a large roasting pan and roast until they begin to brown, about 45 minutes.

3. Meanwhile, combine the remaining 1 teaspoon salt, ½ teaspoon pepper, 1 teaspoon olive oil, and the thyme. Divide this mixture in half and toss the shallots with one half. Place in a small flameproof baking dish and cover. Bake alongside the vegetables. Toss the garlic with the other half of the oil mixture. After 20 minutes, uncover the shallots and add the garlic to that pan. Continue to bake uncovered until both shallots and garlic are soft and brown, about 10 minutes.

4. Remove the shallots and garlic from the pan and set aside. Deglaze the pan by adding ¼ cup of the stock and, using a wooden spoon, scrape up the bits that are stuck to the bottom. Set aside until vegetables finish roasting.

5. Add the roasted shallots and garlic, the beans, and ¼ cup of parsley to the roasted vegetables. Stir in the remaining ¾ cup stock and the reserved shallot-onion glaze. Put all the vegetables into a 2–quart ovenproof casserole.

6. Combine the butter, remaining ¼ cup parsley, cheese, and bread crumbs in a bowl. Sprinkle over the cassoulet.

Cassoulet can be prepared to this point several hours ahead.

7. Bake for 30 minutes, or until the bread crumbs are brown and the beans are hot.

Cannellini with Salsa Verde

My friend Kathy Moselle helped me invent this dish. She'd eaten shrimp with green sauce earlier in the week at a Spanish restaurant in Greenwich Village, and we decided that a green sauce would go well over beans. We created batch after batch of sauce. At first we made it too thin and spicy, then we made it too thick and gluey. We played around with ingredients until we finally got the sauce the way we wanted it. Then we made the mistake of putting it over black beans—not attractive. We eventually came up with this recipe, a vibrant, festive, and delicious bean dish.

SERVES 4
AS AN ENTREE

Preparation time:
20 minutes

Cooking time:
20 minutes

2 shallots, chopped
2 tablespoons olive oil
4 garlic cloves, minced
4 teaspoons flour
¼ cup white wine
½ cup Garden Salad Stock (see page 33) or stock of your choice
2 tablespoons chopped oven-roasted pine nuts (see page 41)

½ cup chopped fresh parsley
¾ teaspoon salt
½ teaspoon freshly ground black pepper
½ cup fresh coriander (cilantro; optional)
2 cups cooked cannellini or other white beans, homemade (see page 35) or canned (see page 153)

1. In a heavy-bottom saucepan, sauté the shallots in the olive oil over medium heat until they begin to color, 3 to 5 minutes. Add the garlic and sauté for 1 minute.

2. Add the flour; stir and cook for 1 minute. Add the wine, stock or water, pine nuts, parsley, salt, and pepper. Cook over medium heat until the sauce has thickened, about 5 minutes. If using coriander, add it now.

3. Process the sauce in either a blender or food processor. (The blender yields a smooth sauce; the food processor, a finely minced sauce. Both are good, but I prefer the texture of the sauce made in the food processor).

Sauce can be prepared to this point several hours ahead.

4. Return the sauce to saucepan and add the beans. Cook just until the beans are heated, 2 to 3 minutes. Or heat the beans separately and serve on top of the sauce. Serve warm.

MENU FOR A HOT BUFFET

VEGETABLE LO MEIN
(PAGE 129)

BLACK BEANS WITH
ROASTED PEPPERS
(PAGE 160)

BRAISED ESCAROLE
WITH GARLIC
(PAGE 217)

WHITE RICE

SOUTHWESTERN SALSA
(PAGE 236)

APPLE COBBLER
(VARIATION OF PEACH
AND CHERRY
COBBLER, PAGE 260)

BLACK BEANS WITH ROASTED PEPPERS

*M*ost black bean dishes rely on ham or other cured meats for their flavor, but this one gets its intense, smoky flavor from roasted peppers and cumin.

1½ cups dried black beans, soaked and drained
3 cups stock of your choice or water

¼ cup dried porcini mushrooms or other dried mushrooms
1 cup warm water

2½ cups chopped leeks, white and
  light green parts
  (about 2 medium)
1 tablespoon olive oil
1 tablespoon minced garlic
1 cup crushed canned tomatoes,
  with juice
1½ teaspoons ground cumin,
  preferably roasted (see page 40)
1 bay leaf
½ teaspoon freshly ground black
  pepper
1 to 2 teaspoons salt
1 unpeeled carrot, diced

½ cup diced celery
1 large roasted yellow or red bell
  pepper (see page 37), diced

GARNISH
4 scallions, chopped; 1 red onion,
  chopped; or 1 bunch fresh
  chives, snipped
1 tablespoon chopped fresh
  oregano
2 tablespoons fresh coriander
  (cilantro)

SERVES 6 AS AN
ENTREE, 8 OR MORE AS
PART OF A BUFFET

Preparation time:
30 minutes

Cooking time:
1 hour and 40 minutes

1. Combine the beans and stock or water in a large pot; cover and simmer for 1 hour.

2. Meanwhile, soak the dried mushrooms in the cup of warm water for 30 minutes. Lift the mushrooms from the soaking water, squeezing them over the water to return any liquid to the cup, and dice. Strain the porcini water through a fine-mesh sieve; reserve.

3. In a large, heavy-bottom saucepan, sauté the leeks in the oil until light brown, about 10 minutes. Add the garlic and sauté until it begins to color, 1 to 2 minutes.

4. Add the tomatoes, and porcini water. Bring to a simmer. Add the beans and their liquid, cumin, bay leaf, black pepper, and chopped mushrooms. Cover and simmer for 30 minutes.

5. Add the salt, carrot, and celery and simmer for 10 minutes. Remove the bay leaf. Add the diced roasted pepper and stir.

6. Garnish with scallions or chives, oregano, and coriander. Serve hot.

These beans can be refrigerated for 2 days. Reheat before serving.

Note: This amount of stock makes a soupy stew. To reduce the liquid, after step 5, remove the cooked beans from the pot and boil down the liquid that remains until you have the amount you want. Add the beans and serve.

To turn this into Black Bean Soup with Roasted Peppers, after removing the bay leaf, puree one-third of the beans in a blender or food processor. Return the beans to the pot and add the roasted peppers.

Black beans and chickpeas have sufficient flavor to be cooked in plain water, without vegetables or seasonings. Soak the beans overnight and discard the soaking water. Then cook 1 cup beans in 2 cups water. Black beans cook in 45 minutes to 1 hour, chickpeas in 1 to 1½ hours.

Always reserve the liquid left after the beans are cooked—usually about ⅓ to ½ cup. This glaze can then be poured over the beans for extra flavor or added to salad recipes along with the cooked beans as a way of cutting down on the amount of oil in the dressing.

CHICKPEAS AND SPINACH

This Middle-Eastern combination, with the earthy, nutty taste of chickpeas and the slightly bitter taste of spinach, is outstanding. An unpretentious dish, serve it with basmati rice or Whole-Grain Fried Rice (page 182) along with a raita (pages 241 to 242) or plain yogurt for a simple family dinner.

Serves 2 as an entree

Preparation time: 20 minutes

Cooking time: 10 minutes

1 pound fresh spinach, washed (see page 91) and tough stems removed
3 garlic cloves, chopped
1 tablespoon olive oil
1 cup chopped scallions, white and green parts
1½ cups cooked chickpeas, home- *made (see page 35) or canned (see page 153)*
1 teaspoon ground cumin, preferably roasted (see page 40)
½ teaspoon salt
¼ teaspoon freshly ground black pepper
2 teaspoons lemon juice

1. Steam the spinach until the leaves are wilted, 1 to 2 minutes. Drain in a colander.

2. In a heavy-bottom saucepan, sauté the garlic lightly in the oil, about 2 minutes. Add the scallions and sauté for 1 minute.

3. Add the drained spinach, chickpeas, cumin, salt, and pepper. Stir,

cover, and cook over low heat until the spinach and chickpeas are heated through, 2 to 3 minutes. Add the lemon juice, stir again. Add more salt and pepper, if needed. Serve hot.

Braised Fava Beans with Fresh Herbs

*F*ava beans are available for only a precious few weeks in the spring. If possible, invite a few friends over to help—shelling beans and telling stories go well together.

SERVES 4 AS PART OF A COMPOSED PLATE

Preparation time: 45 minutes

Cooking time: 15 minutes

1 pound fava beans
1 medium leek, white and green parts, cleaned (see page 32) and chopped (about 1¼ cups)
2 tablespoons olive oil
2 garlic cloves, chopped
1 cup chopped tomato
½ teaspoon salt
¼ teaspoon freshly ground black pepper

¼ cup chopped fresh parsley
1 tablespoon minced fresh oregano
1 tablespoon minced fresh thyme

◄● *For a nonvegetarian variation, add sautéed chopped pancetta or prosciutto along with the garlic.*

1. Bring a medium pot of water to a boil. Add the fava beans and blanch for 1 minute. Cool and peel off the skins.

2. In a heavy-bottom saucepan, sauté the leek in the olive oil until it softens, 3 to 5 minutes. Add the garlic and brown slightly, 3 to 4 minutes. Add the tomato and fava beans, cover, and simmer for 10 minutes.

3. Remove the lid from the pot. Add the salt, pepper, and herbs, and simmer for 1 minute more. Serve hot or warm.

GINGER LENTIL STEW

*L*ike most ten-year-olds, my son Todd couldn't sit still for more than five minutes. When it came time to plan our vacation, I picked out a farm in Pennsylvania that encouraged the guests to help with farm chores, thinking this would teach Todd about rural life and be a wonderful opportunity to use some of his bountiful energy.

In early July, bubbling with enthusiasm, we set out from Manhattan in our old Datsun. Within an hour of arriving, I realized we were the only "guests" at the farm. By the next day I knew why.

At this time of the year, in this part of Pennsylvania, microscopic insects swarm around the horses—and any part of us that was bare—making riding impossible. Plus, the owner of the farm had recently retired from farming, so there were no chores to be done. A disastrous vacation for an active child!

The only good thing I remember was a wonderful spicy lentil stew with a unique ginger kick. Here's my version. To turn the stew into a hearty soup, add an additional cup of stock.

1 cup chopped leeks, white and light green parts (about 1 small leek)
½ unpeeled carrot, diced
2 celery stalks, diced
1 tablespoon olive oil
1 tablespoon minced fresh ginger
1 tablespoon minced garlic
3 cups Garden Salad Stock (see page 33) or stock of your choice
1 cup lentils, preferably French green lentils

1 teaspoon ground cumin, preferably roasted (see page 40)
¼ teaspoon freshly ground black pepper
¼ teaspoon salt
2 tablespoons soy sauce

1. In a large, heavy-bottom saucepan, sauté the leeks, carrot, and celery in the olive oil over medium heat until they begin to wilt, 5 to 8 minutes. Add the ginger and garlic and sauté for 2 minutes.

2. Stir in the stock, lentils, cumin, and pepper. Cover and cook for 30 minutes.

3. Add the salt and soy sauce and cook until the lentils are soft, another 15 to 30 minutes. Serve with rice.

The stew can be prepared up to 2 days ahead and refrigerated.

Lentil and Potato Stew with Spiced Oil

*T*his lentil stew has become a staple in my life. I eat it several times a month and never grow tired of it. Even my old tennis buddy Rae-Carole Fischer, who swears she's never met a lentil she likes, loves this dish. Turn the stew into a soup by adding more water.

SERVES 6 AS AN ENTREE, 8 OR MORE AS A SOUP

Preparation time: 20 minutes

Cooking time: 45 minutes

6 cups water
1½ cups lentils
1 red or yellow bell pepper, cut into 1-inch squares
2 medium potatoes, peeled or unpeeled, cubed
2 unpeeled carrots, cut into ⅓-inch rounds
1 large Spanish onion, cut into 1-inch pieces
2 celery stalks, cut into 1-inch pieces

¼ cup soy sauce
½ teaspoon freshly ground black pepper
1 bay leaf

SPICED OIL
2 tablespoons olive oil or butter
1 teaspoon ground ginger
1 teaspoon turmeric
1 teaspoon ground cumin, preferably roasted (see page 40)

1. Combine the water, lentils, bell pepper, potatoes, carrots, onion, celery, soy sauce, pepper, and bay leaf in a large pot. Cover and bring to a boil; reduce the heat and simmer for 45 minutes.

2. Meanwhile, warm the oil in a small saucepan over low heat, 1 to 2 minutes. Remove from the heat and add the ginger, turmeric, and cumin. Stir and set aside.

3. When the stew is cooked, add the spiced oil. Season with salt and additional pepper, if needed. Remove the bay leaf. Serve hot.

This stew can be refrigerated for up to 3 days.

MENU FOR A HEARTY WINTER BUFFET
....

LENTIL AND POTATO STEW WITH SPICED OIL (PAGE 165)

VEGETABLE COUSCOUS WITH STEEPED PAPRIKA (PAGE 172)

STIR-FRIED SPINACH (PAGE 229)

CORN BREAD (PAGE 177)

APPLES STEWED IN CALVADOS (PAGE 255)

CREOLE BLACK-EYED PEAS

SERVES 4 AS AN
ENTREE

Preparation time:
20 to 30 minutes

Cooking time:
30 to 40 minutes

I invented this dish for my friend Donald Highsmith, a transplanted Southerner with roots in New Orleans, who's always complained that no one in New York can cook black-eyed peas. (I've never met a Southerner who wasn't a fool for black-eyed peas!) He loves these spicy beans served with rice and Corn Bread (page 177).

4 shallots, chopped
2 medium onions, chopped
3 celery stalks, chopped
1 tablespoon olive oil
6 to 8 garlic cloves, minced
½ to 1 jalapeño pepper, minced
2½ cups cooked black-eyed peas,
    homemade (see page 36) or
    canned (see page 153)
Garden Salad Stock (see page 33)
    or stock of your choice, as
    needed (see Note)

½ teaspoon ground cumin,
    preferably roasted (see page 40)
1 teaspoon salt
¼ teaspoon freshly ground black
    pepper

1. In a deep, heavy-bottom saucepan, sauté the shallots, onions, and celery over medium heat in the olive oil until the onions begin to turn golden, 10 to 15 minutes. Add the garlic and jalapeño pepper and sauté for 2 to 3 minutes.

2. Add the black-eyed peas with some of its cooking liquid or stock to moisten the mixture (see Note). Bring to a simmer and add the cumin, salt, and pepper. Partially cover and keep at a low simmer for 15 to 20 minutes. Add additional bean liquid and stock as needed. Serve hot.

Note: If serving Creole Black-Eyed Peas as a soupy stew over rice, add most or all of the cooking liquid from the black-eyed peas and, if you like, additional stock. If serving as part of a composed plate with other vegetables, add only a few tablespoons of liquid to keep the beans from drying out while they cook.

RED BEAN SAUCE

This delicious recipe comes from Dominique Richard, an excellent cook as well as a gifted homeopathic practitioner. These flavorful beans, with just a suggestion of garlic, have become a primary part of my diet.

1 cup small red beans or kidney beans, soaked and drained
2 cups water
1 medium onion, quartered
1 unpeeled carrot
1 celery stalk
1 bay leaf
¼ teaspoon freshly ground black pepper
1 tablespoon olive oil
1 tablespoon chopped garlic
1 teaspoon dried oregano
1 tablespoon chopped fresh sage, or 1 teaspoon dried
⅛ teaspoon freshly ground black pepper
½ teaspoon ground cumin, preferably roasted (see page 40)
1 teaspoon salt

1. In a medium saucepan, combine the beans, water, onion, carrot, celery, bay leaf, and pepper; cook until the beans are soft, 45 minutes to 1 hour. Remove the bay leaf, onion, carrot, and celery. Drain beans and reserve cooking liquid.

2. Place a skillet over high heat for 1 minute, then add the olive oil. Reduce the heat to low, add the garlic, and stir. Add the oregano, sage, pepper, cumin, and salt. Sauté until the garlic begins to color, about 2 minutes.

3. Put the contents of the skillet, the beans, and ¼ cup of the cooking liquid into a food processor or blender. Process until the beans are smooth (see Note). Add additional cooking liquid—up to ½ cup—to achieve the desired consistency. Serve hot.

The bean sauce can be prepared several hours ahead and gently reheated, adding a little stock or water if needed.

Note: If you prefer, puree only some of the beans for a chunky consistency or leave all the beans whole.
   This sauce can also be a dip if you use less liquid.

SERVES 4 AS AN ENTREE

Preparation time: 30 minutes

Cooking time: About 1 hour

MENU FOR A SIMPLE DINNER

ASPARAGUS AND CARROT VINAIGRETTE (PAGE 89)

BASMATI RICE WITH LEEKS AND CAULIFLOWER (PAGE 186)

RED BEAN SAUCE (PAGE 167)

BAREFOOT CONTESSA'S LOW-FAT GINGER CAKE (PAGE 246)

PAN-SEARED TOFU

SERVES 4 AS PART OF A
COMPOSED PLATE,
6 AS PART OF A BUFFET

In advance:
2 hours for the tofu
to drain and 1 day
to marinate

Preparation time:
15 minutes

Cooking time:
10 minutes

I have had the good fortune to eat many a delicious meal at The Autumn Cafe in Oneonta, New York, with my son Todd Hartman, a glass artist, who lives in Oneonta. The restaurant has mostly a vegetarian menu, and they were kind enough to share this recipe with me.

The tofu can marinate for up to three days. I often make this recipe and then cook the amount of tofu I want each day, leaving the rest refrigerated in the marinade.

1 pound firm tofu (see Note)
¼ cup soy sauce
1 cup water
¼ teaspoon dried oregano
¼ teaspoon dried tarragon
¼ teaspoon dried dill
¼ teaspoon dried thyme
1 tablespoon peanut oil

1. Place the tofu on a towel and let dry for 1 hour. Cut into slices ⅜ inch thick, then place the slices on a dry towel to drain for another hour.

2. Combine the soy sauce, water, and herbs. Submerge the tofu in this liquid and refrigerate for at least 24 hours. If the liquid doesn't completely cover, baste several times over the next day.

Can be prepared to this point up to 3 days ahead and refrigerated.

3. Drain the tofu before frying. Place an iron skillet over high heat for 3 to 5 minutes. Add ½ tablespoon of the oil and add half of the tofu slices. Do not crowd the pan. Sear over high heat until the tofu is brown and crusty, about 2 minutes each side. Repeat the procedure with the remaining oil and tofu slices. Serve immediately.

Note: Tofu can be found in the produce section of most supermarkets.

Chapter 10

GRAINS

Following the advice of nutritionists, these days my meals are frequently built around grains. It's a rare week when I don't have cooked brown rice and at least one other cooked grain in my refrigerator with which to make Whole-Grain Fried Rice. It's this dish, with its endless variations, that I eat most often. All grains are low in fat, and like other foods derived from plants, have no cholesterol. Whole grains have an abundance of vitamins, minerals, fiber, and carbohydrates. With their mild, earthy flavors, they act as a perfect backdrop for a variety of seasonings and embellishments.

I also eat lots of white rice. While I love the rich nutty flavor of basmati rice and the perfumed scent of jasmine rice, any long-grain white rice can be cooked exactly the same way with excellent results.

I went to Boston one weekend to attend a seminar in macrobiotic philosophy and cooking. I had been catering and teaching cooking for more than twelve years. But it was here that I finally learned how to wash grains properly. Place the grain in a bowl and cover it with cold water by a few inches. Swish the grain around with your hands to allow the "natural grains of nature"—also known as dirt—to float to the top. Pour off the water and place the grain in a strainer to drain it.

As I like them firm, I cook the grains in less water than most packages or other recipes call for. Since I also prefer most grains dry and separate, I cook them for a relatively short time and then let them "relax" (sit covered, off the heat in the cooking pot).

Using a heavy-bottom saucepan with a tight-fitting cover, I bring the water to a rolling boil over high heat. I add the drained grain and stir briefly with chopsticks or a wooden spoon. Once the water has returned to a rolling boil, I stir it again. Then I cover the pot and turn the heat to very low. I let the grain simmer for the specified time before checking to see if it's done. It's properly cooked when steam holes—the Chinese call them "fish eyes"—appear. Then I let the grain relax.

If I'm going to char the grains, I spread them out in a shallow roasting pan or plate to cool and further dry for several hours. When the grains are dry and separate, I cover and refrigerate them for up to five days. The secret to perfect charring—which deepens the naturally nutty flavor of rice and other grains—is to first cook and thoroughly cool the grains, at least a few hours ahead.

I also enjoy couscous, a fast-cooking granulated semolina popular throughout northern Africa. When well-seasoned and studded with vegetables, couscous makes a terrific featured entree, side dish, or first course.

Recently I've created a number of polenta dishes. Polenta, a cornmeal porridge, is revered in many parts of northern Italy. When first cooked, it has the consistency of mashed potatoes. When allowed to cool, it hardens and can be fried or broiled. Topped with a vegetable or meat stew, pasta sauces, or spicy beans, polenta is an outstanding change-of-pace from pasta.

WASHING AND COOKING GRAINS

Grains that Need Washing

All whole grains, brown rice, and Asian white rice should be washed. American white rice doesn't need washing.

Proportion of Grain to Cooking Water

1 cup grain to 1½ cups water

2 cups grain to 2¾ cups water

3 cups grain to 3 cups water (this one-to-one ratio continues for any amount larger than 3 cups)

Cooking and Relaxing Time

Whole grains, including brown rice, should cook for 30 minutes, then relax for 30 minutes. All white rices, including basmati, converted, and Japanese short-grain, should cook for 15 minutes, then relax for 15 minutes.

Vegetable Couscous with Steeped Paprika

SERVES 6 AS AN
ENTREE, 8 TO 12 AS
PART OF A COMPOSED
PLATE OR A BUFFET

Preparation time:
20 minutes

Cooking time:
5 minutes

Alexandra Branyon, a gifted playwright and long-time friend, has been enormously influential in expanding my vegetarian horizons. I turn to her when I'm having a hard time coming up with the final touch for a dish.

It was Alexandra's suggestion to steep the paprika in vegetable stock (just as you steep saffron) to bring out its eye-catching color and warm flavor.

•→ *I like to serve this couscous with grilled swordfish and a green vegetable.*

1¾ cups vegetable stock (see page 30) or stock of your choice
1 tablespoon paprika
1½ teaspoons salt
⅛ teaspoon cayenne pepper
1 cup couscous
1 tablespoon olive oil
½ cup chopped red onion
3 scallions, white and green parts cut into ¼-inch rounds
½ unpeeled carrot, cut in large dice
½ cup diced red bell pepper
½ cup diced yellow bell pepper
1 cup diced tomato
¼ cup chopped fresh parsley

MENU FOR LUNCH OR A LIGHT DINNER
. . . .

VEGETABLE
COUSCOUS WITH
STEEPED PAPRIKA
(PAGE 172)

RAITA WITH MIXED
VEGETABLES
(PAGE 242)

CABBAGE
VINAIGRETTE
(PAGE 237)

SLOW-COOKED RICE
PUDDING (PAGE 253)

1. In a saucepan with a tight-fitting cover, bring the stock to a boil. Dissolve the paprika, salt, and cayenne pepper in it. Return the stock to a boil.

2. Remove the stock from the heat and add the couscous. Stir, cover, and allow to stand about 15 minutes.

3. Heat a skillet for 1 minute; add the olive oil, then the onion and scallions. Sauté until the onion begins to color, about 2 minutes. Add the carrot and peppers and sauté for 1 minute. Add the tomato and sauté 1 minute more. Add the remaining ½ teaspoon salt and the remaining ¼ teaspoon pepper, then stir. Add the parsley and stir again. Remove from the heat.

4. Add the couscous to the skillet and fluff it as you mix it with the

vegetables. Serve immediately or at room temperature.

Couscous can be refrigerated for 1 day. Return to room temperature before serving.

Curried Couscous with Vegetables and Chickpeas

My brother Ken has gone through different cooking phases. College was his "Indian" period, when I learned to appreciate the infinite varieties of curry tastes from him. I steep the curry powder in this dish as I do for the Vegetable Couscous with Steeped Paprika (page 172). The dish needs only condiments to accompany it.

3 teaspoons olive oil
1 tablespoon curry powder
2½ cups vegetable stock (see page 30) or stock of your choice
1 cup couscous
½ cup peeled and quartered shallots
1 unpeeled carrot, cut into ⅓-inch-thick circles
2¼-inch-thick slices fresh ginger, with peel

1 cup sliced button mushrooms
1 cup snow peas, strings removed (about 3 ounces)
1 teaspoon salt
¼ teaspoon freshly ground black pepper
½ cup cooked chickpeas, homemade (see page 35) or canned (see page 153)

1. In a wok or a small cast-iron skillet, heat 1 teaspoon of the olive oil over low heat. Remove from the heat and stir in the curry powder. Set aside.

2. Bring 2 cups of stock to a boil in a large saucepan. Add the curried olive oil mixture and stir. Add the couscous, stir, and cover immediately. Allow to sit for 5 minutes.

3. Meanwhile, place a wok or skillet over high heat for 1 minute. Add the remaining 2 teaspoons oil. Immediately add the shallots, reduce the heat to medium, and stir-fry until the shallots begin to char, 1 to 2 minutes.

MENU WITH A MOROCCAN ACCENT

GINGER LENTIL STEW (PAGE 164)

CURRIED COUSCOUS WITH VEGETABLES AND CHICKPEAS (PAGE 173)

HARISSA (PAGE 240)

RAITA WITH CUCUMBER AND MINT (PAGE 241)

MOROCCAN ORANGES (PAGE 258)

◄• *This savory entree can also be used as a side dish with grilled fish or chicken.*

SERVES 6 AS AN ENTREE, 8 TO 12 AS PART OF A COMPOSED PLATE OR A BUFFET

Preparation time: 30 minutes

Cooking time: 15 minutes

4. Add the carrot and ginger; stir-fry until they begin to char, 1 to 2 minutes. Add the mushrooms and stir-fry for 1 minute. Add the peas and stir-fry for 1 minute more. Remove the ginger.

5. Heat the remaining ½ cup stock, salt, and pepper in a large saucepan. Add the chickpeas and simmer for 2 to 3 minutes.

6. Combine the couscous, vegetables, and chickpeas with the seasoned stock. Serve hot or warm.

SERVES 4 AS A SIDE DISH OR AS PART OF A COMPOSED PLATE, 8 AS PART OF A BUFFET

Preparation time: 20 minutes

Cooking time: 5 minutes

Couscous with Sautéed Brussels Sprouts and Tomatoes

When I was a kid I hated Brussels sprouts. As I got older I was still resistant, until I tasted them combined with tomatoes. Today I love sprouts prepared in many different ways.

This unconventional couscous is both pretty and tasty. It's good as part of a buffet, as a side dish with beans, or as a light lunch dish with a salad of bitter greens.

1½ cups Garden Salad Stock (see page 33) or stock of your choice
½ teaspoon salt
¼ teaspoon freshly ground black pepper
¾ cup couscous
1 cup diced Brussels sprouts

1 tablespoon olive oil
2 garlic cloves, chopped
1 cup cherry tomatoes, cut in half
½ cup sliced scallions, white and green parts
¼ cup fresh parsley

1. In a medium saucepan with a tight-fitting cover, bring the stock to a boil. Add the salt and pepper. Remove from the heat and add the couscous. Stir, cover, and allow to stand for at least 5 minutes.

2. Meanwhile, in a large, heavy-bottom pot sauté the Brussels sprouts in the olive oil over medium-high heat until they soften and turn bright green, 3 to 4 minutes. Add the garlic and cherry tomatoes; sauté 3 to 4 minutes more.

3. Add the scallions and sauté for 2 minutes. Remove from the heat. Add the couscous and parsley; toss. Serve hot or at room temperature.

Kasha with Chinese Charred Peppers and Zucchini

This is another tempting way to use charred peppers and zucchini. Roasting the kasha in a skillet before adding the liquid improves the aroma and consistency of this healthful and flavorful grain.

SERVES 6 AS A
SIDE DISH

Preparation time:
10 minutes, plus 30
minutes to soak the
mushrooms and 15
minutes for kasha
to relax

Cooking time:
25 minutes

¼ cup dried porcini mushrooms
1 cup cold water
1½ cups kasha (see Note)
1 egg, beaten
2¼ cups mushroom stock (see page 32) or stock of your choice

1 teaspoon salt
½ cup grated Parmesan cheese
1 tablespoon olive oil
2 cups chopped onions
1½ cups Chinese Charred Peppers and Zucchini (page 220)

1. Soak the mushrooms in the water for 30 minutes. Lift them from the soaking water. Squeeze them over the water to return any liquid to the cup, and dice. Strain the soaking water through a fine-mesh sieve and save.

2. Wash and drain the kasha. Mix the kasha and the beaten egg in a bowl. Place a 10-inch stainless-steel skillet over high heat for 1 minute. Turn heat to low, add the kasha, and dry roast for 3 to 4 minutes or until the egg has dried up and the kasha starts to take on a roasted aroma.

3. Combine the porcini soaking water, stock, and salt and add to skillet containing kasha. Bring to a rapid boil over high heat. Stir and turn heat to low. Cover and simmer for 15 minutes. Remove from the heat and allow to relax, covered, for 15 minutes. Uncover, mix in the cheese, and cover again.

4. Place a wok or cast-iron skillet over high heat for 1 minute. Add the oil, then the onions. Lower the heat and sauté until the onions begin to brown, 3 to 4 minutes. Remove from the heat.

5. Add the kasha and the peppers and zucchini. Toss, and serve at room temperature.

Note: To make Rice with Chinese Charred Peppers and Zucchini, substitute 3 cups of cooked rice for the kasha.

CURRIED BULGUR WHEAT PILAF

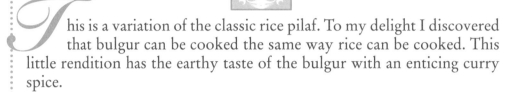

This is a variation of the classic rice pilaf. To my delight I discovered that bulgur can be cooked the same way rice can be cooked. This little rendition has the earthy taste of the bulgur with an enticing curry spice.

SERVES 6 AS
A SIDE DISH

Preparation time:
30 minutes

Cooking time:
10 minutes, plus
20 minutes for bulgur
to relax

1 teaspoon butter
2 tablespoons chopped walnuts
1½ cups vegetable stock (see page 30) or stock of your choice
2 teaspoons curry powder
1 teaspoon salt
⅛ teaspoon cayenne pepper
1 cup bulgur wheat
⅓ cup chopped shallots (about 2 shallots)
1 tablespoon olive oil

1. Preheat the oven to 325°F. Melt the butter and toss with the walnuts. Roast for 5 to 10 minutes, or until nicely browned.

2. In a small saucepan, bring the stock to a boil. Add the curry powder, salt, and pepper; turn off the heat, and let steep 5 minutes.

3. Wash and drain the bulgur.

4. In a large, heavy-bottom saucepan with a tight-fitting cover, sauté the shallots in the olive oil until they soften and are lightly brown, about 5 minutes. Add the bulgur and stir a few minutes, until the grains are coated with oil and shallots. Add the curry-infused stock, stir, and bring to a boil over high heat. Cover, and turn heat to low; simmer 20 minutes. Turn off the heat and allow bulgur to relax for 20 minutes. Place bulgur in a bowl and top with roasted nuts. Serve hot or at room temperature.

CORN BREAD

*L*iving in Manhattan, where you can buy some of the best breads in the world, I don't bake my own—except for corn bread. There's nothing like the taste of homemade corn bread as it comes from the oven. Over the years I've tried a number of recipes, but I always come back to this one.

¼ cup corn oil
1½ cups cornmeal
½ cup all-purpose flour
1 teaspoon baking powder
1 teaspoon baking soda

¼ teaspoon salt
2 tablespoons sugar
1 cup buttermilk
1 egg

1. Preheat the oven to 400°F.

2. Using a little of the corn oil, grease a 10-inch cast-iron skillet, and place it in the oven.

3. In a large bowl, sift together the cornmeal, flour, baking powder, baking soda, salt, and sugar.

4. In a separate bowl, mix the buttermilk, remaining oil, and egg. Combine with the dry ingredients and stir briefly with a fork until just combined.

5. Add the batter to the hot greased skillet. Bake until the bread pulls away from the sides of the pan, or until a cake tester inserted into the center comes out clean, 20 to 30 minutes. Serve hot or at room temperature.

BASIC POLENTA

*P*olenta is an Italian cornmeal porridge that can be served soft or allowed to solidify and then broiled or fried.

Although a few cooks like to use finely ground cornmeal for polenta,

YIELDS ABOUT 3 CUPS;
SERVES 4 TO 5

Cooking time:
20 minutes

like most chefs I prefer the coarse-grained meals that come from Italy or France.

Though you have to hang around the kitchen when you cook polenta, you don't have to give it your undivided attention. Stirring every couple of minutes is sufficient.

Polenta makes an excellent base for Ragout of Wild Mushrooms (page 199), Braised Fennel and Peppers (page 197), Spinach with Scallions and Feta (page 203), Creole Black-Eyed Peas (page 166), Black Beans with Roasted Peppers (page 160), and any other well-seasoned bean dishes.

4 cups water
1½ teaspoons salt

1 cup coarse-grained yellow corn-
*   meal*

1. Bring the water and salt to a boil in a heavy saucepan. Lower the heat so the water is just simmering.

2. Pour the cornmeal in a slow and steady stream into the water. Stir almost continuously until all the cornmeal is absorbed. This takes about 3 minutes.

3. Turn the heat to very low and using a large wooden spoon or paddle, stir the cornmeal thoroughly in a figure-eight every 2 to 3 minutes. The polenta is done when it adheres to itself and pulls away from the sides of the pot, 20 to 25 minutes. Serve immediately or allow to solidify and slice for Grilled Polenta (see below).

"The discovery of a new dish does more for the happiness of mankind than the discovery of a new star."

—ANTHELME BRILLAT-SAVARIN,
The Physiology of Taste

GRILLED POLENTA

For a change from pasta, try this polenta as a first course. Cover it with or put atop any sauce you would use on pasta. Particularly good are Pizziola Sauce (page 144), Marsala and Wild Mushrooms (page 134), and Chino Caponata (page 53). The Ragout of Wild Mushrooms (page 199); the Chinese Mushroom, Green Bean, and Tomato Stew (page 200); and the Braised Fennel and Peppers (page 197) all make superb toppings for Grilled Polenta.

Serve plain or on top of the Basic Tomato Sauce (page 34) as part of a composed plate or as a side dish to any featured entree, especially an Italian one.

SERVES 4 TO 5 AS A
FIRST COURSE OR
SIDE DISH

Preparation time:
5 minutes, plus
30 minutes for the
polenta to cool

Cooking time:
5 minutes

1 recipe Basic Polenta (page 177), hot	2 teaspoons olive oil or melted butter

1. Lightly grease a 9 x 5-inch loaf pan with oil or butter.

2. Pour the polenta into the pan and allow it to cool and solidify at room temperature, about 30 minutes.

3. Preheat the broiler. Remove the polenta from the pan and cut into ¾-inch-thick slices. Place them on a greased heatproof dish. Brush both sides with the oil or melted butter and broil close to the heat for a few minutes on each side until the polenta is crusty, about 5 minutes. Serve immediately.

 Grilled polenta is traditionally served alongside roasted quail or duck.

MIXED WILD MUSHROOMS WITH GRILLED POLENTA

This rich, multipurpose mushroom mix is one of my favorite dishes. In addition to having it with grilled polenta, I serve it over toasted, sliced brioche as a side dish, and combine it with an equal amount of wild rice as a stuffing for tomatoes and chicken.

SERVES 4 TO 5 AS A
SIDE DISH OR FIRST
COURSE

Preparation time:
15 minutes, plus
30 minutes to soak
mushrooms

Cooking time:
25 minutes

½ cup dried porcini mushrooms
1 cup cold water

SEASONING SAUCE
2 teaspoons cornstarch
2 tablespoons medium-dry sherry
2½ tablespoons soy sauce
1 teaspoon molasses

2 tablespoons peanut oil
1 cup chopped leeks, white and light green parts (about 1 small leek)
¾ pound assorted fresh wild mushrooms (cremini, portobello, blond or black chanterelles, morels, pieds de moutons), *cut into large pieces*
1 recipe Grilled Polenta (page 178) (see Note)

1. Soak the porcini in the cold water for 30 minutes. Lift the mushrooms from the soaking water, squeezing them over the water to return any liquid to the cup, and dice. Strain the porcini water through a fine-mesh sieve.

2. Reduce the porcini water over low heat until only 2 tablespoons remain, about 15 minutes. Allow to cool.

3. Make the seasoning sauce by dissolving the cornstarch in the sherry. Stir in the reduced porcini water, soy sauce, and molasses. Set aside.

4. Heat a wok or large cast-iron skillet over high heat until it smokes, 2 to 3 minutes. Add the peanut oil and then immediately add the leeks; stir-fry for 3 to 4 minutes.

5. Add the porcini and the fresh mushrooms and stir-fry for 3 to 4 minutes more.

6. Restir the seasoning sauce and add it to the wok all at once, continuing to stir until the sauce has thickened and has thoroughly glazed the mixture, about 30 seconds.

7. Put the polenta on a serving plate. Top with the mushroom mix. Serve at once.

Note: Broil the Grilled Polenta during the last few minutes the Mixed Wild Mushrooms are cooking. If necessary, the mushrooms can wait for a few minutes while you broil the polenta.

CREAMY POLENTA WITH MASCARPONE AND GORGONZOLA

*T*his dish was inspired by a wonderful recipe from Danny Meyer, the owner of the Union Square Cafe. The mascarpone adds rich creaminess; the gorgonzola, its distinctive blue-cheese pungency.

Serves 6 as an entree

Preparation time: 5 minutes

Cooking time: 25 minutes

2 cups water
2 cups low-fat milk
1 cup yellow cornmeal
2 tablespoons mascarpone

1½ teaspoons salt
¼ teaspoon white pepper
2 ounces gorgonzola, crumbled
    (½ cup)

1. Bring the water and milk to a boil in a wide, heavy-bottom saucepan. Add the cornmeal in a slow and steady stream. Stir almost continuously until all the cornmeal is absorbed, about 3 minutes.

2. Turn the heat very low and using a large wooden spoon or paddle, stir the cornmeal thoroughly in a figure-eight every 2 to 3 minutes. The polenta is done when it adheres to itself and pulls away from the sides of the pot, 20 to 25 minutes.

3. Preheat the broiler.

4. Remove the saucepan from the heat. Add the mascarpone, salt, and pepper and stir. Serve now, or pour the polenta into an ovenproof dish and dot evenly with gorgonzola. Broil the polenta a few inches from the heat until the cheese begins to brown, 1 to 2 minutes. Serve immediately.

Note: This is excellent when sprinkled with chopped toasted walnuts just before serving.

MENU FOR A WINTER DINNER PARTY

....

GRILLED SHIITAKE MUSHROOMS ON ARUGULA (PAGE 64)

....

CREAMY POLENTA WITH MASCARPONE AND GORGONZOLA (PAGE 180)

....

BROCCOLI DI RAPE WITH GARLIC (PAGE 212)

....

WHITE BEANS WITH A LIGHT TOUCH OF TOMATO (PAGE 154)

....

APPLE CRISP (PAGE 254)

SPICY POLENTA WITH CRISPY GARLIC AND CHEESE

My friend Vicky Lyons loves food from the Southwest. After one of her frequent trips to New Mexico, she came back raving about a spicy polenta with chunks of fried garlic that she ate at a small, out-of-the-way restaurant whose name she couldn't remember. This is the dish we created from her description.

6 garlic cloves, sliced or coarsely
   chopped
1 tablespoon olive oil
4 cups water
1½ teaspoons salt
1 cup coarse-grained yellow cornmeal
¼ teaspoon freshly ground black
   pepper

1 to 2 tablespoons slivered roasted
   poblano, jalapeño, or serrano
   pepper, or any combination (see
   page 38)
¼ cup shredded sharp cheddar
   cheese (1 ounce)

SERVES 4 AS A LIGHT ENTREE, 6 TO 8 AS PART OF A COMPOSED PLATE

Preparation time: 15 minutes

Cooking time: 25 to 30 minutes

1. In a small skillet, sauté the garlic in the olive oil until it turns golden brown, 3 to 5 minutes. Set aside.

2. Bring the water and salt to a boil in a large, heavy saucepan. Lower the heat so the water is just simmering.

3. Pour the cornmeal in a slow and steady stream into the water. Stir almost continuously until all the cornmeal is absorbed; this takes about 3 minutes.

4. Turn the heat very low and using a large wooden spoon or paddle, stir the cornmeal thoroughly in a figure-eight every 2 to 3 minutes. As the polenta begins to pull away from the sides of the pot, about 20 to 25 minutes, add the ground black pepper, garlic, roasted peppers, and cheese. Stir for 30 seconds to melt the cheese. Serve immediately or let the polenta cool and then sauté or broil it.

WHOLE-GRAIN FRIED RICE

*I*f I had to point to one dish as essential to my diet, it would be this fried rice. It's also the most popular grain dish in my catering business.

Most people eat brown rice because it's good for them, but they eat Whole-Grain Fried Rice because it tastes great. Some clients have even called it sexy.

Serves 4 as a side dish, 2 as an entree

Preparation time: 10 minutes

Cooking time: 10 minutes

4 teaspoons peanut or other vegetable oil
2 cups cold or room-temperature cooked brown rice, or a combination of cooked whole grains (see Note)
1 unpeeled carrot, sliced into thin rounds

2 scallions, white and green parts sliced into ⅛-inch rounds
1 tablespoon soy sauce
1 teaspoon roasted sesame seeds (see page 40)

1. Heat a wok or large cast-iron skillet over high heat until it smokes, 2 to 3 minutes. Add 1 tablespoon of the peanut oil.

2. Immediately add the rice and stir-fry until all the grains are coated with oil. To scorch the rice as it browns, repeatedly press it with the back of a spatula and flip every minute or so for 4 to 5 minutes.

3. Remove the rice from the wok. Add the remaining teaspoon of oil, then the carrot and scallions. Stir-fry for 1 minute. Return the rice to the wok or skillet and add the soy sauce. Stir-fry a few seconds, tossing the rice with the soy sauce, until the soy sauce has evenly colored the rice, about 1 minute. Empty the wok or skillet onto a serving platter and sprinkle with roasted sesame seeds. Serve hot or at room temperature.

Note: I could write a chapter on whole-grain fried rice dishes. Combine any number of cooked grains with cooked white or brown rice and add your choice of vegetables. My favorite combination of grains at the moment is one-third each wheat berries, short-grain brown rice, and short-grain sweet brown rice. These three grains can be cooked together.

Health food stores carry 1-pound packages of mixed grains, any of which can be used in this dish.

Among the vegetable combinations I choose the most often are:

- *Mung bean sprouts, red and yellow bell pepper, snow peas, and scallions*
- *Red bell peppers, zucchini, and sugar-snap peas*
- *Bok choy, red bell pepper, and leeks*
- *Green beans, corn, red bell peppers, and onions*

Middle-Eastern Rice and Spinach

This Middle-Eastern recipe was given to me by Janis Carr, chef for the last fifteen years at Grace's Market, a wonderful food store in Manhattan with an excellent selection of high-quality produce and cheese. It's easy to prepare and tastes terrific.

1 garlic clove, chopped
2 scallions white and green parts cut into ¼-inch rounds
1 tablespoon olive oil
1½ cups water
1 cup long-grain white rice
1 pound spinach (1 large bunch or two small bunches) washed (see page 91) and thick stems removed, chopped
1 teaspoon salt
⅓ teaspoon freshly ground black pepper
⅓ cup freshly grated Parmesan cheese
2 tablespoons oven-roasted pine nuts (see page 41)

*Serves 2 as an entree,
4 as a side dish*

Preparation time: 20 minutes, plus 15 minutes for rice to relax

Cooking time: 25 minutes

*SERVES 6 AS AN
ENTREE*

*Preparation time:
10 to 15 minutes,
plus 15 minutes for
rice to relax*

*Cooking time:
1 hour*

1. In a heavy-bottom saucepan, sauté the garlic and scallions in the olive oil until the garlic just begins to color and the scallions soften, 2 to 3 minutes.

2. Add the water and bring to a boil. Add the rice, spinach, salt, and pepper. Stir, cover, and turn the heat to low. Simmer for 15 minutes.

3. Remove pot from the heat and allow the rice to relax, covered, for 15 minutes.

4. Stir in the cheese. Transfer to a serving platter and sprinkle with the roasted pine nuts. Serve hot or at room temperature.

MIDDLE-EASTERN RICE AND LENTILS

*T*his creation of Janis Carr's is characteristic of the many rice and lentil mixtures offered throughout the Middle East and makes a tasty, easy-to-fix dinner.

*1 cup lentils
1 cup canned tomatoes, crushed
1 bay leaf
½ teaspoon ground cumin, preferably roasted (see page 40)
1½ cups vegetable stock (see page 30) or stock of your choice*

*¼ teaspoon freshly ground black pepper
1½ teaspoons salt
1½ cups water
1 cup white rice
½ tablespoon olive oil
1 Spanish onion, sliced*

1. Bring the lentils, tomatoes, bay leaf, cumin, vegetable stock, and pepper to a simmer over high heat in a 4-quart saucepan. Stir, cover, turn the heat to low, and simmer until the lentils are cooked through and have ab-

sorbed the liquid, 45 minute to 1 hour. Add 1 teaspoon of the salt during the last 5 minutes of cooking. Remove the bay leaf.

Lentils can be prepared a day ahead and refrigerated. Gently reheat before serving.

2. In a medium saucepan with a tight-fitting lid, bring the water to a rolling boil. Stir in the rice and add the remaining ½ teaspoon of salt. Return to a boil, cover, and turn the heat to low. Simmer for 15 minutes. Remove from the heat and allow the rice to relax, covered, for 15 minutes.

3. Meanwhile, in a skillet, sauté the onion in the olive oil over medium heat until golden, about 5 minutes.

4. Place the rice on a plate; put the lentils on top of the rice and the onion on top of the lentils. Serve hot or at room temperature.

Rice with Chinese Charred Peppers and Zucchini

I always make more Chinese Charred Peppers and Zucchini than I need so that I'll have some left over with which to make this dish. With just a bowl of hearty soup, like Black Bean Soup with Sherry (page 78), and a salad you can put together a tasty and satisfying meal.

SERVES 4 AS AN ENTREE, 6 AS A SIDE DISH, 8 TO 12 AS PART OF A BUFFET

Preparation time: 10 minutes, plus 30 minutes for the mushrooms to soak and 15 minutes for rice to relax

Cooking time: 15 minutes

¼ cup dried porcini mushrooms
1 cup cold water
1½ cups white rice
1½ cups vegetable stock (see page 30) or stock of your choice
1 teaspoon salt

2 tablespoons olive oil
2 cups chopped onions
1½ cups Chinese Charred Peppers and Zucchini (page 220)
½ cup grated Parmesan cheese

1. Soak the mushrooms in cold water for 30 minutes. Lift them from the soaking water. Squeeze them over the water to return any liquid to the cup; dice. Strain the soaking water through a fine-mesh sieve and reserve.

2. Combine the rice, porcini soaking water, stock, and salt in a large,

heavy-bottom saucepan. Bring to a rapid boil over high heat, stir, and turn the heat to low. Cover and simmer for 15 minutes. Remove from the heat and allow to relax, covered, for 15 minutes.

3. Place a wok or cast-iron skillet over high heat for 1 minute. Add the oil, then the onions. Lower the heat and sauté until the onions begin to brown, 3 to 4 minutes. Remove from the heat and add the rice and the peppers and zucchini. Toss. Add the cheese and toss again. Serve at room temperature.

Basmati Rice with Leeks and Cauliflower

*T*his recipe, along with the one for Red Bean Sauce, was given to me by Dominique Richard. For a simple, heavy and colorful meal, I spread the Red Bean Sauce on a white plate and then pile this basmati rice dish on top.

SERVES 8 AS THE BASE FOR BEANS, 10 TO 12 AS A SIDE DISH

Preparation time: 10 minutes

Cooking time: 30 minutes

*G*rains, including white and brown rice, are too moist when first cooked. To make the grains drier and fluffier, let them "relax" by leaving them in their cooking pot off the heat, covered. With a gas range, turn the flame off and leave the pot on the burner; with an electric, remove the pot from the hot burner.

2 cups basmati rice
2¾ cups water
1½ teaspoons salt
4 cardamom pods
3 cups leeks, white and light green parts, sliced ½ inch thick (about 3 small)
1 tablespoon olive oil
½ teaspoon ground anise or fennel seed

1 head cauliflower, broken into small florets
½ teaspoon freshly ground black pepper
1 cup vegetable stock (see page 30) or water
1 recipe Red Bean Sauce (page 167)

1. Wash and drain the rice. In a medium saucepan with a tight-fitting lid, bring the water to a rolling boil. Stir in the rice and add 1 teaspoon of the salt. Return to a boil. Add the cardamom pods, cover, and turn the heat to low. Simmer for 15 minutes. Remove from the heat and allow the rice to relax covered, for 15 minutes.

2. Meanwhile, in a large heavy-bottom saucepan, sauté the leeks in the olive oil until they soften, about 5 minutes. Add the anise or fennel and stir for a few seconds. Add the cauliflower and toss.

3. Stir in the remaining ½ teaspoon salt, pepper, and stock. Bring to a simmer. Cover and simmer over medium heat until the stock has evaporated and the cauliflower is just cooked through, 4 to 5 minutes.

4. Stir the rice into the vegetables.

5. Spread the Red Bean Sauce on individual plates and top with the rice, leek, and cauliflower mixture. Serve hot or at room temperature.

SAFFRON HERB RICE

*S*erve this colorful and savory rice with any bean dish or as part of a composed plate with two or more vegetable dishes, such as Asparagus with Brown Butter and Lemon (page 211) and Tomatoes Stuffed with Herbs and Cheese (page 68).

1½ cups vegetable stock (see page 30) or stock of your choice
¼ teaspoon saffron threads
¼ cup minced shallots, or 1 cup minced Spanish onion
1 tablespoon olive oil

1 cup basmati rice (see Note)
1 teaspoon salt
¼ teaspoon freshly ground black pepper
½ cup chopped fresh parsley

SERVES 4 AS A SIDE DISH OR AS PART OF A COMPOSED PLATE

Preparation time: 10 minutes, plus 30 minutes for the saffron to steep and 15 minutes for rice to relax

Cooking time: 20 minutes

1. In a medium pot, bring the stock to a simmer; remove from the heat. Add the saffron and steep for 30 minutes.

2. In a heavy-bottom saucepan, sauté the shallots in the olive oil until they are soft, 3 to 4 minutes. Add the rice and stir to coat with the oil. Pour in the saffron stock and bring to a simmer. Add the salt and pepper.

3. Turn the heat to low, cover, and simmer for 15 minutes. Check to make sure that all the stock has been absorbed.

4. Turn the heat off and let the rice relax, covered, for 15 minutes.

5. Stir in the parsley and serve immediately.

Saffron Herb Rice is an ideal accompaniment to roasted chicken and grilled fish. I often make it with chicken stock.

Note: This dish can also be made with brown rice. Increase the cooking and relaxing times for the rice to 30 minutes each.

RISOTTO

Risotto is as popular in northern Italy as pasta is in southern Italy. It's always cooked uncovered, with small amounts of stock or other liquid added a little at a time to allow the previous liquid to be absorbed. The result is a rice dish with tender but firm grains and a rich, creamy texture. I make risotto with Arborio, a round, short-grained Italian rice.

Many cooks assume risotto is too difficult to make at home, while in fact it's a fairly simple last-minute dish that can be put together with the ingredients most of us keep on hand. It's best prepared for no more than six.

Risotto takes about twenty minutes to cook. After seventeen minutes I begin to taste one grain of rice every thirty seconds until the risotto is done.

Once you begin your risotto, so long as you return to the pot every minute or two to give it a thorough stir, you can prepare your salad or accompanying vegetable, slice the bread, and have dinner on the table in less than half an hour from start to finish.

TO ENSURE A PERFECT RISOTTO EVERY TIME:

• *Use Arborio rice and never wash it.*
• *Use a wide, heavy-bottom pot.*
• *Never cover the pot.*
• *Your risotto is only as good as the stock you use, so make sure it's rich and flavorful. Nonvegetarians can experiment with chicken and beef stocks.*
• *Add the stock one ladle at a time. Don't let the liquid in the pan totally evaporate before you add more. Keep the heat under the rice at medium and the liquid at a quick simmer.*
• *Keep a pot of stock simmering on a back burner and add a ladle each time the rice appears to have absorbed most of the liquid. You probably won't use all the stock called for in each recipe, but I prefer to heat extra stock rather than run the risk of not having enough.*
• *Stir frequently, especially when the rice is nearly done. However, there's no need to stand in front of the pot and stir continuously while the risotto is cooking.*
• *The rice should be firm but tender, with no hard center core. Remove the risotto from the heat as soon as it's cooked. Serve immediately.*

RISOTTO WITH WILD MUSHROOMS

SERVES 2 TO 3 AS
AN ENTREE,
4 AS A FIRST COURSE

Preparation time:
15 minutes, plus
30 minutes to soak the
mushrooms

Cooking time:
30 minutes

*T*his unbelievably rich-tasting risotto has an intense, almost meaty flavor, but its fat allotment has been kept to a minimum.

¼ cup dried porcini mushrooms
1 cup cold water
4 cups vegetable stock (see page 30) or stock of your choice
1 tablespoon butter or olive oil
¼ cup chopped shallots
1 cup Arborio rice

1 portobello mushroom, sliced
1¼ teaspoons salt
¾ teaspoon freshly ground black pepper
½ cup white wine
½ cup grated Parmesan cheese

1. Soak the porcini mushrooms in the cold water for 30 minutes. Lift the mushrooms from the soaking water, squeezing them over the water to return any liquid to the cup, and dice. Strain the porcini water through a fine-mesh sieve and add it to the stock.

2. Heat the stock until it reaches a low simmer, then adjust the heat so that it stays just at the simmering point.

3. Heat the butter over low heat in a wide, heavy-bottom pot. Add the shallots and sauté until they begin to soften, 3 to 4 minutes. Add the rice and stir well to coat the grains. Add the porcini and portobello mushrooms and sauté for 2 minutes.

4. Add a ladle of stock; most soup ladles hold ½ cup. Stir until the liquid is absorbed. Add the salt and pepper. Keep the heat under the rice at medium and the liquid always simmering.

5. After adding 3 or 4 ladles of stock, add the wine. Continue to stir frequently and to add a ladle of stock at a time. When the rice is almost cooked through, in about 20 to 25 minutes, reduce the amount of stock added each time. As soon as the rice is cooked, remove it from the heat. Stir in the grated cheese and serve hot.

MENU FOR A SMALL DINNER PARTY

ASPARAGUS CHOWDER (PAGE 70)

RISOTTO WITH WILD MUSHROOMS (PAGE 189)

GREEN BEANS AMANDINE (PAGE 211)

CHOCOLATE CUSTARD (PAGE 251)

SPINACH RISOTTO

*S*pinach and rice are remarkably compatible. Here they combine to form a wonderfully light, but flavorful risotto.

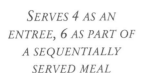

SERVES 4 AS AN ENTREE, 6 AS PART OF A SEQUENTIALLY SERVED MEAL

Preparation time: 20 minutes

Cooking time: 30 minutes

MENU FOR AN INTERNATIONAL DINNER

VEGETABLE SOUP WITH FRENCH PESTO (PAGE 84)

MESCLUN SALAD

SPINACH RISOTTO (PAGE 190)

MOROCCAN ORANGES (PAGE 258)

---

1 small bunch spinach (about ½ pound), thick stems removed
5 to 6 cups vegetable stock (see page 30) or stock of your choice
1 tablespoon olive oil
½ cup coarsely chopped shallots (4 to 6 shallots)

1½ cups Arborio rice
1 teaspoon salt
⅓ teaspoon freshly ground black pepper
¼ cup chopped scallions, white and green parts
⅓ cup grated Parmesan cheese

1. Wash the spinach by submerging and lifting (see page 91) until all the sand and dirt are removed. Do not remove the water that clings to the leaves. Cover and steam just until the spinach is wilted, 2 to 3 minutes.

2. Allow the spinach to cool. Over a bowl, squeeze the spinach dry. Chop it fine and set aside. Add the steaming water from the spinach to the stock.

3. Heat the stock until it reaches a low simmer. Adjust the heat so that the stock stays just at the simmering point.

4. Heat the oil in a separate medium, heavy-bottom pot. Add the shallots and sauté over low heat until they begin to soften, 3 to 4 minutes. Add the rice and stir well to coat the grains.

5. Add a ladle of stock. Stir until the liquid is absorbed. Add the salt and pepper. Continue to stir frequently and to add a ladle of stock at a time. When the rice is close to done, in about 20 to 25 minutes, reduce the amount of stock added each time.

6. As soon as the rice is cooked, remove it from the heat. Add the spinach, scallions, and cheese. Stir. Serve immediately.

Fennel-Leek Risotto

SERVES 4 *AS AN*
ENTREE

Preparation time:
15 minutes, plus 30
minutes for the saffron
to steep

Cooking time:
30 minutes

T'm often asked what my favorite dish is. My answer is, "Something new or something I haven't tasted yet."

Fennel-Leek Risotto is one of my new favorites. It was a challenge to compensate for the absence of chicken or veal stock without adding cream or butter. I achieved the taste I was looking for by using reduced stock and steeping the saffron in it.

5 cups reduced stock of your choice (see Note)
½ teaspoon saffron threads
1½ teaspoons curry powder
2 medium leeks or 1 large leek, white part only, cleaned (see page 32) and chopped (about 2 cups)
2 tablespoons olive oil
1 medium fennel bulb, coarsely diced (about 1½ cups)
1½ teaspoons salt

½ teaspoon freshly ground black pepper
1½ cups Arborio rice
¼ cup white wine
¼ cup chopped fresh parsley
½ cup grated Parmesan cheese

1. Bring the stock to a simmer in a large, heavy-bottom saucepan. Remove from the heat and add the saffron and curry powder. Stir until the curry powder dissolves. Allow to steep for 30 minutes, then reheat.

2. In a wide, heavy-bottom pan, sauté the leeks in the olive oil until they begin to soften, about 2 minutes. Add the fennel and sauté 2 minutes. Add the salt, pepper, and rice.

3. Add the simmering stock, a ladle at a time, stirring frequently. Add 2 or 3 ladles of stock, then add the white wine. Continue to stir and to add a ladle of stock at a time. When the rice is close to done, in about 20 to 25 minutes, reduce the amount of stock added each time.

4. Add the parsley during the last 2 minutes of cooking. As soon as the

rice is cooked, remove it from the heat. Stir in the grated cheese. Serve immediately.

Note: To make the stock, I boil 10 cups of vegetable stock (see page 30) until reduced to 5 cups. If you're using a strong mushroom or chicken stock, you might want to reduce it only by a quarter or a third. Let your taste guide you—you want the stock to be strong, but not over-powering.

Chapter 11

VEGETABLES

*F*resh, in-season vegetables cooked with imagination and care are magnificent. For at least as long as I've been exposed to French cooking, the French have known this. To the best of my knowledge, the British haven't learned it yet. And we Americans have only recently figured it out.

For many years in this country we cooked vegetables to death. Remember limp, soggy broccoli and flat, lifeless cabbage? No? Then you're a lot younger than I am. To disguise these disasters, we buried them under cream sauces.

Then we overcompensated by leaving vegetables nearly raw. But the stalky, undercooked tastes of green beans and carrots also needed concealing. We switched to butter sauces that appeared light but were often even higher in fat than the cream sauces.

VEGETABLES AS THE FEATURED ENTREE

I generally like a light lunch, but at night I want a hearty dinner. While bean and pasta dishes satisfy this desire, many vegetable dishes don't. You'll find that most of the recipes in this section are substantial and filling. For me, they take the place of meat, and while they are much easier to digest than meat, I want them to satisfy the way meat does. A dish like Chinese Mushroom, Green Bean, and Tomato Stew or Eggplant Torte à la Provençal refuels me on a wintery night.

On the other hand, Spinach Soufflé is delicate and airy, and I tend to serve it after a substantial soup like Vegetable Soup with French Pesto (page 84).

The Warm Roasted Vegetables Vinaigrette and the Steamed Vegetables with Three Spicy Chinese Sauces are light dishes I serve during the summer as part of a buffet or sit-down outdoor meal.

Relegated to the role of extras beside the standing rib roast, fried chicken, or grilled fish, even properly cooked greens, cauliflower, and potatoes haven't—until recently—earned much attention. But today, with doctors emphasizing the nutritional importance of plant-based foods and well-known chefs prizing them for their versatility and flavor, vegetables of all kinds are taking center stage.

With dishes like Roasted Portobello Mushrooms, Stir-Fried Bok Choy with Seared Onions, Braised Fennel and Peppers, Hashed Brussels Sprouts with Fresh Oregano, and Spinach Soufflé, vegetables finally receive the celebrity status they deserve.

For convenience I've divided this section into three parts:
• *Vegetable dishes I serve as the featured entree*
• *Vegetable dishes I combine with other foods to create a composed plate or serve as an accompaniment to a featured entree*
• *Stir-fried vegetables, to be served either as the featured entree or as part of a composed plate*

EGGPLANT TORTE À LA PROVENÇAL

Among my friend Sigun Coyle's numerous talents is French cooking. This is one of the many scrumptious recipes she has shared with me over the years of our close friendship.

The lusty flavors and informal feel of Provence are captured in this dish.

2 medium eggplants (about 1 pound each), cut into ½-inch rounds
2 teaspoons salt

SEASONED OIL
⅓ cup olive oil
1 garlic clove, chopped
1 teaspoon chopped fresh thyme, or ⅓ teaspoon dried

2 medium potatoes, about ½ pound

each, peeled and cut into ⅜-inch rounds
2 medium tomatoes, cut into ⅜-inch-thick rounds
1 medium red onion, cut into ⅜-inch rounds
¼ teaspoon freshly ground black pepper
A few sprigs of fresh thyme (optional)
¾ cup torn fresh basil leaves

1. Sprinkle the eggplant slices with 1 teaspoon salt and set aside for 1 hour. Rinse and pat the eggplant slices dry using paper towels.

2. For the seasoned oil, in a separate bowl, combine the oil, garlic, and thyme.

3. Preheat the oven to 350°F.

SERVES 6 TO 8 AS A FEATURED ENTREE

Preparation time: 20 minutes, plus 1 hour to salt eggplant

Cooking time: 1 hour and 15 minutes

MENU FOR A DINNER PARTY

"CREAM" OF CARROT SOUP (PAGE 71)

MESCLUN, BLUE CHEESE, AND PEARS (PAGE 97)

EGGPLANT TORTE À LA PROVENÇAL (PAGE 195)

PASTA RISOTTO (PAGE 142)

POACHED PEARS AND CHERRIES IN PORT (PAGE 261)

*SERVES 5 AS A FEATURED
ENTREE, 7 TO 8
AS AN APPETIZER,
12 TO 15 AS PART OF
AN ANTIPASTO*

*Preparation time:
20 minutes, plus
1 hour to salt the
eggplant and preheat
barbecue*

*Cooking time:
5 to 10 minutes*

4. Place a large cast-iron skillet over high heat for 3 minutes. While the skillet is heating, brush the eggplant slices with the seasoned oil. Sauté the eggplant over high heat until it is crusty and dark, 2 to 3 minutes each side. Sauté as many slices as comfortably fit in the pan and then repeat the process. Do not crowd the skillet. Turn the heat down if the eggplant is browning too quickly.

5. Lightly oil an ovenproof baking pan. Overlap the eggplant, potato, tomato, and onion slices, leaving ½ inch of each uncovered. Repeat the layers until all the vegetable slices have been used.

6. Add the remaining 1 teaspoon salt and the pepper to the remaining seasoned oil and brush the vegetables with this mixture. Place the thyme and basil in-between the layered vegetables. Bake uncovered for 1 hour. Serve hot or at room temperature.

This torte can be refrigerated for 1 day. Reheat before serving.

STUFFED GRILLED EGGPLANT ROLLS

These eggplant rolls are equally at home at a sophisticated dinner and a summer barbecue. The rosemary-goat cheese stuffing can also be used on toast rounds as an hor d'oeuvre.

Save the end slices of the eggplant; they're too small to roll. Brush them with olive oil and grill them.

ROSEMARY-GOAT CHEESE STUFFING
1 teaspoon olive oil
2 teaspoons minced fresh rosemary
*½ cup soft fresh goat cheese
(2 ounces)*
½ cup cottage cheese
*1 tablespoon minced oil-cured
black olives*

*1½ tablespoons diced drained oil-
packed dried tomatoes*

*2 medium eggplants (about 1
pound each) sliced lengthwise
into ¼- to ⅓-inch pieces
(approximately 15 center slices)*
Olive oil, for brushing eggplant

1. To make the stuffing, combine the olive oil, rosemary, goat cheese, cottage cheese, olives, and dried tomatoes.

Can be prepared up to 1 day ahead and refrigerated.

2. Sprinkle the eggplant slices with salt and allow them to drain for 1 hour. Rinse the eggplant and pat dry. Brush lightly with olive oil on both sides.

3. Meanwhile, make a fire in the barbecue and allow it to burn down so the coals are white-hot, about 30 minutes (see Note).

4. Grill the eggplant until well-charred and cooked through, 3 to 4 minutes each side.

5. Spread 1 tablespoon of the cheese stuffing on each slice of grilled eggplant. Roll the eggplant slices starting from the small end. Serve warm or at room temperature.

Note: Stuffed Grilled Eggplant Rolls can also be prepared in an oven. Broil the eggplant slices on both sides about 6 inches from the heat until well-charred, 2 to 4 minutes on each side. Remove from the oven and stuff.

MENU FOR SUNDAY DINNER

Stuffed Cherry Tomatoes (page 54)

Braised Fennel and Peppers (page 197)

Saffron Herb Rice (page 187)

Swiss Chard with Shallots (page 216)

Ricotta Torte (page 248)

Braised Fennel and Peppers

I got the idea for this light but flavorful stew from a little out-of-the-way restaurant in Italy, where the preparation of fennel is an art form.

1 medium red onion, sliced
4 garlic cloves, chopped
1 tablespoon olive oil
1 medium fennel bulb, cut lengthwise into ⅜-inch strips
1 red bell pepper, cut into ⅜-inch-thick strips
3 plum tomatoes, cut in quarters lengthwise
2 fresh thyme sprigs
⅓ cup white wine
1 teaspoon salt
¼ teaspoon freshly ground black pepper

1. In a medium skillet, sauté the onion and garlic in the olive oil until the garlic begins to color, 2 to 3 minutes. Add the fennel and red pepper; sauté for 2 minutes.

Serves 4 as a featured entree

Preparation time: 20 minutes

Cooking time: 35 minutes

◄● *For a nonvegetarian meal, this is great on top of, or under, poached or broiled striped bass, swordfish, or red snapper.*

2. Add the tomatoes, thyme, wine, salt, and pepper. Cover and bring to a simmer over high heat. Turn the heat to low and simmer until the vegetables are soft and the sauce is reduced to a glaze, about 30 minutes. If the vegetables are soft, but the sauce too thin, remove the cover and cook over low heat for a few minutes. Serve hot.

Can be prepared 1 day ahead and refrigerated. Reheat gently before serving.

Roasted Portobello Mushrooms

Because of their rich taste, I think of portobello mushrooms as vegetarian steak. Inspired by a recipe of Jamie Leeds, a former sous-chef at the Union Square Cafe, this is one of the easiest entrees I've ever made.

If I have the barbecue going, I grill these for one minute on each side before or after I roast them. This adds a wonderful charred taste.

1 tablespoon balsamic vinegar
3 tablespoons olive oil
1 teaspoon salt
¼ teaspoon freshly ground black pepper
¼ cup chopped fresh marjoram
2 tablespoons minced shallot
4 medium portobello mushrooms (5- to 6-inch diameter)

1. Combine the vinegar, oil, salt, pepper, marjoram, and shallots in a bowl.

2. Remove the stems from the mushrooms (see Note). Place in bowl and spoon the marinade over; marinate for 1 hour.

3. Preheat the oven to 400°F.

4. Place the mushrooms in an ovenproof dish and spoon any remaining marinade over them. Roast for 20 minutes. Serve hot with any marinade left in the roasting pan spooned over them.

SERVES 4 AS A FEATURED ENTREE

Preparation time: 5 to 10 minutes, plus 1 hour to marinate

Cooking time: 20 minutes

MENU FOR AN EASY-TO-MAKE COMPANY DINNER

SIMPLE BRUSCHETTA (PAGE 63)

ROASTED PORTOBELLO MUSHROOMS (PAGE 198)

STIR-FRIED SPINACH (PAGE 229)

FUSILLI WITH ROASTED PEPPERS AND SHALLOTS (PAGE 139)

FRESH FRUIT AND CHEESE

Note: Save the stems of the portobello mushrooms to use in Mushroom Stock (page 32), Braised Mushrooms (page 219), and Fresh Pasta with Black Chanterelles (page 135).

RAGOUT OF WILD MUSHROOMS

*SERVES 4 AS A
FEATURED ENTREE*

*Preparation time:
30 minutes,
plus 30 minutes to
soak mushrooms*

*Cooking time:
15 to 20 minutes*

I love the rich, earthy taste of mushrooms. This ragout can be served on rice, alongside polenta, or as the topping for pasta or a baked potato.

*2 tablespoons dried porcini
   mushrooms*
½ cup cold water
*½ cup coarsely chopped shallots (4
   to 6 shallots)*
1 tablespoon olive oil
4 garlic cloves, chopped
*3½ cups, (10 oz.) assorted fresh
   mushrooms, such as shiitake,
   portobello, cremini, and button,
   cut into 1-inch pieces*
1 teaspoon salt

*1 teaspoon freshly ground black
   pepper*
2 fresh thyme sprigs
1 cup diced plum tomatoes
*¼ cup tomato sauce, preferably
   homemade (see page 34)*
½ cup red wine
*1 teaspoon Porcini Powder
   (optional; page 42)*

1. Place the porcini mushrooms in a bowl and cover with the cold water. Soak until soft, about 30 minutes. Remove the mushrooms from the water, squeezing the water back into the bowl. Pour the liquid through a fine sieve and reserve. Coarsely chop the mushrooms and set aside.

2. In a medium skillet, sauté the shallots in olive oil until they soften, about 2 minutes. Add the garlic and sauté until light brown, 2 to 3 minutes. Add the fresh and reconstituted mushrooms and toss well.

3. Add the salt, pepper, thyme, tomatoes, tomato sauce, wine, porcini soaking water, and Porcini Powder, if using. Bring to a simmer over high heat. Turn heat to low, cover, and simmer until the mushrooms are cooked, 10 to 15 minutes. If the mushrooms are cooked through but the

sauce is too thin, uncover and simmer for a few minutes until the sauce has thickened. Remove the thyme. Serve hot.

The ragout can be prepared 1 day ahead and refrigerated. Reheat gently before serving.

SERVES 4 AS A
FEATURED ENTREE

Preparation time:
20 to 30 minutes, plus
30 minutes to soak
the mushrooms

Cooking time: 2 hours

CHINESE MUSHROOM, GREEN BEAN, AND TOMATO STEW

A robust, slow-cooked winter stew with a rich meaty flavor. This is a good dish in which to use those large older green beans that take forever to become tender.

1 cup dried Chinese mushrooms
1 cup cold water
2 medium leeks, white and light
   green parts, cleaned (page 32)
   and coarsely chopped (about 2½
   cups)
1 tablespoon olive oil
½ pound whole green beans, stem
   ends removed
1 (28-ounce) can whole Italian
   plum tomatoes, with juice

1 cup red wine
1 teaspoon dried oregano
½ teaspoon dried thyme
1 bay leaf
1 teaspoon salt
⅓ teaspoon freshly ground black
   pepper
1 teaspoon sugar

1. Soak the mushrooms for at least 30 minutes in cold water. Drain and reserve the soaking water. Remove and discard the stems. Cut caps into thick slices.

2. In a large pot, sauté the leeks in the olive oil over medium heat until they begin to soften, about 3 minutes.

3. Add the beans, mushrooms, and tomatoes with their liquid. Stir in the wine, ½ cup mushroom soaking water, oregano, thyme, bay leaf, salt, pepper, and sugar.

4. Using a wooden spoon, break up the tomatoes as you stir. Cover and cook over low heat for 1 hour. Uncover and cook for 1 hour more. The beans should be soft and the sauce dark red and thick. Remove the bay leaf. Serve hot.

Refrigerate for up to 3 days. Reheat before serving.

PEPPERS STUFFED WITH LIGHTLY CREAMED VEGETABLES

I fall back on this dish in winter, when many vegetables are not available; these ingredients are easily obtainable year-round. The peppers look particularly attractive when served in the center of a plate with small portions of white beans and green vegetables placed around them.

4 red or yellow bell peppers
½ cup chopped shallots
(4 to 6 shallots)
1 tablespoon olive oil
1 tablespoon butter
2 cups cleaned and chopped leeks, white and green parts (about 2 medium)
½ cup chopped unpeeled carrots
2 cups chopped button mushrooms
½ cup white wine
½ cup vegetable stock (see

page 30) or stock of your choice
1 tablespoon chopped fresh sage, or 1 teaspoon poultry seasoning
½ cup chopped fresh parsley
1 cup chopped tomato (1 large)
2 teaspoons salt
½ teaspoon freshly ground black pepper
2 tablespoons heavy cream
½ cup cooked rice
Bread crumbs
Butter

1. Preheat the oven to 375°F.

2. Slice ½ inch off the tops of the peppers. Remove the seeds and membranes. Rub a little olive oil on the outside of the peppers and sprinkle a little salt on the insides.

3. Roast the peppers for 15 minutes, then allow them to cool.

4. Meanwhile, in a medium skillet sauté the shallots in the oil and butter

SERVES 4 AS A FEATURED ENTREE, 8 AS A SIDE DISH

Preparation time: 30 minutes

Cooking time: 45 minutes to 1 hour

◂◦ Cut the peppers in half vertically before stuffing them if you wish to serve them as part of a composed plate or as a side dish with chicken or steak.

MENU FOR A SPECIAL
OCCASION FOR TWO

. . . .

*GRILLED SHIITAKE
MUSHROOMS ON
ARUGULA (PAGE 64)*

*SUMMER (OR WINTER)
TOMATO SOUP
(PAGES 75, 76)*

*SPINACH SOUFFLÉ
(PAGE 202)*

*CHOCOLATE ANGEL
FOOD CAKE
(PAGE 247) SERVED
WITH STRAWBERRIES
WITH RASPBERRY
SAUCE (PAGE 261)*

for 2 minutes. Add the leeks and sauté for 2 minutes. Add the carrots, and sauté for 2 minutes more. Add the mushrooms and sauté for 1 minute.

5. Stir in the wine, stock, sage, and parsley and cook for 2 minutes. Add the tomatoes, salt, and pepper and cook for 2 more minutes. Add the cream and stir. Toss well with the rice.

6. Stuff the peppers with the vegetable-rice stuffing. Top with bread crumbs, and dot lightly with butter.

Can be prepared up to 2 hours ahead.

7. Bake at 375°F. until the bread crumbs are browned and the rice and vegetables have been heated through, 20 minutes.

SPINACH SOUFFLÉ

A special treat for a small, intimate dinner party. Have your guests at the table before the soufflé comes out of the oven; like most soufflés, this one falls within seconds.

*SERVES 2 AS AN
ENTREE, 4 AS A FIRST
COURSE OR AS PART OF
A SEQUENTIALLY
SERVED MEAL*

*Preparation time:
30 to 40 minutes*

*Cooking time:
35 minutes*

3 tablespoons chopped shallots
1 tablespoon butter
*1 large bunch spinach, washed (see
    page 91) and thick stems re-
    moved*
¾ teaspoon salt

BÉCHAMEL SAUCE
1 tablespoon butter
1½ tablespoons flour
½ cup low-fat milk

*1 teaspoon finely chopped fresh
    thyme*
*¼ teaspoon freshly ground black
    pepper*
¼ teaspoon grated nutmeg
2 egg yolks

4 egg whites
Pinch of cream of tartar
*2 tablespoons grated Parmesan
    cheese*

1. Preheat the oven to 400°F.

2. In a medium skillet, sauté the shallots in butter over medium heat un-

til the shallots have softened, 2 to 3 minutes. Add the washed spinach with the water still clinging to the leaves and ¼ teaspoon salt. Cook until the water evaporates, about 3 minutes. Set aside.

3. For the béchamel, use a medium saucepan to melt the butter over low heat. Add the flour and stir with a wooden spoon for a couple of minutes to dissolve. In another medium saucepan, heat the milk until hot but not boiling. Add the milk all at once to the flour mixture and stir rapidly with a wire whisk until the sauce has thickened. Add the thyme, remaining ½ teaspoon salt, pepper, and nutmeg. Remove from the heat.

4. Mix 2 tablespoons of the sauce into the egg yolks to warm them. Immediately add the yolks to the sauce. Continue to beat until the eggs are incorporated.

Both the spinach mixture and the sauce can be prepared several hours ahead and refrigerated. Return to room temperature before continuing.

5. Combine the spinach and the sauce in a large bowl. Set aside.

6. Butter a 4-cup soufflé dish.

7. Beat the egg whites until frothy. Add the cream of tartar and beat until stiff peaks form. Mix one-fourth of the egg whites into the spinach mixture. Fold in the remaining egg whites gently, then pour into the soufflé dish and sprinkle with the cheese.

8. Put the soufflé into the oven and reduce the temperature to 375°F. Bake until the top turns golden and cracks, about 30 minutes. Serve immediately.

SPINACH WITH SCALLIONS AND FETA

*T*he taste of this dish is reminiscent of a traditional Greek spinach pie. However, not only does this version contain only a fraction of the calories and fat, but the spinach tastes far fresher because it's only lightly cooked.

Serve with rice, as a topping for pasta, or as a stuffing for a baked potato.

MENU FOR AN EASY, INFORMAL MEAL

Spinach with Scallions and Feta (page 203)

Steamed basmati rice

Raita with Cucumber and Mint (page 241)

Coarse-Grain bread

Moroccan Oranges (page 258)

SERVES 2 AS AN ENTREE, 4 AS A SIDE DISH OR WITH PASTA

Preparation time: 20 minutes

Cooking time: 5 minutes

1 tablespoon olive oil
*1 small bunch scallions, white and
  green parts chopped (about
  1½ cups)*
*1 large or 2 small bunches spinach
  (about 1 pound), washed
  (see page 91) and thick stems
  removed*

2 tablespoons chopped fresh thyme
½ teaspoon salt, or more to taste
*¼ teaspoon freshly ground black
  pepper*
*½ teaspoon ground cumin, prefer-
  ably roasted (see page 40)*
*½ cup diced or crumbled feta
  cheese (2 ounces)*

1. Heat the olive oil in a heavy-bottom saucepan over high heat. Add the scallions; they will begin to brown immediately. Lower the heat and add the spinach. Cover and cook until the spinach has wilted, 1 to 2 minutes. Drain any liquid left in the bottom of the pan.

2. Add the thyme, salt, pepper, and cumin. Stir, then add the cheese. Remove from the heat and keep covered until the cheese softens and melts slightly, 2 to 3 minutes. Serve immediately.

Baked Acorn Squash Stuffed with Nuts and Apples

*Serves 2 as a
featured entree*

❧

*Preparation time:
15 minutes*

❧

Cooking time: 1 hour

*L*ook for acorn squash with dark green skins that have "the kiss of the sun"—a large spot of orange. Although not a guarantee, it is an indication that the flesh will be deep orange and sweet.

1 medium acorn squash
1 large apple, peeled and chopped
1 to 2 teaspoons honey
1 teaspoon lemon juice

*1 to 2 tablespoons chopped walnuts
  (optional)*
*¼ teaspoon ground cinnamon
  (optional)*

1. Preheat the oven to 350°F.

2. Cut the acorn squash in half and remove the seeds. Bake the squash upside down for 30 minutes.

3. Meanwhile, combine the apple, honey, lemon juice, nuts, and cinnamon. Fill the squash halves with this mixture and bake for another 30 minutes, or until the squash is soft. Serve hot.

TOMATOES STUFFED WITH SWISS CHARD, RICE, AND CHEESE

N o matter how often I make this dish, I never tire of it. If Swiss chard is unavailable, I substitute spinach or bok choy. I might use basmati rice, long-grain white rice, or brown rice.

6 medium to large tomatoes
Salt
1 tablespoon olive oil
¼ cup chopped shallots (2 to 3 shallots)
1 cup washed (see page 91) and chopped Swiss chard, tightly packed
1½ cups cooked white rice

1 tablespoon soy sauce
2 tablespoons oven-roasted pine nuts (see page 40)
1 tablespoon chopped fresh oregano, or 1 teaspoon dried
½ cup grated cheddar cheese (2 ounces)

1. Preheat the oven to 350°F.

2. Cut a ½-inch slice from the top of each tomato. Scoop out the seeds and pulp, leaving the shell intact. Sprinkle the inside of the tomatoes with salt and turn them upside down on a roasting rack to drain while you prepare the stuffing.

3. Heat a wok or large cast-iron skillet over a high heat for 1 minute. Add the oil and shallots, then reduce the heat to low. Sauté until the shallots are soft, 2 to 3 minutes. Add the chard and sauté until wilted, 2 to 3 minutes more. Add the rice, soy sauce, pine nuts, and oregano. Remove from the heat.

4. Stuff the tomatoes, and place them in a shallow greased roasting pan with a little space between them.

SERVES 6 AS A FEATURED ENTREE

Preparation time: 15 minutes

Cooking time: 15 to 20 minutes

For a nonvegetarian meal, I enjoy these stuffed tomatoes as a side dish with grilled fish, chicken, or a chop.

MENU FOR A FAMILY DINNER

TOMATOES STUFFED WITH SWISS CHARD, RICE, AND CHEESE (PAGE 205)

GREEK ROASTED POTATOES (PAGE 221)

ZUCCHINI WITH FRESH HERBS (PAGE 225)

APPLES STEWED IN CALVADOS (PAGE 255) AND GINGER COOKIES (PAGE 262)

Can be prepared to this point early in the day. Cover and refrigerate. Return to room temperature.

5. Bake uncovered until the tomatoes are cooked through, 10 to 12 minutes. Remove the tomatoes from the oven and turn the oven to broil. Sprinkle the cheese over the tops of tomatoes and broil until the cheese has melted, 1 to 2 minutes. Watch carefully—they burn quickly. Serve immediately.

Mixed Vegetables al Forno

*L*arge chunks of vegetables are baked together in a covered heavy ovenproof pot or casserole, creating their own savory gravy. Vary them according to what you like and what's in season. Serve over orzo or rice.

SERVES 4 AS AN ENTREE, 6 TO 8 AS A SIDE DISH, 8 OR MORE AS PART OF A BUFFET

Preparation time: 20 to 30 minutes

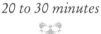

Cooking time: 1½ hours

1 medium onion, sliced
4 garlic cloves, smashed and coarsely chopped
2 medium yellow summer squash, sliced 1 inch thick
1 medium zucchini, sliced 1 inch thick
1 medium to large portobello mushroom, cut into 1-inch squares

¾ cup green beans, stem ends removed and cut into 2-inch-long pieces (3 ounces)
6 plum tomatoes, quartered
1 tablespoon fresh thyme leaves, or 1 teaspoon dried
½ teaspoon salt
1 to 2 teaspoons olive oil

1. Preheat the oven to 350°F.

2. Put the onion, garlic, squashes, mushroom, beans, tomatoes, thyme, and salt in a large ovenproof pot with a lid. Drizzle with the olive oil, cover, and bake for 1½ hours. Serve warm or hot.

The vegetables can be kept covered in their pot at room temperature for several hours. Reheat gently.

All-American Succotash

*T*his is my Uncle Morris's favorite dish. (That's the uncle who won't have anything to do with my "fancy cooking.") He says it's the best succotash he's ever had.

3 ears corn, or 3 cups frozen kernels
2 pounds fresh lima beans (about 2 cups) (see Note)
1 medium leek, cleaned (see page 32) and chopped, white and green parts (approximately 1¼ cups)

1 tablespoon olive oil
2 cups chopped tomatoes (about 2 large)
1 teaspoon salt
½ teaspoon freshly ground black pepper
½ cup chopped fresh parsley, coriander, basil, or a mixture

1. Cut the corn from their husks and remove the lima beans from their pods.

2. In a large skillet, sauté the leek in the oil until it wilts, 2 to 3 minutes. Add the corn, lima beans, tomatoes, salt, and pepper.

3. Bring to a simmer over high heat. Cover and turn the heat to low, then simmer for 10 minutes. Add the parsley. Serve hot or at room temperature.

Note: Since fresh lima beans are in season only for a few weeks at the end of each summer, you may want to use frozen ones. If so, defrost them and then add them during the last few minutes of cooking.

Warm Roasted Vegetables Vinaigrette

*W*hen summer comes, these flavorful vegetables are often on my party table. Serve with rice as an entree, pass around with toothpicks as an hors d'ouevre, or serve them the way I most often do—as part of a buffet.

Serves 6 as a featured entree, 10 to 12 as part of a buffet

Preparation time: 30 minutes

Cooking time: 15 minutes

"*It does not require much historical research to uncover the fact that nobody knows if the Pilgrims really ate turkey at the first Thanksgiving dinner. The only thing we know for sure about what the Pilgrims ate is that it couldn't have tasted very good. Even today, well-brought-up English girls are taught by their mothers to boil all veggies for at least a month and a half, just in case one of the dinner guests turns up without his teeth.***"**
—Calvin Trillin,
Third Helpings

½ *pound shallots*
2 *red bell peppers*
1 *yellow bell pepper*
6 *medium zucchini*
2 *medium yellow summer squash*
1½ *tablespoons olive oil*

VINAIGRETTE
1½ *tablespoons lemon juice*
1½ *tablespoons balsamic vinegar*

1 *teaspoon Dijon-style mustard*
⅓ *teaspoon salt*
¼ *teaspoon freshly ground black
   pepper*
½ *teaspoon lemon zest*
1½ *tablespoons olive oil*

1. Preheat the oven to 500°F.

2. Peel the shallots but leave them whole. Cut the red and yellow peppers into 1½-inch squares. Cut the zucchini and yellow squash into 1½-inch-thick slices. Toss all with the olive oil.

3. Place the vegetables in a large roasting pan; make sure they aren't crowded. Roast until they begin to char, about 30 minutes.

4. For the vinaigrette, mix the lemon juice, vinegar, mustard, salt, pepper, and lemon zest with the olive oil. Pour the vinaigrette over the hot vegetables and gently toss. Serve at room temperature.

STEAMED VEGETABLES WITH THREE SPICY CHINESE SAUCES

*M*y friend Adrienne Jamiel is a vegan—someone who eats no dairy products or eggs. She's also a personal sports trainer. When Adrienne comes over, she corrects my floor routine and I teach her how to make dishes like this.

The sauces can be made up to a week ahead. During the summer the vegetables can be steamed hours ahead and then served cold or at room temperature. In the winter I prefer to serve the vegetables warm or hot.

Vegetables can be varied depending on what you like and what's available. Quantities can easily be adjusted for the season, the number of people coming for dinner, and the amount of additional food you're serving.

For a sit-down dinner, put the vegetables on one large platter or several small ones and the sauces in separate bowls. Place these on the dining room table along with lots of rice.

If the theme of your meal is not Chinese, you might try a different selection of sauces: good choices include Porcini Vinaigrette (page 49), Mustard Vinaigrette (page 60), Curried Roasted Garlic Spread (page 59), Yogurt and Chickpea Dip (page 54), and the Tahini Vinaigrette (page 89).

I like to add a few "little dishes" such as Raita with Coriander (page 241), Black Bean Salsa (page 234), and Mango-Lime Chutney (page 239).

SERVES 8 TO 12 AS AN ENTREE, UP TO 20 AS AN APPETIZER OR AS PART OF A BUFFET

Preparation time: 45 minutes

Cooking time: 20 minutes

SPICY SESAME SAUCE
⅓ cup tahini
½ cup steeped Chinese black tea
2½ tablespoons soy sauce
1 teaspoon chili oil (see page 43)
1 tablespoon Oriental sesame oil
1 tablespoon sugar
1 tablespoon red wine vinegar

SOY AND RICE VINEGAR SAUCE
½ cup soy sauce
¾ cup rice vinegar
1 tablespoon balsamic vinegar
2 tablespoons minced fresh ginger
1 teaspoon Oriental sesame oil
1 teaspoon chili oil (see page 43)
1 teaspoon sugar

PICKLED GINGER SAUCE
¼ cup rice vinegar
2 tablespoons chopped pickled ginger
2 teaspoons sugar
1 teaspoon Oriental sesame oil
½ teaspoon chili oil (see page 43)
1 tablespoon chopped scallion
2 tablespoons chopped fresh coriander (cilantro; optional)

1 head cauliflower
1 head broccoli
1 pound asparagus
1 pound carrots
1 pound green beans

1. For the sesame sauce, combine the tahini, tea, soy sauce, chili oil, sesame oil, sugar, and vinegar. Set aside.

Spicy Sesame Sauce can be prepared 1 week ahead. Refrigerate.

2. For the vinegar sauce, combine the soy sauce, rice vinegar, balsamic vinegar, ginger, sesame oil, chili oil, and sugar. Set aside.

Soy and Rice Vinegar Sauce can be prepared 1 week ahead. Refrigerate.

3. For the ginger sauce, combine the vinegar, ginger, sugar, sesame oil, and chili oil.

"*Vegetables can be the glory of any meal when lovingly cooked.***"**
—JULIA CHILD,
The Way to Cook

The sauce can be prepared to this point up to 1 week ahead.

4. Add the scallion and coriander just before serving.

5. Remove the core of the cauliflower. Break into florets, then steam 4 to 5 minutes.

6. Remove the thick stalk from the broccoli. Break into florets, then steam 4 to 5 minutes.

7. Remove the tough part of the asparagus and discard. Steam for 4 to 5 minutes.

8. Clean the carrots and cut them on the diagonal. Steam for about 5 minutes.

9. Remove the stem ends from the beans. Steam for 3 to 5 minutes.

10. Arrange the vegetables attractively on a large white platter. Serve with the sauces. Vegetables can be hot, at room temperature, or cold.

VEGETABLES AS PART OF A COMPOSED PLATE OR AS SIDE DISHES

The vegetable recipes in this section can be used to accompany either a vegetarian or a meat or fish featured entree; as part of a buffet or an antipasto; or combined with other dishes to create a composed plate. None of them is substantial enough to be served as a featured entree. However, if you and your family have a passion for, say, asparagus, you might want to think about serving a large portion with a baked potato on the side and a hearty soup like Vegetable Soup with French Pesto (page 84) to begin the meal.

For information on how to design a vegetarian composed plate, see page 20.

> *"Prior to World War II, those who didn't over-cook their vegetables were considered to be part of a lunatic fringe— adjudged almost as quirky as folks who dunked their bodies in the surf in January or (heaven forbid) slept in the nude!"*
>
> —BERT GREENE
> *Greene on Greens*

Asparagus with Brown Butter and Lemon

I adore asparagus and eat them regularly when they're in season. I generally prepare them as simply as possible. Buy asparagus that have tight tips and moist ends. This brown butter and lemon sauce is wonderful on Brussels sprouts, broccoli, string beans, and carrots.

1 pound asparagus, tough ends removed

BROWN BUTTER AND LEMON SAUCE
1 tablespoon butter

½ teaspoon salt
¼ teaspoon freshly ground black pepper
1 tablespoon lemon juice

1. Steam the asparagus for 4 to 5 minutes, or until tender.

2. Meanwhile, brown the butter in a saucepan over low heat, 3 to 5 minutes. Add the salt and pepper. Allow the salt to dissolve, about 30 seconds, then add the lemon juice. Stir. Pour the sauce over the asparagus. Serve hot.

Green Beans Amandine

W ith beans available all year—and tasty either hot or at room temperature—they appear often on my home and catering menus. This simple recipe is good for ordinary beans and outstanding for the tender thin French beans known as *haricots verts*.

3 tablespoons chopped raw almonds (see Note)
1 teaspoon butter, melted
½ pound green beans, stem ends removed

1 large garlic clove, minced
2 teaspoons olive oil
½ teaspoon salt
⅛ teaspoon freshly ground black pepper

SERVES 4 AS A SIDE DISH OR AS PART OF A COMPOSED PLATE, 6 AS PART OF A BUFFET

Preparation time: 10 minutes

Cooking time: 5 minutes

MENU FOR A FAMILY SPRING DINNER

ASPARAGUS WITH BROWN BUTTER AND LEMON (PAGE 211)

MEDITERRANEAN WHITE BEANS (PAGE 154)

SAFFRON HERB RICE (PAGE 187)

RAITA WITH CORIANDER (PAGE 241)

PEACHES IN RED WINE (PAGE 259)

SERVES 4 AS A SIDE DISH OR AS PART OF A COMPOSED PLATE, 6 AS PART OF A BUFFET

Preparation time: 20 minutes

Cooking time: 15 minutes

1. Preheat the oven to 325°F.

2. Toss the almonds with the butter in a baking dish and roast until they're dark brown, about 10 minutes. Set aside.

3. Steam the beans for 4 to 6 minutes, depending on how big and tough they are. I usually taste one to see if it's done.

4. While the beans are steaming, sauté the garlic in the olive oil in a large skillet over low heat. When the garlic just begins to turn golden, add the salt and pepper and stir. Add the beans and stir again for 1 minute. Sprinkle with the roasted almonds. Serve hot.

Note: Instead of topping the beans with roasted almonds, you can cut fresh shiitake mushrooms into thin strips and brush them with olive oil. Heat a wok or cast-iron skillet, add the mushrooms, and then blacken the mushrooms by cooking them over high heat for 1 minute on each side. Scatter these blackened shiitakes over the beans.

*SERVES 4 AS A SIDE
DISH OR AS PART OF A
COMPOSED PLATE*

*Preparation time:
10 minutes*

*Cooking time:
10 minutes*

BROCCOLI DI RAPE WITH GARLIC

I'm amazed how many people love this bitter vegetable as much as I do. Blanching is a critical step; without it broccoli di rape is stringy and far too bitter.

An excellent side dish with any Italian pasta.

*1 bunch broccoli di rape
4 garlic cloves, minced
½ teaspoon salt*

*1 tablespoon olive oil
¼ teaspoon freshly ground black
    pepper*

➧ *Those who are not
vegetarian can substi-
tute chicken stock for
the steaming water for
a delicious variation.*

1. While the broccoli di rape is still tied, remove 3 to 4 inches of the stems with a single cut; discard. Cut the remaining portion into 2-inch pieces and wash by submerging and lifting.

2. Steam the broccoli for 2 minutes. Drain and reserve any juices. Immerse broccoli in ice water for 1 minute, then drain again.

3. In a large, heavy-bottom pot, sauté the garlic and salt in the olive oil over low heat until the garlic is golden and the salt is dissolved, 2 to 3 minutes. Add the broccoli di rape, turn the heat to high, and sauté for 1 minute.

4. Add ⅓ cup of steaming juices and cook uncovered over a low heat for 2 minutes. Add the pepper, and serve hot or warm.

HASHED BRUSSELS SPROUTS WITH FRESH OREGANO

This recipe was inspired by the hashed Brussels sprouts I ate at the Union Square Cafe in New York City.

Chopping the sprouts and quickly sautéing them before braising them in lemon and wine changes both their flavor and texture. I've seen the most adamant "I-hate-Brussels-sprouts" eaters go for second and third helpings of these.

2 cups (1 pint) Brussels sprouts
1 tablespoon olive oil
1 garlic clove, chopped
2 tablespoons white wine
1½ tablespoons lemon juice

1 tablespoon chopped fresh oregano
Salt and freshly ground black pepper to taste

1. Cut the Brussels sprouts in half vertically, then coarsely chop them.

2. Heat the olive oil for 1 minute over medium-high heat in a large skillet. Add the Brussels sprouts and the garlic and sauté until the sprouts begin to char, 1 to 2 minutes.

3. Turn the heat to medium-low. Add the wine and lemon juice and partially cover. Cook until the sprouts are easily pierced with a fork but not soft, about 3 minutes. Add the oregano and cook for 30 seconds. Add salt and pepper. Serve hot or warm.

After steaming vegetables, reserve the liquid to use in stocks, to cook grains, to boil pasta, or to drink with a splash of umeboshi vinegar, a sour plum vinegar available at Asian markets and in health food stores.

SERVES 4 AS A SIDE DISH OR AS PART OF A COMPOSED PLATE

Preparation time: 10 minutes

Cooking time: under 10 minutes

MENU FOR A WINTER DINNER

WINTER TOMATO SOUP (PAGE 76)

HASHED BRUSSELS SPROUTS WITH FRESH OREGANO (PAGE 213)

CREOLE BLACK-EYED PEAS (PAGE 166)

STEAMED WHITE RICE

APPLES STEWED IN CALVADOS (PAGE 255)

Red-Cooked Cabbage

The Chinese consider the color red lucky. One frequently finds that when ingredients are cooked in soy sauce, the final dish is called red-cooked, even though its color isn't red.

With its appealing salty-sweet taste, this cabbage is good with a hearty bean stew.

2 teaspoons cornstarch
2 tablespoons dry sherry
1 medium onion, cut into large dice
4 slices fresh ginger, approximately
    1 inch long, ½ inch wide,
    ¼ inch thick
2 garlic cloves, crushed

1 tablespoon peanut oil
2 pounds napa cabbage, cut into 1-
    inch pieces
2 tablespoons soy sauce
1 teaspoon sugar
¼ teaspoon freshly ground black
    pepper

1. Dissolve the cornstarch in 1 tablespoon of the sherry and set aside.

2. In a wok or large skillet, sauté the onion, ginger, and garlic in the oil over medium heat until the garlic begins to color, 3 to 4 minutes. Add the cabbage and toss.

3. Stir in the soy sauce, sugar, remaining 1 tablespoon of sherry, and the pepper. Cover and cook until the cabbage is wilted, 10 to 15 minutes. Uncover and remove the ginger.

4. Restir the cornstarch mixture and add, stirring with a wooden spoon or chopstick until the liquids have thickened and the cabbage is glazed, about 30 seconds. Serve hot.

Cabbage, Carrots, and Sauerkraut

Serve this unusual vegetable combination with any hearty bean dish, like Black Beans with Roasted Peppers (page 160) or Ginger Lentil Stew (page 164), and white rice. The sauerkraut adds zest to the cabbage and carrots without dominating them.

2 unpeeled carrots, shredded
2 teaspoons Oriental sesame oil
½ head cabbage, savoy or regular,
    shredded (about 8 cups)

½ cup sauerkraut, drained

SERVES 4 TO 6 AS A
SIDE DISH OR AS PART
OF A COMPOSED PLATE

Preparation time:
15 minutes

Cooking time:
15 minutes

1. In a large skillet, sauté the carrots in the oil until they soften, 2 to 3 minutes.

2. Add the cabbage and toss, then stir in the sauerkraut. Sauté, tossing every couple of minutes, for 10 minutes. Serve hot or at room temperature.

CARROT AND RICE PUREE

*L*ast year one of my guests tasted this dish and then pushed it aside, convinced it was loaded with cream and butter. It's hard to believe how low in fat this buttery, sensuously sweet puree is.

8 to 10 unpeeled carrots, cut into
    1-inch chunks
⅓ cup white rice
½ cup vegetable stock (see page 30)
    or stock of your choice
⅓ cup low-fat milk

¼ teaspoon five-spice powder
    (see Note)
1 tablespoon butter
1 teaspoon salt
½ teaspoon freshly ground black
    pepper

SERVES 6 AS A SIDE
DISH OR AS PART OF A
COMPOSED PLATE

Preparation time:
15 minutes

Cooking time:
30 minutes

1. Bring the carrots, rice, and stock to a boil in a medium saucepan. Reduce the heat and simmer, covered, for 30 minutes. Add the milk a few seconds before removing the pan from the heat.

2. Pour the contents of the pan into a food processor (or pass the solids through a food mill) and add the five-spice powder, butter, salt, and pepper. Puree—the consistency will be thick, similar to mashed potatoes. Serve hot.

This puree can be prepared several hours in advance and reheated in a bain-marie, a water bath. To make your own bain-marie, put the puree in a small saucepan and then put the saucepan into a skillet filled to a depth

of 1 inch with water. Turn the heat to high until the water boils, then turn it down to medium and heat just until the puree is warmed through.

Note: Five-spice powder is a combination of fennel, cinnamon, cloves, Sichuan pepper, and anise. It's available in many supermarkets. Cinnamon can be substituted.

SWISS CHARD WITH SHALLOTS

*I*f you have the luxury of growing your own Swiss chard, harvest it when it is four to eight inches tall by cutting it two inches above the root. It will continue to grow from early summer to the end of fall. With such young chard, you don't have to bother separating the ribs from the leaves or first steaming it before sautéing.

Most of the chard we buy, however, needs to be blanched to make it tender enough to eat.

1 bunch Swiss chard, stems and
   leaves
1 tablespoon olive oil
1 to 2 shallots, chopped
1 garlic clove, minced

½ teaspoon salt
1 teaspoon cider vinegar
¼ teaspoon freshly ground black
   pepper

1. Wash the Swiss chard by first spraying it with cold water and then submerging and lifting. Make sure to wash thoroughly; chard tends to be sandy. Shake dry.

2. Remove the center rib with a paring knife. Cut the ribs on the diagonal into 1½-inch pieces. Steam the ribs for 3 to 4 minutes.

3. Meanwhile, stack the leaves on top of each other. Make a single lengthwise cut down the center of the leaves, and then cut across into 1½-inch pieces. Add the leaves to the ribs and steam for an additional 3 to 4 minutes. Reserve the water in the steamer.

4. While the chard is steaming, heat the olive oil in a wok or cast-iron skillet. Sauté the shallots and garlic until the garlic is golden, 2 to 3 min-

utes. Add the salt and stir until the salt dissolves, just a few seconds.

5. Add the chard and toss. Add ¼ cup of the reserved steaming water and cook the chard uncovered over a low heat until tender, about 5 minutes. Add the vinegar and pepper. Toss. Serve hot.

BRAISED ESCAROLE WITH GARLIC

A lthough escarole can be eaten in salads as you would other bitter greens, I usually prefer it lightly cooked. This simple dish is ideal alongside Spaghetti with Tomatoes, Basil, and Parsley (page 149); Pasta Caponata (page 143), and other entrees with an Italian accent.

SERVES 4 AS A SIDE DISH OR AS PART OF A COMPOSED PLATE

Preparation time: 15 minutes

Cooking time: 12 to 13 minutes

1 bunch escarole
4 garlic cloves, crushed
1 tablespoon olive oil
½ teaspoon salt
¼ cup vegetable stock (see page 30)

or stock of your choice
Lemon juice (optional)
⅛ teaspoon hot red pepper flakes (optional)

1. Cut ½ inch of the base off the escarole. Wash by submerging the escarole in a large bowl of water. Lift out, drain, then spin-dry. Cut into 1-inch pieces.

2. In a medium skillet, sauté the garlic over low heat in the olive oil until golden, 2 to 3 minutes. Add the salt and stir until it dissolves.

3. Add the escarole, turn the heat to high, and toss well. Add the stock, cover, and simmer over a low heat for 10 minutes.

4. Place the sautéed escarole on a plate and sprinkle with lemon juice and hot red pepper flakes, if desired. Serve hot.

FENNEL

ennel is a pale green, feathery-topped vegetable with an enlarged bulblike base that looks similar to celery. When raw it has a crunchy texture like celery and a mild licorice taste. When cooked, its flavor is delicate and haunting.

Italians have used fennel extensively since the time of the Ancient Romans. They serve it in any course, appetizer through dessert. If fennel is new to you, I urge you to try it. You're in for a wonderful new taste.

Fennel is widely available from spring through fall. Choose bulbs that look shiny—never those with brown or splitting outer leaves.

FENNEL AND ONION CONFIT

SERVES 6 AS A SIDE DISH OR AS PART OF A COMPOSED PLATE

Preparation time: 15 minutes

Cooking time: 50 minutes

y students refer to this confit as the sleeper of the year because none of them believed that a dish this simple could be so good. I serve it hot or at room temperature, as part of an hors d'oeuvre platter, on a buffet table, and as a side dish. The mild aniselike taste of fennel harmonizes magically with the onions and fresh oregano.

1 medium fennel bulb
1 Spanish onion
1 tablespoon olive oil
½ teaspoon salt
¼ teaspoon freshly ground black pepper

Up to ¼ cup vegetable stock (see page 30) or water
2 tablespoons minced fresh oregano

➤ *For a nonvegetarian meal, serve it with Carrot and Rice Puree (page 215) and grilled fish, roasted chicken, or a pork roast.*

1. Slice the fennel and onion vertically into long strips ¼ inch thick.

2. Heat the olive oil in a large, heavy-bottom pan. Add the onion and sauté over medium-high heat until it begins to brown, about 5 minutes.

3. Turn the heat to low. Add the fennel, salt, and pepper. Partially cover

the pan with a lid. Stir once or twice, adding 2 or 3 tablespoons of stock or water if the onion is sticking, and cook until the fennel is soft and brown, the onion slightly caramelized, about 45 minutes.

4. Add the oregano 1 or 2 minutes before removing from the heat. Serve warm or at room temperature.

This confit can be refrigerated for several days. Reheat before serving.

BRAISED MUSHROOMS

These mushrooms are a great side dish, an outstanding omelet filling (without sesame seeds), and a delightful appetizer on buttered toast rounds. I also add them to other dishes, like stir-fried vegetables.

SERVES 4 AS A SIDE DISH OR AS PART OF A COMPOSED PLATE, 6 TO 8 AS AN APPETIZER

Preparation time: under 10 minutes

Cooking time: 10 minutes

1 pound portobello, cremini, or button mushrooms
1 tablespoon olive oil
1½ tablespoons soy sauce

2 scallions, chopped
1 tablespoon roasted and ground sesame seeds (see page 40)

1. Remove and discard the sandy ends of the mushroom stems. Wash the mushrooms under a light spray of cold water. Chop the stems and caps.

2. Place a wok or large cast-iron skillet over high heat for 1 minute. Add the oil around the sides of the wok or pan, and turn the heat to medium. Add the chopped mushrooms and stir-fry until they give up their juices, about 5 minutes. If the mushrooms are browning too fast, lower the heat.

3. Add the soy sauce. Turn the heat to low and simmer for 2 minutes.

4. Remove wok or skillet from the heat, add the scallions, and stir. Sprinkle with the sesame seeds. Serve hot.

CHINESE CHARRED PEPPERS AND ZUCCHINI

*YIELDS 2 CUPS; SERVES
6 AS A SIDE DISH OR
AS PART OF A
COMPOSED PLATE*

*Preparation time:
20 minutes, plus
1 hour to salt
vegetables*

*Cooking time:
5 minutes*

This is an all-purpose recipe. I toss these vegetables into salads, add them to vinaigrette, serve over rice, scatter over slices of goat cheese and then surround with asparagus, and serve with pasta.

1 cup large-diced red bell pepper
*1 cup large-diced yellow bell pep-
    per*
2 cups sliced zucchini
1 teaspoon salt

SEASONING SAUCE
1 tablespoon soy sauce
2 teaspoons red wine vinegar
½ teaspoon chili oil (see page 43)
½ teaspoon sugar

1 tablespoon peanut oil

To char food is to scorch it deliberately, usually with intense heat.
    Charring can be done in the oven or on top of the stove, with oil or without. Vegetables being charred in the oven should be turned occasionally; those on top of the stove should be flipped once in a while and pressed frequently with the back of the spatula.

1. Put the peppers and zucchini in a bowl and sprinkle with salt. Allow to sit at room temperature for 1 hour.

2. Submerge salted vegetables in cold water, drain, and spin- or drain dry. Make sure to dry well or the vegetables will not char properly.

3. To make the seasoning sauce, combine the soy sauce, vinegar, chili oil, and sugar. Set aside.

4. Place a wok or large cast-iron skillet over high heat until it smokes, 2 to 3 minutes. Add the oil. Immediately add the peppers and zucchini. Press down occasionally with the back of a spatula to aid the charring. Cook until the peppers and zucchini are scorched in places and soft, about 5 minutes. If they appear to be scorching too rapidly, reduce the heat.

5. Add the seasoning sauce and stir for a few seconds until absorbed. Serve at room temperature.

Chinese Charred Peppers and Zucchini can be refrigerated for up to 5 days. Return to room temperature before serving.

Greek Roasted Potatoes

*T*hese easy-to-make, crusty little potato cubes have a mild lemon tang.

10 new potatoes
1 tablespoon olive oil
1 tablespoon fresh lemon juice

1 tablespoon fresh oregano
  (optional)
1 teaspoon salt

1. Preheat the oven to 425°F.

2. Cut the potatoes in sixths. Do not peel. Place the potatoes in a bowl of cold water to cover for 15 minutes. Drain in a colander.

3. Place the drained potatoes in a large bowl. Mix with the olive oil, water, and lemon juice and salt.

4. Place a large cast-iron skillet over high heat for 2 minutes. Turn off heat.

5. Crumple a paper towel and moisten a small area of it with a little olive oil by turning the bottle upside down while holding the paper against the opening. Being careful not to burn your fingers, wipe the bottom of the hot skillet with the oil.

6. Add the potatoes to the skillet and place in the oven. Bake until the potatoes are crispy and brown on the outside and soft on the inside, about 45 minutes. Shake the pan once or twice to keep the potatoes from sticking and to help them brown more evenly. Do not crowd the potatoes or they will steam instead of becoming crusty.

7. Five minutes before removing the potatoes from the oven, sprinkle with oregano. Serve hot.

SERVES 2-4 AS A SIDE DISH OR AS PART OF A COMPOSED PLATE

*Preparation time:
5 minutes*

*Cooking time:
45 minutes*

◄● *Use these potatoes instead of French fries with hamburgers, steak, or chicken for a wonderful, low-fat change-of-pace.*

BALSAMIC-GLAZED SUMMER SQUASH

*SERVES 6 AS A SIDE
DISH OR AS PART OF A
COMPOSED PLATE*

*Preparation time:
10 minutes*

*Cooking time:
15 minutes*

My friend Toby Liebmann swore she couldn't stand to look at another zucchini last August; however, her vegetable patch was still brimming with them.

We invented this dish in a successful attempt to give summer squash or zucchini an entirely new flavor. The unique sweet-sharp taste of balsamic vinegar works magic on this bland vegetable.

*1 medium leek, white and light
   green parts, cleaned (see page
   32) and sliced
   (about 1¼ cups)*
1 tablespoon olive oil
*4 medium yellow summer squash
   or zucchini, sliced ¼ to ⅓ inch
   thick*

½ teaspoon salt
*¼ teaspoon freshly ground
   black pepper*
2 tablespoons balsamic vinegar

1. In a large skillet, sauté the leek in the olive oil over medium heat until it begins to brown, 7 or 8 minutes.

2. Add the squash and fry until they soften, 3 or 4 minutes.

3. Add the salt, pepper, and vinegar. Continue to cook until the vinegar evaporates and the squash is glazed and beginning to brown, 4 to 5 minutes. Serve hot or at room temperature

GRILLED SUMMER SQUASH WITH PEPPERS AND OREGANO

Barbecues and summer go hand-in-hand for me. Grilled vegetables like this one are ideal as part of a vegetarian buffet.

If you have a barbecue grill, allow the fire to burn down until you have white-hot charcoals; this takes about 30 minutes. If you're using a gas grill, preheat it to 350°F. This dish can also be made in a broiler.

1½ teaspoons salt
1 medium yellow bell pepper, cut into thick strips
1 red bell pepper, cut into thick strips
2 small zucchini, cut diagonally into ¼-inch-thick slices
2 small yellow summer squash, cut diagonally into ¼-inch-thick slices

Olive oil, for brushing the vegetables
3 tablespoons olive oil
1 tablespoon lemon juice
¼ teaspoon freshly ground black pepper
2 to 3 tablespoons chopped fresh oregano
2 tablespoons chopped fresh parsley

1. Start the fire in the barbecue. Allow the fire to burn down until the coals are white-hot.

2. Sprinkle the salt over the yellow and red peppers, zucchini, and squash and allow to stand for 10 minutes. Rinse and pat dry with paper towels.

3. Brush vegetables lightly with olive oil, and grill for 2 to 3 minutes on each side. (If using a broiler, broil 6 to 8 inches from the heat.) Vegetables should be nicely charred, but not burned.

4. Place the vegetables on a serving plate. Mix the olive oil, lemon juice, black pepper, and oregano in a bowl and pour the mixture over the grilled vegetables. Sprinkle with the chopped parsley. Serve hot or at room temperature.

SERVES 6 TO 8 AS A SIDE DISH OR AS PART OF A COMPOSED PLATE, 10 TO 12 AS PART OF A BUFFET

Preparation time: 20 minutes, plus 10 minutes to salt the vegetables

Cooking time: 10 minutes

◄● *This squash is an excellent accompaniment to steak or hamburger.*

Mashed Sweet Potatoes and Butternut Squash

*W*hen sweet potatoes and butternut squash are paired, each augments the flavor of the other. The squash softens the intense sweetness of the potatoes, and the potatoes add succulent moistness to the squash.

2 medium sweet potatoes
1 medium butternut squash, halved and seeds removed
¼ teaspoon salt
⅛ teaspoon freshly ground black pepper

½ teaspoon ground cinnamon
½ teaspoon freshly grated nutmeg
½ teaspoon ground ginger
1 tablespoon lemon juice
2 tablespoons brown sugar

SERVES 10 TO 12 AS A SIDE DISH OR AS PART OF A COMPOSED PLATE

Preparation time: 10 to 15 minutes

Cooking time: 1 hour and 45 minutes

◄● *Serve with Thanksgiving turkey.*

1. Preheat the oven to 350°F.

2. Place the sweet potatoes in the oven and bake for 30 minutes.

3. Put the butternut squash halves upside down on a cookie sheet, place in oven to bake with the sweet potatoes until both are soft, 45 minutes more. Allow to cool slightly. Leave oven at 350°F.

4. Scoop the flesh from the shells of the squash and sweet potatoes. Mash together with the salt, pepper, cinnamon, nutmeg, ginger, lemon juice, and brown sugar.

This puree can be prepared up to 2 days ahead and refrigerated.

4. Place mashed mixture in a baking dish and cover. Bake for 30 minutes. Serve hot.

Sweet Potato and Pear Gratin

*I*t sounds incongruous, but the sweetness of the sweet potatoes and pears contrast delightfully with the sharp saltiness of the Parmesan cheese topping. For a striking presentation, alternate the sweet potatoes and pears in concentric circles on a large gratin pan. To save time, simply toss the sweet potatoes and pears together.

Serves 4 to 6 as a side dish or as part of a composed plate

Preparation time: 20 to 30 minutes

Cooking time: 45 to 50 minutes

Good with any kind of roasted meat or poultry.

¼ *cup orange juice*
¼ *cup lemon juice*
¼ *teaspoon ground cinnamon*
¼ *teaspoon ground allspice*
2 *tablespoons brown sugar*
2 *medium sweet potatoes, peeled or unpeeled*

2 *ripe pears, preferrably Bartlett or Comice, peeled or unpeeled*
¼ *cup grated Parmesan cheese*
¼ *cup dried bread crumbs (see page 48)*
Pinch of freshly ground black pepper

1. Preheat the oven to 375°F.

2. In a large bowl, combine the orange juice, lemon juice, cinnamon, allspice, and brown sugar. Set aside.

3. Cut the sweet potatoes and pears in half and remove the cores from the pears. Slice both ⅓ inch thick and arrange in a single layer of alternating slices in a gratin pan. Pour the orange juice mixture evenly over the top.

4. Combine the cheese, bread crumbs, and pepper. Sprinkle over the sweet potatoes and pears.

5. Cover the pan with a lid or aluminum foil and bake for 40 minutes or until the sweet potatoes are soft.

6. Uncover and raise the temperature of the oven to 450°. Bake an additional 5 to 10 minutes, until the topping is lightly browned and most of the liquid in the pan has evaporated. Be careful not to burn the topping. Serve hot or warm.

ZUCCHINI WITH FRESH HERBS

I was proud of my mother and father when I was very small for winning the Sunday-night Samba contests at Tavern on the Green, a sprawling restaurant and club in Manhattan's Central Park. My mother was always dressed to the hilt, looking like a professional ballroom dancer in her brightly colored skirts that nipped in at her tiny waist and flared out and twirled around her as she danced. My father looked distinguished and calm in his conservative blue suit, more the elder statesman. To me, my parents were as grand as Ginger Rogers and Fred Astaire.

My mother's flamboyant style in dress and dance didn't extend to her cooking. She served zucchini plain with just salt and pepper—she didn't believe in using herbs. But with her grace and style, I could forgive her anything—even plain boiled zucchini. Years later she admitted that she liked this zucchini far better than her own.

SERVES 4 TO 6 AS A SIDE DISH OR AS PART OF A COMPOSED PLATE

Preparation time: 20 minutes

Cooking time: 10 to 12 minutes

1 tablespoon olive oil
1 cup chopped onion
1 medium zucchini (about 1 pound), cut into 1-inch-thick slices
1 teaspoon salt

¼ teaspoon freshly ground black pepper
3 tablespoons chopped fresh chives
3 tablespoons chopped fresh basil
3 tablespoons chopped fresh parsley

1. Heat the oil in a cast-iron skillet. Sauté the onion over medium heat until brown, 5 to 7 minutes.

2. Turn the heat to high and add the zucchini. Sauté until they begin to brown, about 5 minutes. Add the salt and pepper.

3. Remove from the heat. Add the chives, basil, and parsley. Stir. Serve hot.

SERVES 4 AS PART OF A COMPOSED PLATE, 6 AS PART OF A BUFFET

Preparation time: 15 minutes

Cooking time: 10 minutes

CHARRED BEAN SPROUTS WITH SCALLIONS AND CARROTS

Today fresh mung bean sprouts, wonderfully crisp and tender, are available all year long in Asian food stores and in the produce section of many supermarkets. Sprouts should be eaten raw or cooked only briefly. Charring them keeps them from wilting.

I keep sprouts in the refrigerator, wrapped in paper towels for a day or two. Do not substitute canned, which are limp and tasteless.

Serve these Sprouts with Whole-Grain Fried Rice (page 182), Vegetable Lo Mein (page 129), Braised Mushrooms (page 219), or any other dish with Oriental overtones.

1 pound fresh mung bean sprouts
2 teaspoons Oriental sesame oil
½ teaspoon salt

2 unpeeled carrots, julienned
4 scallions, white and green parts
   shredded or julienned

1. Heat a wok until extremely hot and smoking, 3 to 5 minutes.

2. Add the bean sprouts. Char them by pressing down occasionally with the back of the spatula. Char for 2 minutes on one side. Flip the sprouts and char the other side. Remove the sprouts from the wok.

3. Turn the heat to low and add the sesame oil, salt, and carrots. Stir-fry for 2 minutes. Add the scallions and stir-fry 1 minute more.

4. Add the charred sprouts and toss for 30 seconds. Serve hot.

STIR-FRIED VEGETABLES

My early training in Chinese cooking has had an enormous influence on how I cook and eat. Without question, stir-frying is my favorite method of cooking.

I love being able to prepare the ingredients hours in advance and then spend just minutes cooking. I love the rhythm and movements of stir-frying. Most of all, I love the clean, healthy taste of stir-fried vegetables.

To stir-fry means to cook food rapidly, constantly tossing it, over a high heat in a small amount of oil for a short time. Everything happens at once. Tools and ingredients must be lined up and ready to go. From the instant the first ingredients are added to the sizzling wok, there's no turning back—no time to cut more vegetables or fetch the scallion from the refrigerator.

THE FOLLOWING ARE TIPS I GIVE MY STUDENTS FOR SUCCESSFUL STIR-FRY COOKING:

• *Put the ingredients on a tray in the order in which you will add them to the wok.*
• *Choose a flat-bottom steel wok with a wooden handle to avoid the metal ring necessary under a round-bottomed wok. (This ring raises the wok from the heat and lessens the heat that reaches it.) If you don't have a wok, a cast-iron skillet, although harder to lift because of its weight, works well.*
• *Use the highest possible heat. The success of stir-fry dishes depends on the intensity of the heat.*
• *Have someone read the recipe to you as you stir-fry.*
• *Heat the wok for 1 minute or more (times are specified in the recipes) before you add the oil. Then heat the oil for 1 minute before adding the food. This keeps the food from sticking to the wok. For most dishes the oil should be hot but not smoking.*
• *Peanut oil is preferred for stir-frying, as it can be heated to a higher temperature without smoking or burning.*
• *Set a steady rhythm when you stir-fry: one-two, one-two, always reaching the bottom of the center of the wok with your metal spatula so the food cooks evenly.*
• *Restir any seasoning sauces and binders just before adding them to the wok. When adding the binder to a sauce that has few solids, pour it in a steady stream into one spot. Using a wire whisk, briskly whisk that spot for 10 seconds; then using a figure-eight motion, incorporate the binder into the entire sauce.*

When adding the binder to a sauce with many ingredients, pour it over the top and toss as you would a salad until the sauce thickens. This takes about 30 seconds. Be sure to reach the food at the bottom in the center of the wok.
• *Serve the finished dish immediately. Never reheat stir-fried food.*

SERVES 4 AS PART OF A
COMPOSED PLATE,
6 AS PART OF A BUFFET

*Preparation time:
15 minutes*

*Cooking time:
6 to 8 minutes*

SICHUAN GREEN BEANS

Years ago I deep-fried these beans in 2 cups of oil. Now I steam them. The taste is fresher, less greasy, and fewer vitamins are lost.

For a special occasion, make this dish with *haricots verts*.

1 pound green beans (haricots verts, *if available*)

SEASONING SAUCE
*1 teaspoon soy sauce
½ teaspoon chili oil (see page 43)
1 teaspoon honey
1 tablespoon medium-dry sherry*

1 teaspoon sesame oil

*1 tablespoon peanut oil
1 teaspoon minced fresh ginger
1 scallion, white and green parts, chopped
1 garlic clove, chopped*

1. Cut the stem ends off the beans and discard. Steam the beans for 3 to 4 minutes. Submerge in ice water to stop the cooking; drain.

2. In a bowl, combine the soy sauce, chili oil, honey, sherry, and sesame oil; set aside.

3. Place a wok or large cast-iron skillet over a high heat until it smokes, 2 to 3 minutes. Add the peanut oil. Immediately add the ginger, scallion, and garlic; stir-fry for 1 minute. Add the beans and stir-fry 1 to 2 minutes.

4. Restir the seasoning sauce. Add all at once and stir continuously until the sauce is absorbed, about 30 seconds. Serve hot or warm.

Variation: For Sichuan Asparagus, replace the beans with 1½ pounds asparagus. Use only the tender part of the asparagus and cut into 2-inch pieces.

MENU FOR A SIMPLE ASIAN MEAL

MISO SOUP (PAGE 72)

STIR-FRIED BOK CHOY WITH SEARED ONIONS (PAGE 229)

STEAMED WHITE OR BROWN RICE

SICHUAN GREEN BEANS (PAGE 228)

MIXED BERRIES WITH ALMOND CREAM (PAGE 256)

Stir-Fried Bok Choy with Seared Onions

*SERVES 4 AS PART OF A
COMPOSED PLATE, 6 AS
PART OF A BUFFET*

*Preparation time:
20 minutes*

*Cooking time:
10 minutes*

Bok choy is a mild vegetable with wide, tender dark green leaves and white stalks that have a celerylike crunchiness. It's available year-round in Asian food stores and most supermarkets.

This basic stir-fry goes well with any Chinese dish.

SEASONING SAUCE
1 teaspoon cornstarch
2 tablespoons dry sherry
1 tablespoon soy sauce
1 tablespoon peanut oil
1 medium to large Spanish
*   onion, sliced*

1 slice fresh ginger, ¼ inch thick,
*   unpeeled*
1 garlic clove, crushed
5 to 6 cups slant-cut bok choy,
*   white and green parts separated*
*   (1 medium bunch)*
1 tablespoon roasted unhulled
*   sesame seeds (see page 40)*

1. To make the seasoning sauce, combine the cornstarch, sherry, and soy sauce; set aside.

2. Place a wok or large cast-iron skillet over high heat for 1 minute. Add the oil, then the onion. Stir-fry the onion for 5 minutes, turn the heat to medium if onion is browning too fast. During the last minute of cooking the onion, however, the heat should be high so it turns dark brown and crispy.

3. Add the ginger and garlic and stir-fry for 30 seconds. Add the white part of the bok choy and stir-fry for 1 minute. Add the green part and stir-fry for 1 minute more.

4. Restir the seasoning sauce and add it to the wok. Continue to stir-fry until the sauce has formed a glaze around the vegetables, about 1 minute. Place vegetables on a platter and sprinkle on the sesame seeds. Serve immediately.

Stir-Fried Spinach

Madame Grace Zia Chu, my first Chinese cooking teacher, taught me this simple way to prepare spinach in 1967.

SERVES 4 AS PART OF A
COMPOSED PLATE,
6 AS PART OF A BUFFET

Preparation time:
15 minutes

Cooking time:
5 minutes

Now, more than twenty-five years later, it's still my favorite way to pre-pare spinach.

2 pounds spinach, washed (see page 91) and thick stems removed
1 tablespoon peanut oil
1 teaspoon salt
1 garlic clove, crushed

¼ teaspoon freshly ground black pepper
1 teaspoon roasted sesame seeds, for garnish (see page 40)

1. After the spinach is washed, drain and spin-dry.

2. Place a wok or iron skillet over high heat until it smokes, 2 to 3 min-utes. Add the oil, then the salt and garlic. Turn the heat to low to allow the salt to dissolve and the garlic to lightly brown, 1 minute.

3. Add the spinach and stir-fry until wilted, about 2 minutes.

4. Put the spinach on a platter. Sprinkle with the pepper and roasted sesame seeds.

STIR-FRIED SUGAR SNAPS WITH SHIITAKE MUSHROOMS

SERVES 4 AS PART OF A
COMPOSED PLATE,
6 AS PART OF A BUFFET

Preparation time:
10 minutes

Cooking time:
5 minutes

*T*he crisp texture of the sugar-snap peas is retained during the brief stir-frying. This is another simple stir-fry that takes just minutes to prepare.

2 teaspoons peanut oil
⅓ teaspoon salt
¼ teaspoon freshly ground black pepper
¼ teaspoon sugar
1 cup thickly sliced fresh shiitake

mushrooms (about 2 ounces)
½ pound sugar-snap peas or snow peas (about 2½ cups), strings re-moved
½ teaspoon Oriental sesame oil

⦿ The combination of sugar-snap peas and shiitake mushrooms is particularly good with steak.

1. Place a wok or large cast-iron skillet over high heat for 1 minute. Add

the peanut oil and turn the heat to low. Add the salt, pepper, and sugar. Stir for a few seconds to dissolve.

2. Add the mushrooms and stir-fry for 2 minutes over medium heat.

3. Add the peas and stir-fry until they soften, about 2 minutes. Remove from the heat and add the sesame oil. Serve hot or at room temperature.

STIR-FRIED VEGETABLES WITH PEPPERS

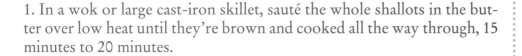

This recipe is limited only by your imagination and your grocer's selection of seasonal vegetables. The shallots are left whole and cooked slowly so they will soften and caramelize.

½ cup shallots, peeled
½ tablespoon butter

SEASONING SAUCE
1 teaspoon cornstarch
1 tablespoon dry sherry
1 tablespoon soy sauce
1 tablespoon miso (optional)
¼ cup vegetable stock (see page 30)
or stock of your choice

½ tablespoon peanut oil
2 cups non-leafy green vegetable
(see Note)
½ cup diced red bell pepper
½ teaspoon chili oil (see page 43)
½ teaspoon Oriental sesame oil

1. In a wok or large cast-iron skillet, sauté the whole shallots in the butter over low heat until they're brown and cooked all the way through, 15 minutes to 20 minutes.

2. Prepare the seasoning sauce by dissolving the cornstarch in the sherry. Add the soy sauce, miso, and stock. Mix well. Set aside.

Can be prepared to this point up to 3 hours ahead. Leave the shallots in the wok. Do not refrigerate.

3. Turn the heat to high under the shallots for 1 minute. Add the peanut oil.

MENU FOR A CHINESE MEAL

STIR-FRIED SUGAR SNAPS WITH SHIITAKE MUSHROOMS (PAGE 230)

WHOLE-GRAIN FRIED RICE (PAGE 182)

PAN-SEARED TOFU (PAGE 168)

GINGER COOKIES (PAGE 262)

SERVES 2 AS AN ENTREE, 4 AS PART OF A COMPOSED PLATE, 6 AS PART OF A BUFFET

Preparation time: 25 minutes

Cooking time: 20 minutes

Immediately add the green vegetable and stir-fry until almost cooked through, usually a minute or two. Add the pepper and stir-fry for 2 minutes.

4. Restir the seasoning sauce. Add it to the wok all at once. Stir continuously until the sauce thickens, about 30 seconds. Add chili and sesame oils. Stir briefly and serve hot.

Note: Blanch vegetables like broccoli, green beans, carrots, cauliflower, and asparagus. Cabbage, zucchini, yellow squash, snow peas, sugar-snaps, and all members of the onion family should not be blanched.

Chapter 12

"LITTLE DISHES": SALSAS, CHUTNEYS, AND RAITAS

These "little dishes" transform a simple meal of beans and rice, vegetables and couscous, or roasted potatoes and spinach into an adventuresome foray into ethnic eating. Chutneys and raitas add an Indian accent, salsas a south-of-the-border tone.

Requiring only a few minutes to prepare, these fresh salsas and chutneys—with their exotic mixtures of hot, sweet, salty, and sour—have replaced the rich and often bland sauces of yesteryear. We've switched from the waltz to the tango.

There's a murky line between salsas and chutneys. *Salsa* means "sauce" in Spanish, but it has come to signify the spicy little dishes made with tomatoes, cucumbers, chile peppers, and vinegar or lime juice. Often made with fruit, chutneys are usually hot and sweet at the same time.

Raitas are combinations of yogurt, aromatic spices, and vegetables or fruit. They cool the palate and balance the fieriness of Indian curries. Raitas are among the few condiments that go well with both spicy and bland food. The three recipes in this chapter are for savory raitas, but raitas can also be made with bananas, raisins, and sweet seasonings.

Any of the salsas in this chapter can be made with poblano, jalapeño, or serrano peppers. While I like my food well seasoned, I'm not partial to its being blisteringly hot. Therefore I often use poblano peppers, which are milder than jalapeño. Jalapeños in turn are milder than serranos.

YIELDS 2 CUPS

Preparation time: 15 minutes

❧ *This salsa is an excellent accompaniment to grilled salmon, bluefish, or any other simply grilled fish.*

Black Bean Salsa

This tangy salsa enhances any vegetarian buffet that features a pasta or grain salad, such as Warm Pasta Salad with Arugula and Goat Cheese (page 116) or Roasted Barley Salad (page 119).

1 cup cooked black beans, homemade (see page 162) or canned (see page 153)
1 cup diced tomato (1 large)
¼ cup chopped red onion

2 tablespoons lime juice
⅛ teaspoon Tabasco sauce
½ cup chopped fresh coriander (cilantro)

1. Combine the beans, tomato, onion, lime juice, and Tabasco.

Can be prepared to this point up to 3 hours ahead.

2. Add the coriander.

ITALIAN SALSA

YIELDS 2 CUPS

*Preparation time:
20 minutes*

This tasty condiment enhances the flavors of beans and grains. Try it over field greens instead of salad dressing.

7 plum tomatoes
2 tablespoons olive oil
1 tablespoon lime juice
1 tablespoon balsamic vinegar
½ teaspoon salt
*¼ teaspoon freshly ground black
  pepper*
¼ cup chopped fresh chives
2 tablespoons minced fresh basil

◀● *I use this salsa to dress up plain baked or grilled fish or chicken.*

1. Blanch the tomatoes. Peel them and then cut in half. Squeeze the juice and seeds out and dice.

2. Place tomatoes in a bowl. Add the oil, lime juice, vinegar, salt, pepper, chives, and basil. Mix well.

This salsa can be prepared up to 3 hours ahead.

MEDITERRANEAN SALSA

YIELDS 1 CUP

*Preparation time:
5 minutes, plus
30 minutes to sit*

Good with any grain dish, this salsa is great with Middle-Eastern Rice and Spinach (page 183) and Curried Couscous with Vegetables and Chickpeas (page 173). I often serve this bright and lively, but not spicy, salsa as a tomato salad when I'm bored with the available lettuce.

3 plum tomatoes, diced
2 scallions, white and green parts
   chopped
1 tablespoon drained capers, with 1
   teaspoon liquid

1 teaspoon rice vinegar
Salt and freshly ground black pepper to taste

Combine the tomatoes, scallions, capers and liquid, vinegar, salt, and pepper. Let sit at room temperature for at least 30 minutes.

This salsa can be prepared up to 2 hours ahead.

YIELDS 1½ CUPS

*Preparation time:
15 minutes*

SOUTHWESTERN SALSA

The secret to this simple salsa is to finely dice the ingredients so the flavors blend well. If you like your salsa fiery hot, use up to four hot peppers instead of the one called for in this recipe.

4 plum tomatoes
½ cup chopped scallions, white and
   green parts
1 jalapeño pepper
½ cup chopped fresh coriander
   (cilantro)

½ teaspoon salt
1 tablespoon sherry vinegar

1. Cut the tomatoes in half and squeeze them lightly to release the seeds. Discard the seeds.

2. Finely chop the tomatoes, scallions, jalapeño, and coriander. Mix in a bowl with the salt and vinegar.

The salsa can be prepared up to 2 hours in advance.

Sweet Red Pepper and Cucumber Salsa

This salsa has a light, clean taste and is a nice change from tomato-based salsas. Try this with the Black Beans with Roasted Peppers (page 160) or Noodles with Spicy Sesame Sauce (page 118).

*YIELDS 1½ TO
2 CUPS*

*Preparation time:
10 minutes, plus
30 minutes to sit*

1 medium cucumber, peeled, seeded,
   and diced
½ teaspoon salt
1 red bell pepper, diced

½ to 1 jalapeño or
   poblano pepper, minced
2 scallions, white and green parts
   chopped
Juice of 1 lime

 *This salsa is great
with grilled meat, poul-
try, or fish.*

Combine the cucumber, salt, red pepper, jalapeño pepper, scallions, and lime juice. Let sit at room temperature for at least 30 minutes.

This salsa can be prepared up to 2 hours ahead.

Cabbage Vinaigrette

*SERVES 8 TO 12
AS A SIDE DISH*

*Preparation time:
15 to 20 minutes,
plus at least 6 hours
to marinate*

Janis Carr of Grace's Market in New York City was kind enough to share his imaginative variation of cold slaw. It's easy to toss together and great for family or parties. I make this slaw anytime I have extra cabbage—even if I don't have all the other ingredients on hand. A bit of carrot, pepper, and onion is all you need.

¼ head green cabbage, shredded
   (about 5 cups)
¼ small head of cauliflower,
   chopped
½ cup diced red bell pepper
1 unpeeled carrot, diced
1 small zucchini, diced
½ cup diced red onion
¼ cup chopped fresh parsley

DRESSING
¼ cup tarragon or rice vinegar
½ tablespoon salt
¼ cup olive oil
1¼ teaspoons freshly ground black
   pepper
½ teaspoon dried oregano

1. Mix all the vegetables in a large bowl.

2. To make the dressing, mix the vinegar and salt in a bowl. Add the oil, black pepper, and oregano and whisk to blend. Pour the dressing over the vegetables and toss. Allow to remain at room temperature for 6 hours, or refrigerate overnight, before serving. Serve cold or at room temperature.

Cabbage Vinaigrette can be refrigerated for 3 days.

PICKLED RADISHES

*Y*ields 1½ cups

Preparation time: 10 minutes, plus 30 minutes to drain radishes

Serve as part of an antipasto, with a hearty bean dish, or with Spicy Polenta with Crispy Garlic and Cheese (page 181).

1 bunch radishes, stems and leaves removed
1 teaspoon coarse salt

1 tablespoon rice vinegar
Freshly ground black pepper to taste

1. Cut the radishes into thin circles. Combine with the salt in a glass bowl and set aside for at least 30 minutes.

2. Drain off the liquid that is left in the bowl and then thoroughly rinse the radishes in water to remove as much of the salt as possible. Press dry with paper towels.

3. Combine the radish slices with the vinegar and mix. Sprinkle liberally with freshly ground black pepper. Serve cold or at room temperature.

The radishes can be prepared up to 3 hours ahead.

MANGO-LIME CHUTNEY

Excellent with beans and cold pasta salads. If you like your chutney hot, add one or two minced chili peppers.

1 ripe mango, coarsely chopped
1 tablespoon maple syrup
1½ tablespoons lime juice
½ teaspoon finely minced lime zest

1 teaspoon minced fresh ginger
½ teaspoon salt
½ teaspoon ground cumin, preferably roasted (see page 40)
4 to 6 drops Tabasco sauce

Combine the mango, maple syrup, lime juice, lime zest, ginger, salt, cumin, and Tabasco in a bowl. Let sit at room temperature for at least 1 hour to let the flavors blend.

This chutney can be prepared up to 3 hours ahead.

YIELDS ½ CUP

Preparation time: 15 minutes, plus 1 hour to blend flavors

◄● *Try this chutney with roasted chicken or grilled meat.*

STEWED PEARS WITH CRANBERRIES

This not-too-sweet fruit compote goes well with black beans or any spicy bean dish. For a piquant variation, add two tablespoons of diced crystallized ginger a few minutes before the pears are done cooking. Sometimes I add a little more sugar and serve these pears as a dessert.

6 pears, Bosc or other firm variety, peeled, cored, and chopped in large chunks
½ cup unfiltered apple juice
¼ teaspoon five-spice powder or

ground allspice
¼ teaspoon ground cinnamon
½ lemon, juiced
2 tablespoons sugar
½ cup fresh cranberries (see Note)

1. In a large pot, cook the pears, apple juice, five-spice powder, cinnamon, lemon juice, and sugar over low heat until pears are soft but not

SERVES 8 TO 12 AS A CONDIMENT

Preparation time: 25 minutes

Cooking time: 35 to 50 minutes

◄● *I particularly like these pears at Thanksgiving dinner with roasted turkey, or at Christmas with baked ham.*

mushy, 30 to 45 minutes.

2. Add the cranberries and cook until the cranberries begin to burst, about 5 minutes. Serve warm, at room temperature, or cold.

Can be prepared up to 2 days ahead and refrigerated.

Note: ¼ cup dried cranberries can be substituted for the fresh. Omit the sugar and add them along with the pears.

YIELDS ¼ CUP

*Preparation time:
15 minutes, plus 1
hour to soak peppers*

*Cooking time:
5 minutes*

HARISSA

This is a nontraditional version of a fiery sauce that's served throughout northern Africa as an accompaniment to couscous. Place a dab on your plate as you would a spicy mustard.

3 large dried hot chile peppers
   (see Note)
2 garlic cloves
2 tablespoons chopped red onion or
   scallion

1 teaspoon ground cumin,
   preferably roasted (page 40)
1 teaspoon ground coriander
2 tablespoons olive oil

1. Bring enough water to cover the peppers—about 2 cups—to a boil.

2. Put the peppers in a glass bowl and cover with the boiling water. Cover the bowl and let the peppers soak at room temperature until very soft, about 1 hour.

3. While the peppers are soaking, sauté the garlic, onion, cumin, and coriander in the olive oil over medium heat for 1 to 2 minutes. Drain the peppers and reserve the soaking water. Remove the stems and seeds from the peppers.

4. Combine all the ingredients in a blender or food processor. Add 1 to 2 tablespoons of the pepper soaking water. Pulse on and off until all the ingredients are chopped fine, but there is still some texture.

Harissa can be refrigerated for at least 1 week.

Note: I use New Mexico dried peppers, available in my local supermarket. They're 5 to 6 inches long and 1 inch wide.

As a precaution, remember to wear rubber gloves so you don't get the oils from the hot peppers on your hands, and be careful not to put your hands near your eyes.

RAITA WITH CORIANDER

YIELDS 1 CUP

Preparation time: 10 minutes, plus 30 minutes to blend flavors

Serve this raita and the two that follow not only with curries but also with rice, couscous, and spinach dishes. Offer it as part of a buffet with Fiery Black-Eyed Pea Salad (page 108) or with Black Bean, Corn, and Red Pepper Salad (page 107).

¼ cup loosely packed chopped fresh coriander (cilantro)
1 cup plain nonfat yogurt
1 teaspoon sherry vinegar

¼ teaspoon freshly ground black pepper
½ teaspoon salt

 All raitas, sweet or savory, are excellent with highly seasoned meat or chicken dishes.

Combine the coriander, yogurt, vinegar, pepper, and salt in a bowl. If possible, let flavors blend for 30 minutes.

RAITA WITH CUCUMBER AND MINT

YIELDS 2 CUPS

Preparation time: 10 minutes, plus 1 hour to blend flavors

¾ cup shredded or finely chopped peeled and seeded cucumber (about ½ a large cucumber)
1 cup plain nonfat yogurt
1 tablespoon lemon juice, lime juice, or rice vinegar

2 tablespoons chopped fresh mint
⅛ teaspoon white pepper
1 teaspoon ground cumin, preferably roasted (see page 40)
Salt to taste

1. Lightly salt the cucumber, then rinse well under cold running water. Dry in a clean cotton or linen towel, squeezing firmly to remove as much moisture as possible.

2. Mix the cucumber and yogurt in a bowl. Add the lime juice, mint, white pepper, and cumin. Stir. Let sit at room temperature for at least 1 hour.

This raita can be prepared a day ahead and refrigerated.

3. Taste and add salt if needed. Serve cold or at room temperature.

Yields 2½ cups

Preparation time: 15 minutes, plus at least 1 hour to blend flavors

Raita with Mixed Vegetables

2 cups plain nonfat or low-fat yogurt
2 tablespoons sour cream
1 kirby cucumber, peeled, seeded, and diced
1 ripe plum tomato, seeded and diced

2 tablespoons diced red onion
¼ cup diced red bell pepper
1 tablespoon lemon juice
½ teaspoon salt
¼ teaspoon ground cumin, preferably roasted (see page 40)

Combine the yogurt, sour cream, cucumber, tomato, onion, red pepper, lemon juice, salt, and cumin in a bowl. Serve cold or at room temperature. Can be eaten immediately, but tastes even better an hour or two later.

Can be prepared up to 1 day ahead and refrigerated.

Chapter 13

DESSERTS

*A*ll my life I've had a sweet tooth. For me desserts are the climax of the meal, the sumptuous finale, the course that destroys the resolve of even the most health-conscious eater. Anything with that much power has my deepest respect.

For those of us who watch our weight, dessert time can feel like the low point of the meal as we glumly watch others indulge themselves. Feeling virtuous but cheated, we long for the meal to be over. Sometimes we splurge only to feel unhappy later at having broken our promises to ourselves.

When I began writing this cookbook I couldn't imagine what dessert, other than raw fruit, would meet my standard of taste without running up a huge "fat bill."

As I went through my files, however, I realized that several of the desserts I rely on at home and for my catering business had little or no fat. I hadn't thought about it before. I ate these desserts because I loved them, not because they were good for me.

But what about custard, chocolate soufflé, fruit cobbler, and Italian cheesecake? Could these be made reasonably low in fat without giving up their wonderful flavors and rich creaminess? The answer is a resounding yes, indeed. You can feel righteous and still eat desserts like Chocolate Soufflé, Pumpkin Crème Brûlée, Slow-Cooked Rice Pudding, or Peach and Cherry Cobbler.

Only those desserts I'm proud to serve to my guests and clients are included here. If any of my testers said, "Gee, for a low-fat dessert, that's pretty good," I tossed the recipe out.

I've also included my favorite chocolate recipe, a sinfully rich Drop-Dead Chocolate Cake. I believe that once in a while it's a good idea to indulge in what we fancy—and to savor every morsel without worrying about health or weight.

Drop-Dead Chocolate Cake

*T*his cake got its name when a student who had missed the class in which I taught this recipe called her friend for instructions. Her classmate omitted an important point: the cake is *supposed* to fall. I returned home that day to find a frantic message on my answering machine

saying "Karen, this is Shari. I followed the directions exactly, but the cake dropped dead."

The cake is also drop-dead delicious. I indulge in this decadently rich treat infrequently. But when I do, it's with total delight and not a twinge of guilt.

*YIELDS ONE 8-INCH
ROUND CAKE*

*Preparation time:
20 minutes,
plus time to cool*

*Cooking time:
45 minutes*

Cocoa powder
8½ ounces semisweet chocolate, broken into small pieces
¾ cup plus 1 tablespoon sugar
1 cup (2 sticks) unsalted butter, cut into small pieces
6 large eggs
2½ tablespoons all-purpose flour

1. Preheat the oven to 350°F.

2. Butter and sprinkle cocoa powder into an 8-inch springform pan. (The pan should have sides at least 2 inches high.) Tap out any cocoa that doesn't adhere.

3. In a double boiler, heat the chocolate and sugar until the chocolate melts. Add the butter gradually, using a wooden spoon to stir frequently until the butter is incorporated. Remove from the heat and allow to cool to room temperature.

4. Separate the eggs. Set the whites aside.

5. Beat the yolks into the cooled chocolate mixture until combined. Add the flour and stir well.

6. In a separate bowl, beat the egg whites until stiff but not dry. Using a rubber spatula, fold the egg whites into the chocolate mixture.

7. Pour the batter into the prepared pan. Place the pan on the middle rack in the oven and bake until the cake has risen and the crust is beginning to crack, about 45 minutes. The inside of the cake will be soft and have a slightly puddinglike consistency. Remove the cake from the oven and let cool before unmolding. Serve at room temperature, either alone, with chantilly cream, or with ice cream and berries.

This cake can be prepared a day ahead and kept at room temperature, covered with aluminum foil.

Barefoot Contessa's Low-Fat Ginger Cake

*Yields one 9-inch
round cake*

*Preparation time:
20 to 30 minutes,
plus time to cool*

*Cooking time:
30 minutes*

*I*f you want to go to culinary heaven, head straight for Barefoot Contessa in East Hampton, New York. Among their fabulous selection of prepared foods are a variety of low-fat dips, soups, and cakes. Ina Garten was kind enough to share this wonderful recipe with me.

¼ cup vegetable oil
½ cup molasses
¼ cup honey
1 large egg
1 tablespoon baking soda
1 cup all-purpose flour
1 cup whole wheat flour
1 tablespoon ground ginger
½ tablespoon ground cinnamon
1 teaspoon freshly grated nutmeg

½ teaspoon salt
¼ cup finely minced crystallized
   ginger
½ cup dried currants
½ cup buttermilk

GLAZE
¼ pound confectioners' sugar
2 tablespoons fresh lemon juice

1. Preheat the oven to 350°F. Grease a 9-inch springform pan with oil or butter.

2. In a large bowl, stir together the oil, molasses, and honey. Using a wire whisk, beat an egg into this mixture until it is well incorporated.

3. In a separate bowl, combine the baking soda, flour, whole-wheat flour, ginger, cinnamon, nutmeg, salt, crystallized ginger, and currants.

4. Add the dry ingredients, alternating with the buttermilk, to the molasses mixture, stirring with a wooden spoon until all the ingredients are combined.

5. Pour the batter into the prepared pan. Bake until the sides of the cake pull away from the pan or a cake tester inserted into the center of the cake comes out clean, about 30 minutes. Do not overbake.

6. Allow the cake to cool for 1 hour in the pan.

7. While the cake is cooling, make the glaze by stirring the confectioners'

sugar and lemon juice together until the sugar dissolves.

8. Remove the cake from the pan. Pour the glaze over the top of the cake. Let cool.

CHOCOLATE ANGEL FOOD CAKE

The taste of Chocolate Angel Food Cake is paradoxically light and rich. Close to fat-free, it's wonderful served by itself or with the Strawberries with Raspberry Sauce (page 261), Moroccan Oranges (page 258), or any fresh fruit.

About 1 cup cake or unbleached all-purpose flour
1¾ cups superfine sugar
¼ teaspoon salt
½ cup Dutch-process cocoa
¼ cup plus 1 tablespoon hot espresso

2 teaspoons vanilla extract
2 cups egg whites (approximately 16 large eggs)
2 teaspoons cream of tartar

1. Preheat the oven to 350°F.

2. Place a 1-cup dry measure on a sheet of waxed paper. Sift the flour into the cup until the cup is overflowing. Never shake or tap the cup; this compresses the flour and you end up with more flour than the recipe calls for. Sweep the back of a knife across the top of the flour to make it even with the top of the measuring cup. Sift the flour again, this time with ¾ cup of the sugar and the salt. Set aside.

3. In a medium bowl, combine the cocoa and espresso. Stir until smooth; add the vanilla. Set aside.

4. In a large mixing bowl, beat the egg whites until frothy. Add the cream of tartar and beat until soft peaks form. Gradually beat in the remaining 1 cup sugar. Beat until very stiff peaks form when the beater is slowly raised. Remove 1 heaping cup of stiff egg white and place it on top of the cocoa mixture. Set aside.

YIELDS ONE 10-INCH CAKE

Preparation time: 1 hour, plus time to cool

Cooking time: 40 minutes

MENU FOR A DESSERT BUFFET

CHOCOLATE ANGEL FOOD CAKE (PAGE 247)

RICOTTA TORTE (PAGE 248)

MOROCCAN ORANGES (PAGE 258)

POACHED PEARS AND CHERRIES IN PORT (PAGE 261)

FRESH FRUIT

Cake and icing recipes occasionally call for superfine sugar, which is hard to find and expensive. Make your own by grinding granulated sugar (regular table sugar) in a food processor.

Never substitute confectioners' sugar, which has added cornstarch.

5. Sift the flour-sugar mixture over the remaining egg whites ¼ cup at a time. Fold in. Using a rubber spatula, turn the bowl a quarter of the way around after each stroke—about 15 strokes between each quarter-cup of added flour should be enough to completely incorporate the flour and egg whites without breaking the egg whites down.

6. Stir together the egg whites and cocoa mixture and fold into the batter. Pour into a 10-inch ungreased tube pan. (The cake will not rise if the pan has been greased.) Using the rubber spatula, cut through the middle of the batter to level it.

7. Bake until a cake tester inserted in the center comes out clean and the cake springs back when lightly pressed, about 40 minutes. The surface will have deep cracks, like a soufflé. Invert the pan on its legs or hang it over the neck of a wine or glass soda bottle until the cake has thoroughly cooled, 1 to 2 hours.

8. Remove the cake from the pan.

Tastes best the day it is made and the next, but leftovers can be eaten for 4 more days. Never refrigerate.

RICOTTA TORTE

I prefer this rich, creamy dessert when it's made with whole-milk ricotta, but it's still good when made with part-skim ricotta. Since I'm not partial to raisins, I usually leave them out. For a different flavor, substitute orange rind and juice for the lemon.

YIELDS ONE 8- OR 9-
INCH CAKE

Preparation time:
20 minutes,
plus time to cool

Cooking time:
30 to 40 minutes

1 tablespoon melted butter
¼ cup graham cracker crumbs
1 pound whole-milk or part-skim
   ricotta cheese
5 large egg yolks

½ cup sugar
½ teaspoon salt
1 teaspoon grated lemon rind
1 tablespoon fresh lemon juice
½ cup raisins (optional)

1. Preheat the oven to 325°F.

2. Combine the butter and graham cracker crumbs in a bowl. Sprinkle the mixture over the bottom of an 8- or 9-inch pie pan.

3. Mix the ricotta cheese, egg yolks, sugar, salt, lemon rind, and lemon juice. Add the raisins if you're using them.

4. Pour the cheese mixture over the graham cracker crumbs. Bake until golden, 30 to 40 minutes. Serve at room temperature, either alone or with fresh berries.

Best the same day, but can be made up to 2 days ahead and refrigerated. Do not refrigerate if you are going to eat it the same day.

CHOCOLATE SOUFFLÉ

SERVES 6

*Preparation time:
20 to 25 minutes*

*Cooking time:
20 to 25 minutes*

When I want deep-down chocolate satisfaction—the kind I thought came only from the richest, densest chocolate dessert—I make this soufflé. No one ever suspects it of being a lighter version of my original.

If you prepare the chocolate base in advance, beating the whites and assembling the final dish takes only a few minutes.

*Confectioners' sugar
1 tablespoon unsalted butter
1 tablespoon all-purpose flour
⅔ cup low-fat milk
2 ounces (2 squares) good-quality*

*bittersweet chocolate, chopped
into small pieces
2 large egg yolks
3 large egg whites
¼ cup granulated sugar*

1. Preheat the oven to 350°F.

2. Grease a 2-quart soufflé dish. Sprinkle with confectioners' sugar.

3. In a small saucepan, melt the butter over low heat. Add the flour and stir for 2 minutes.

4. Meanwhile, in a separate saucepan, warm the milk over low heat. Add the chocolate and stir until the chocolate melts. Remove from the heat.

5. Beat the egg yolks lightly. Add a little of the warm chocolate mixture to the yolks and stir, then add the yolks to the chocolate mixture. Allow to cool.

The chocolate base can be prepared to this point several hours in advance and left at room temperature.

6. Beat the egg whites until soft peaks form. Add the granulated sugar gradually and continue to beat until stiff but not dry. Fold into the chocolate mixture. Pour this batter into the prepared soufflé dish.

7. Bake until the soufflé has risen and cracked, 25 to 30 minutes. Serve immediately, with confectioners' sugar sifted over the top.

BAKED EGG CUSTARD

SERVES 4

Preparation time: 15 minutes, plus time to cool

Cooking time: 30 minutes

My mother's former career in vaudeville was good training for her later pursuit of ballroom dancing, but it did nothing to prepare her to cook or take care of a house and two kids.

When the occasional maternal urge hit my mother, she made what seemed to me the world's best custard. I can't imagine where she learned to prepare it. Both the Baked Egg Custard and the Chocolate Custard that follows were my favorite childhood desserts. To this day, when life becomes frantic or stressful, I prepare one, sit wrapped in a robe, and slowly savor it.

2 cups low-fat milk
2 large eggs
¼ cup sugar

1 teaspoon vanilla extract
⅛ teaspoon grated nutmeg

1. Put a kettle of water on to boil; preheat the oven to 400°F.

2. Heat the milk until it is warm.

3. Crack the eggs and remove the connective tissue that separates the yolk from the white. Beat the eggs and add the sugar slowly, continuing to beat until the sugar dissolves. Add the warm milk, vanilla, and nutmeg to the egg mixture.

4. Butter four 1-cup custard cups (see Note). (I use the inexpensive Pyrex ones.) Pour in the custard, leaving ½ inch of space at the top of each. Place the filled custard cups in a shallow roasting pan and put the pan on the center of the lower oven rack. Pour the boiling water into the roasting pan to a depth of ½ inch. Lower oven temperature to 350°F.

5. Bake until the custard is solid and a sharp paring knife or a cake tester comes out clean, about 30 minutes. Serve at room temperature.

Tastes best the day made, but can be refrigerated for a day or two. Do not return to room temperature.

Note: If you prefer, bake the custard in a 1-quart dish, as long as the mixture is at least 1¼ inches thick; measure by inserting a chopstick. The thickness of the custard determines the baking time. A thicker mixture will take longer.

CHOCOLATE CUSTARD

SERVES 4

*Preparation time:
30 minutes,
plus time to cool*

*Cooking time:
35 minutes*

1 tablespoon boiling water
2 ounces (2 squares) semisweet
   chocolate
2 cups low-fat milk

2 large eggs
⅓ cup sugar
1 teaspoon vanilla extract

1. Put a kettle of water on to boil; preheat the oven to 350°F.

2. Put the boiling water and chocolate into a double boiler. (Actually, I never use a double boiler. I put the chocolate in a small saucepan and then put the saucepan into a skillet filled to a depth of 1 inch with water. I turn the heat to high until the water boils, then I turn it down to low. This is my improvised *bain-marie*. It works just fine and it's one less pot to buy and store.) Stir until the chocolate melts. Set aside to cool.

3. Heat the milk until it's warm.

4. Meanwhile, crack the eggs and remove the connective tissue that sepa-

rates the yolk from the white. Beat the eggs and add the sugar slowly, continuing to beat until the sugar dissolves. Add the milk and vanilla to the egg mixture.

5. Butter four 1-cup custard cups. Pour in the custard, leaving at least ½ inch of space at the top of each. Place the filled custard cups in a shallow roasting pan and place the pan in the oven on the center of the lower rack. Pour the boiling water into the roasting pan to a depth of ½ inch.

6. Bake until the custard is solid and a sharp paring knife or a cake tester comes out clean, about 30 minutes. Serve at room temperature.

Tastes best the day made, but can be refrigerated for a day or two. Do not return to room temperature.

Serves 6

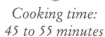

Preparation time: 10 to 25 minutes plus 1 hour to chill

Cooking time: 45 to 55 minutes

Pumpkin Crème Brûlée

I'm convinced no broiler can ever make a proper *brûlée*. By the time the sugar melts, it's burnt.

One day I read that a blowtorch was a good way to scorch a sugar topping. Blowtorch? The idea of using one intimidated me. I had visions of exploding in a fireball of custard. Finally I bought the dreaded contraption and a pair of safety goggles at a local hardware store in Amagansett. My friend Jed Schutz, an artist and a construction worker, came over to hold my hand—literally and figuratively—and taught me how to scorch sugar without incinerating it or myself.

If you don't have a blowtorch, or aren't inclined to use yours on custard, serve this pumpkin custard without the scorched sugar. I love it both ways.

1 small pumpkin, or 1 cup canned or frozen pumpkin puree (see Note)
2 cups low-fat milk
2 tablespoons maple syrup
½ cup brown sugar
4 large eggs, lightly beaten

½ teaspoon ground cinnamon
½ teaspoon ground ginger
½ teaspoon freshly grated nutmeg
1 teaspoon vanilla extract
Superfine sugar

1. If using a fresh pumpkin, cut in half and remove the seeds. Slice into 1-inch-wide wedges and peel. Dice the peeled wedges into 1-inch cubes.

2. Steam the pumpkin until easily pierced with a poultry skewer, 7 to 9 minutes. Pass through a food mill or mash well. Set aside 1 cup of the pumpkin puree and freeze the rest in 1-cup portions for future custards.

3. Preheat the oven to 325°F. Butter a 1-quart soufflé dish or six 1-cup custard cups.

4. In a large saucepan, heat the milk, maple syrup, and brown sugar over low heat until the sugar dissolves, about 5 minutes.

5. Beat the eggs with a wire whisk and strain to remove the membrane between the white and the yolk. Beat into the warm milk mixture. Add the pumpkin puree, cinnamon, ginger, nutmeg, and vanilla.

6. Pour mixture into the soufflé dish or custard cups. Bake until a knife inserted into the center of the custard comes out clean, about 40 minutes.

7. Refrigerate for at least 1 hour, and up to 1 day. Sift superfine sugar on top of the cold custard. Using a blowtorch, quickly brown the sugar. Serve warm, or at room temperature as a simple custard.

Best the day made. Can be refrigerated for 3 to 4 days as a custard. Brûlées can be kept for 1 or 2 days, but the topping will soften.

Note: If using canned puree, omit steps 1 and 2. While you only need 1 cup puree, the smallest can I could find is 1 pound, yielding 3½ cups. Save the rest for more custards.

SLOW-COOKED RICE PUDDING

This recipe comes from my brother Ken Korsh, a photographer, who began to bake while he was in college. Ken started his cooking career flipping hamburgers at the American Museum of Natural History in New York City, and he worked at many food jobs until he became the *chef de legumes* at Le Pavillon and later at La Côte Basque. The secret to the rich creaminess of this pudding is the slow cooking.

SERVES 8

*Preparation time:
5 minutes*

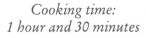

*Cooking time:
1 hour and 30 minutes*

1 quart low-fat milk
¼ cup white rice
⅓ cup sugar

1 large egg, beaten
1 teaspoon vanilla extract
Ground cinnamon (optional)

1. In a heavy pot, bring the milk, rice, and sugar to a boil. Lower the heat and simmer, partially covered, for 1 hour and 30 minutes, stirring every 10 to 15 minutes to keep the pudding from scorching. Remove the pot from the heat.

2. Mix the egg with a little of the hot pudding. Add the warmed egg and the vanilla to the pot; stir.

3. Spoon the pudding into individual serving bowls, or into a large bowl, and sprinkle with cinnamon. It will continue to thicken as it cools. Serve warm, at room temperature, or cold.

Refrigerate for up to 4 days. Return to room temperature before serving.

SERVES 8 TO 10

Preparation time: 20 to 30 minutes

Cooking time: 1 hour

APPLE CRISP

Any apple dessert—apple pies, baked apples, stewed apples, or apples crowned with a light crumb topping like this crisp—you name it, I love it. They go well after any kind of food, they're never too heavy, and unless drowned in sugar and butter, the tart-sweet taste of apple bursts through.

Turn this into an Apple-Pear Crisp by substituting 4 ripe pears for half the apples.

CRUMB TOPPING
½ cup all-purpose flour
¼ cup sugar
¼ cup (½ stick) butter, softened
Zest of ½ lemon
¼ cup chopped walnuts

8 to 10 apples
¼ cup sugar
1½ teaspoons ground cinnamon
⅛ teaspoon freshly grated nutmeg
1 teaspoon vanilla extract
1 tablespoon all-purpose flour

1. Preheat the oven to 350°F.

2. Using your fingers, make the topping by crumbling together the flour, sugar, and butter. Add the lemon zest and walnuts. Set aside.

3. Peel, core, and slice the apples into eighths. Toss the apple slices with the sugar, cinnamon, nutmeg, vanilla, and flour.

4. Put the apple mixture into a 9-inch round baking dish with high sides. Distribute the crumb topping over the apples. Bake until the topping is brown and crusty, about 1 hour. Serve warm or at room temperature.

Tastes best the day made, but can be refrigerated for 1 day. Return to room temperature.

APPLES STEWED IN CALVADOS

SERVES 6 TO 8

Preparation time: 20 minutes

Cooking time: 20 to 30 minutes

My parents had a cook named Hattie, who could whip up the meanest pot roast, smothered with onions and garlic, and the best potato pancakes except for my grandmother. To go with the potato pancakes, she made a chunky applesauce that I still dream about. This is an adult version my students adore.

Use at least three varieties of apples to get an interesting texture, as some apples take longer to cook than others.

6 apples, peeled, cored, and cut into quarters
½ cup raisins
1 teaspoon ground cinnamon
¼ cup apricot preserves, preferably
sugar-free
¼ cup apple juice (I prefer unfiltered)
2 tablespoons Calvados (see Note; omit if unavailable)

Put the apples, raisins, cinnamon, preserves, apple juice, and Calvados into a heavy pot with a lid. Cook over low heat until the apples are soft, 20 to 30 minutes. Serve warm, at room temperature, or cold, either alone or with low-fat frozen yogurt or vanilla ice cream.

Refrigerate for up to 3 weeks. Return to room temperature before serving.

Note: Calvados is a fine French apple brandy.

SERVES 4

*Preparation time:
5 to 10 minutes*

*Cooking time:
10 to 15 minutes*

◆▸ *This dessert is especially satisfying after a spicy stew, pork roast, or meat or vegetable curry.*

BANANAS BAKED WITH BUTTERED RUM

With only one teaspoon of butter for four servings, you'll be amazed at the richness of this dessert. Good by itself, it can also be served with low-fat vanilla ice cream or frozen yogurt.

1 teaspoon butter	⅛ teaspoon ground cinnamon
1 teaspoon lemon juice	4 firm ripe bananas
2 tablespoons maple syrup	Mint leaves and raspberries for
1 tablespoon dark rum	garnish (optional)

1. Preheat the oven to 400°F.

2. Melt the butter. Combine with the lemon juice, maple syrup, rum, and cinnamon.

3. Peel the bananas and slice in half lengthwise. Put them in a shallow baking dish just big enough to hold them. Spoon the buttered-rum mixture over the bananas.

4. Put the bananas in the oven and bake until they are soft, about 8 minutes.

5. Remove the bananas from the oven and preheat the broiler. Place the bananas under the broiler until they brown slightly and the sauce turns into a glaze, 2 to 4 minutes. Garnish with mint leaves and raspberries, or serve with ice cream or frozen yogurt.

Best when served warm, but can be served at room temperature.

MIXED BERRIES WITH ALMOND CREAM

Over the years, my recipe for this almond cream has evolved. I think you'll be as surprised as I was at how rich and creamy it is even though it's made with low-fat milk.

1 cup blanched almonds
4 cups low-fat milk
½ cup sugar
3 tablespoons cornstarch
4 tablespoons almond-flavored

liqueur
1 cup raspberries
½ cup blueberries
½ cup blackberries

SERVES 8

*Preparation time:
20 minutes plus 5
hours for steeping,
chilling, and
marinating*

*Cooking time:
17 to 20 minutes*

1. Preheat the oven to 325°F.

2. Roast the almonds until they turn light brown, about 15 minutes. Allow the almonds to cool, then pulse them in a food processor until they are finely ground.

3. In a medium saucepan, combine the ground almonds, 3½ cups milk, and sugar. Stirring every minute or two, bring to a simmer over medium-low heat. Remove from the heat, cover, and let the almonds steep for 1 hour.

4. Strain the mixture through a fine-mesh sieve, pressing down hard on the almonds with the back of a spoon to extract all the liquid. Discard the solids left in the sieve.

5. Bring the almond milk to a simmer. Reduce the heat to low. Dissolve the cornstarch in the remaining ½ cup milk. Gradually stir it into the simmering liquid. Simmer 2 to 3 minutes, stirring constantly, until the custard thickens. Add 2 tablespoons of the liqueur. Stir.

6. Strain the custard through a fine-mesh sieve into a bowl. Place a sheet of plastic wrap directly on top of the custard to keep a skin from forming. Chill for at least 4 hours or overnight.

The custard can be made up to 3 or 4 days ahead and refrigerated.

7. Marinate the berries for at least 2 hours in the remaining 2 tablespoons of liqueur.

8. Just before serving, beat the custard well with a wire whisk. Pour the custard over the berries and serve.

Moroccan Oranges

SERVES 8 TO 12

Preparation time: 30 minutes, plus several hours to chill

Cooking time: 1 hour

This dessert has long been a staple of my catering business and a personal favorite. The intensely sweet and tart orange flavor is wonderful alone or with anything chocolate like a simple store-bought chocolate cookie or candy, or the Chocolate Soufflé (page 249) or Drop-Dead Chocolate Cake (page 244).

Try this dessert after a spicy meal or one that features a Middle-Eastern entree like Chickpeas and Spinach (page 162) or Middle-Eastern Rice and Lentils (page 184).

8 navel oranges
½ cup sugar
2 teaspoons vanilla extract

2 tablespoons Grand Marnier
Cherries, raspberries, or strawberries for garnish

1. Peel the zest from 4 of the oranges. Remove any white—the pith is bitter and will ruin the sauce—and, with a sharp knife, cut the orange zest into thin, long, julienne strips. Place in a saucepan, cover the zest with cold water, and bring to a rolling boil. Immediately remove from the heat. Drain. Repeat this process 2 more times. This removes the bitterness from the orange rind.

2. Return the zest to the pot. Cover with cold water and add the sugar. Bring to a boil, then simmer over medium-low heat until the peel is translucent and the sauce is thick and syrupy, about 40 minutes. Add the vanilla and Grand Marnier. Remove from the heat.

3. Remove any remaining pith and the white membrane from around the oranges. Cut crosswise into ¼-inch-thick slices and place the slices in a glass serving bowl. Pour the sauce over the oranges. Refrigerate for several hours. Garnish with the cherries, raspberries, or strawberries, or serve as is. Serve at room temperature.

Tastes best the day made, but can be refrigerated for 1 day. Return to room temperature before serving.

Peaches in Red Wine

Serves 8 to 10

*Preparation time:
15 minutes, plus time
to cool*

*Cooking time:
25 minutes*

During the summer of 1987, a friend and I spent a month in the south of France. Having heard about a spectacular restaurant in Provence, we called ahead for eight o'clock reservations.

At ten we were still driving through the vineyards in the pouring rain, trying to figure out where we'd gone wrong. When we finally arrived, our hosts fussed over us and fed us a magnificent dinner. This dessert alone was worth the ordeal.

*1 cup red wine
½ cup light brown sugar
½ teaspoon ground cinnamon
1 whole clove*

*Pinch of freshly ground black pepper
3 pounds ripe peaches
1 teaspoon vanilla extract*

1. Using a saucepan large enough to cook the peaches in a single layer and deep enough to be able to cover them with a lid, bring the wine and brown sugar to a boil. Stir frequently with a wooden spoon until the sugar dissolves. Add the cinnamon, clove, and pepper. Add the peaches and cover.

2. Turn the heat to medium-low and poach the peaches until they're cooked through, about 10 minutes. Remove the peaches from the sauce. Reduce the sauce until it is the consistency of maple syrup, about 15 minutes. You should have about ⅔ cup of sauce. Add the vanilla.

3. When the peaches are cool enough to handle, remove the skins. Serve the peaches whole, halved, or sliced. Pour the sauce over the peaches. Serve alone or over Baked Egg Custard (page 250), Chocolate Custard (page 251), plain yogurt, frozen vanilla yogurt or ice cream, angel food cake, or sponge cake.

The peaches can be refrigerated for up to 1 week. Return to room temperature before serving.

Peach and Cherry Cobbler

I make this cobbler in different forms throughout the year. In the summer, I also use raspberries, blueberries, plums, or a combination of summer fruits. In the fall, I substitute apples or a combination of apples and pears for the peaches.

6 cups blanched, peeled, and sliced
    ripe peaches
⅓ to ½ cup sugar, depending on
    sweetness of peaches
¾ tablespoon cornstarch
2 tablespoons dried cherries, or 1
    cup pitted fresh Bing cherries,
    loosely packed

CRUST
½ cup all-purpose flour
¾ teaspoon baking powder
⅛ teaspoon salt
1 tablespoon sugar
2 tablespoons unsalted butter
2 tablespoons heavy cream

1. Preheat the oven to 375°F.

2. Lay the peaches in a medium ungreased baking dish. (I use an oval 9 x 11-inch pan.) Toss with the sugar, cornstarch, and cherries.

3. To make the crust, sift together the flour, baking powder, salt, and sugar. Using a pastry blender or your fingers, cut in the butter. Add the cream and stir briefly with a fork. Mix with a light touch.

The dough can be prepared up to 8 hours ahead. Refrigerate only if preparing in advance. You don't need to return the dough to room temperature before continuing.

4. Roll out the dough ⅛ inch thick on a lightly floured board until thin and place over the fruit. It's all right if it doesn't completely cover the peaches. The dough will be crumbly and may break. Don't worry: it will look better when baked.

5. Bake until the crust is well browned, 35 to 45 minutes. Serve warm or at room temperature, plain or with ice cream or whipped cream.

Note: For a real treat, add a tablespoon or so of Pêcher Mignon, peach liqueur, or cognac to the whipped cream during the last minute of whipping.

Poached Pears and Cherries in Port

*H*ere's an elegant dessert with a tart, sophisticated taste that's perfect after a formal dinner. Buy the pears a few days in advance and allow them to ripen at room temperature.

SERVES 6

Preparation time:
15 minutes

Cooking time:
30 to 35 minutes

6 ripe pears, Bartlett or Comice
½ cup water
¼ cup brown sugar
1 cinnamon stick

1 star anise (optional)
¼ cup dried cherries (see Note)
1 cup Port wine

1. Rinse the pears. Using a potato peeler or paring knife, peel the pears and leave them whole; keep the stems intact.

2. In a heavy stainless-steel or enamel saucepan, combine the water, brown sugar, cinnamon, star anise, cherries, and wine. Add the pears. Simmer until the pears are cooked through, but still firm, 15 to 20 minutes.

3. Remove the pears and reduce the liquid to a thick, syrupy glaze, about 15 minutes. Spoon the glaze and the cherries over the pears.

These pears taste best served at room temperature. Make them early in the day and leave covered until ready to serve. Can be refrigerated for 3 days. Return to room temperature before serving.

Note: Dried cherries are becoming increasingly easy to find, but if unavailable either omit or substitute raisins or currants.

Strawberries with Raspberry Sauce

*T*his versatile dessert can also be made with the addition of sections of clementines or other seedless oranges, chunks of fresh pineapple, blueberries, blackberries, or peaches. It's hard to make a mistake.

SERVES 8 TO 12

Preparation time:
5 to 10 minutes,
plus 1 hour to marinate

Serve alone or with Chocolate Soufflé (page 249) or Chocolate Angel Food Cake (page 247). The berries are also excellent as a topping for waffles the next day—if you have any left over.

4 cups strawberries	*1 tablespoon maple syrup*
1 cup raspberries	
1 tablespoon fresh orange juice (see Note)	

1. Wash and remove hulls from the strawberries and put them into an attractive bowl.

2. In a separate bowl, press the raspberries 2 or 3 times with the back of a fork to mash some of them. Stir in the orange juice and maple syrup.

3. Pour the raspberry mixture over the strawberries, mix gently, and cover the bowl with plastic wrap or a clean towel. Allow to remain at room temperature for at least 1 hour. Serve at room temperature.

The raspberries can be prepared up to 4 hours ahead. Refrigerate any leftovers for 1 day.

Note: You may want to adjust the amounts of orange juice and maple syrup depending on the sweetness of the raspberries.

GINGER COOKIES

YIELDS 36 COOKIES

❧

Preparation time: 1 hour, plus 6 hours to chill dough

❧

Cooking time: 10 minutes

For more than five years I worked on getting these ginger cookies precisely as I wanted them—crusty on the outside and soft and chewy on the inside.

I love these cookies. I prepare them for many catering events. I teach my students how to make them, and I bake them for my friends and family. They are so good, I can't imagine ever growing tired of them. But since each cookie has a teaspoon of butter, I usually serve only one or two. They're great with a fruit dessert such as Moroccan Oranges (page 258), Apples Stewed in Calvados (page 255), and Peaches in Red Wine (page 259).

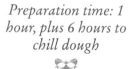

These cookies are easy to make—with one word of caution. Don't omit the step of refrigerating the dough. I did once when I was in a rush. The dough spread over the cookie sheet while it was baking and the result was a giant flat pancake.

Work quickly when making these cookies, as you want the dough to stay cold. On a hot day I preheat the oven, line up the cookie sheets and sugar, and then take only a quarter of the dough out of the refrigerator at a time.

Prepare the dough a day ahead, and you can have delicious, homemade cookies in just minutes.

12 tablespoons (1½ sticks) unsalted
   butter
1 cup brown sugar
1 large egg
¼ cup molasses
2 cups all-purpose flour
2 teaspoons baking soda

½ teaspoon ground cloves
½ teaspoon ground ginger
1 teaspoon ground cinnamon
½ teaspoon salt
2 tablespoons chopped crystallized
   ginger
Granulated sugar

◀● *When measuring flour for this recipe, I like to use a "light" measurement of flour, i.e. take a scoop of flour and place it into the 1 cup measure and level it off.*

1. In a large bowl, beat together the butter, brown sugar, egg, and molasses.

2. In a separate bowl, sift the flour, baking soda, cloves, ginger, cinnamon, and salt.

3. Add the flour mixture and the crystallized ginger to the butter mixture, stirring until it forms a dough.

Prepare to this point at least 6 hours ahead or up to 1 day in advance. Refrigerate until ready to bake.

4. Preheat the oven to 375°F. Lightly grease a cookie sheet with butter.

5. Roll a tablespoon of cold dough quickly in your hands to form a ball. Roll the balls in the granulated sugar to coat them. Place 3 inches apart on a cookie sheet. Do not crowd as the dough will spread.

6. Bake until the cookies are golden brown, about 9 or 10 minutes. Let cool on a rack. Serve at room temperature.

Can be stored in covered container at room temperature for up to 2 days.

CONVERSION CHARTS

LIQUID MEASURES

Fluid Ounces	U.S. Measures	Imperial Measures	Milliliters
	1 tsp.	1 tsp.	5
¼	2 tsp.	1 dessert spoon	7
½	1 T.	1 T.	15
1	2 T.	2 T.	28
2	¼ cup	4 T.	56
4	½ cup or ¼ pint	–	110
5	–	¼ pint or 1 gill	140
6	¼ cup	–	170
8	1 cup or ½ pint	–	225
9	–	–	250 (¼ liter)
10	1¼ cups	½ pint	280
12	1½ cups or ¾ pint	¾ pint	340
15	–	–	420
16	2 cups or 1 pint	–	450
18	2¼ cups	1 pint	500 (½ liter)
20	2½ cups	–	560
24	3 cups or 1½ pints	1¼ pints	675
25	–	–	700
27	3½ cups	1½ pints	750
30	3¾ cups	–	840
32	4 cups or 2 pints or 1 quart	–1¾ pints	900
35	–	–	980
36	4 ½ cups		1000 (1 liter)

SOLID MEASURES

U.S. and Imperial Measures		Metric Measures	
Ounces	Pounds	Grams	Kilos
1	–	28	–
2	–	56	–
3 ½	–	100	–
4	¼	112	–
5		140	–

SOLID MEASURES (CONTINUED)

U.S. AND IMPERIAL MEASURES		METRIC MEASURES	
6	–	168	–
8	½	225	–
9	–	250	¼
12	¾	340	–
16	1	450	–
18	–	500	½
20	1¼	560	–
24	1½	675	–
27	–	750	¾
28	1¾	780	–
32	2	900	–
36	2¼	1000	1
40	2½	1100	–
48	3	1350	–
54	–	1500	1½

OVEN TEMPERATURE EQUIVALENTS

FAHRENHEIT	GAS MARK	CELSIUS	HEAT OF OVEN
225	¼	107	Very Cool
250	½	121	Very Cool
275	1	135	Cool
300	2	148	Cool
325	3	163	Moderate
350	4	177	Moderate
375	5	190	Fairly Hot
400	6	204	Fairly Hot
425	7	218	Hot
450	8	232	Very Hot
475	9	246	Very Hot

INDEX

Numbers in boldface indicate recipes.

U, V

W

Y, Z